SUICIDE RISK ™

VOLUME THREE • SEVEN WALLS AND A TRAP

ROSS RICHIE CEO & Founder • MARK SMYLIE Founder of Archaia • MATT GAGNON Editor-in-Chief • FILIP SABLIK VP of Publishing & Marketing • STEPHEN CHRISTY President of Developm
LANCE KREITER VP of Licensing & Merchandising • PHIL BARBARO VP of Finance • BRYCE CARLSON Managing Editor • MEL CAYLO Marketing Manager • SCOTT NEWMAN Production Design Man
IRENE BRADISH Operations Manager • CHRISTINE DINH Brand Communications Manager • DAFNA PLEBAN Editor • SHANNON WATTERS Editor • ERIC HARBURN Editor • REBECCA TAYLOR
IAN BRILL Editor • CHRIS ROSA Assistant Editor • ALEX GALER Assistant Editor • WHITNEY LEOPARD Assistant Editor • JASMINE AMIRI Assistant Editor • CAMERON CHITTOCK Assistant
KELSEY DIETERICH Production Designer • EMI YONEMURA BROWN Production Designer • DEVIN FUNCHES E-Commerce & Inventory Coordinator • ANDY LIEGL Event Coordinator • BRIANNA HART Executive Assi
AARON FERRARA Operations Assistant • JOSÉ MEZA Sales Assistant • MICHELLE ANKLEY Sales Assistant • ELIZABETH LOUGHRIDGE Accounting Assistant • STEPHANIE HOCUTT PR Ass

SUICIDE RISK Volume Three, August 2014. Published by BOOM! Studios, a division of Boom Entertainment, Inc. and Mike

A catalog record of this book is available from OCLC and from the BOOM! Studios website, www.boom-studios.com, on the Librarians Page.

BOOM! Studios, 5670 Wilshire Boulevard, Suite 450, Los Angeles, CA 90036-5679. Printed in Canada. First Printing. ISBN: 978-1-60886-399-0 eISBN: 978-1-61398-253-2

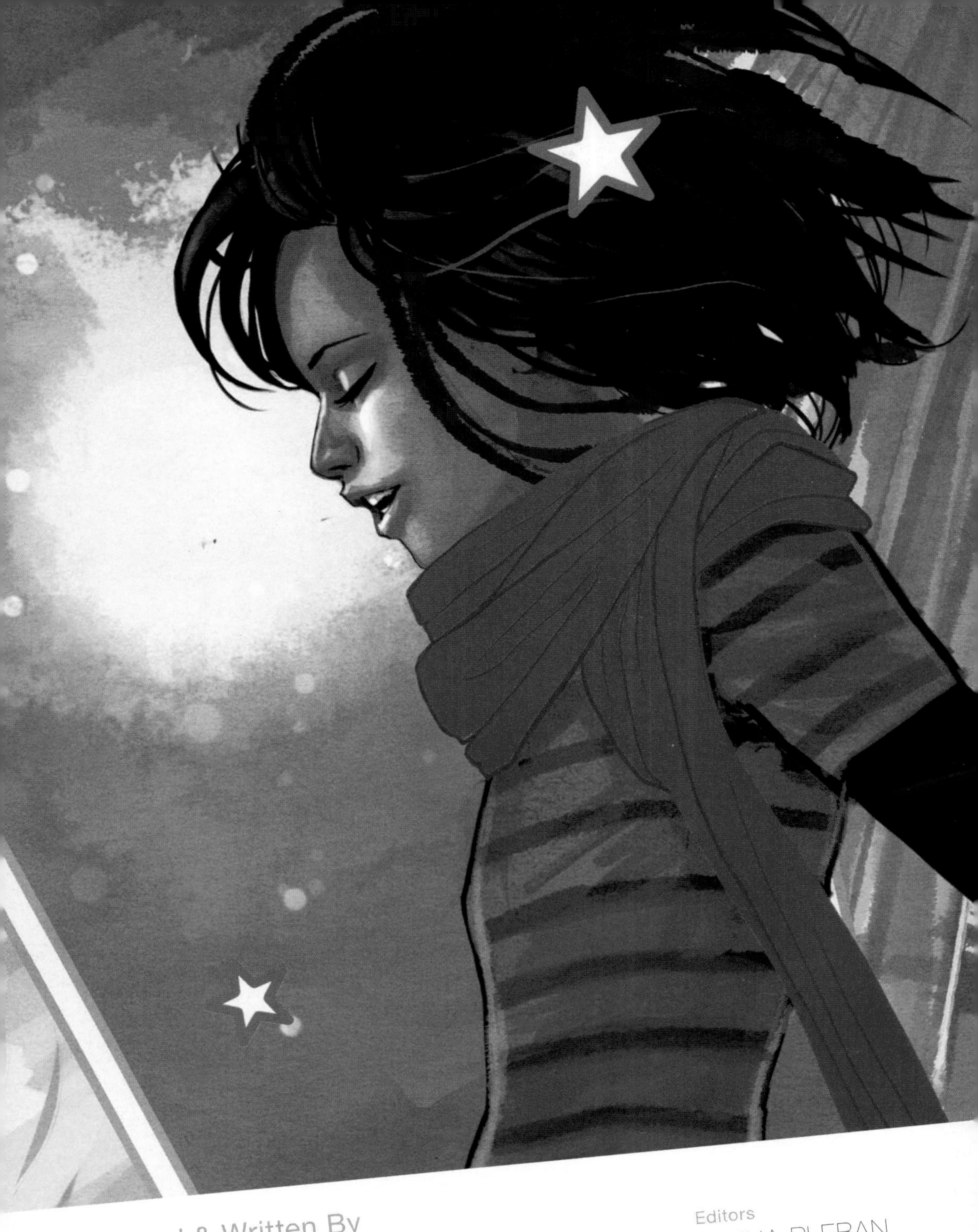

Created & Written By
MIKE CAREY

Art By
LENA CASAGRANDE
(CHAPTERS 11-13)
with ink assists by MICHELE PASTA
(CHAPTER 13)
JORGE COELHO
(CHAPTER 10)

Colors By
ANDREW ELDER
(CHAPTERS 11-13)
KELLY FITZPATRICK
(CHAPTER 10)

Letters By
ED DUKESHIRE

Editors
DAFNA PLEBAN
MATT GAGNON

Cover By
TOMMY LEE EDWARDS

Trade Design By
EMI YONEMURA BROWN

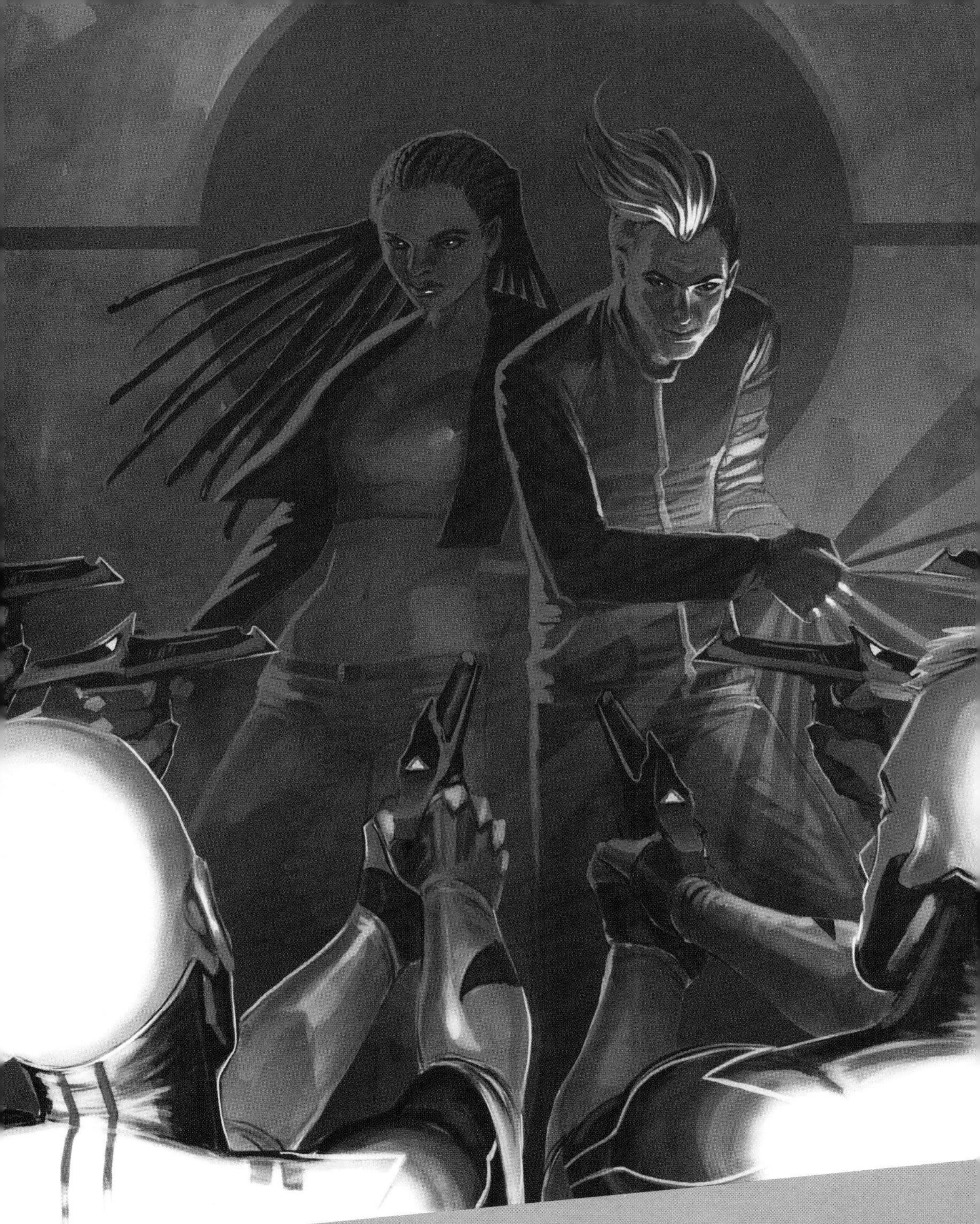

"A LIFE THAT'S **CRASH-LANDED** LEAVES
A SMOKE TRAIL THEY CAN FOLLOW."
Chapter 10

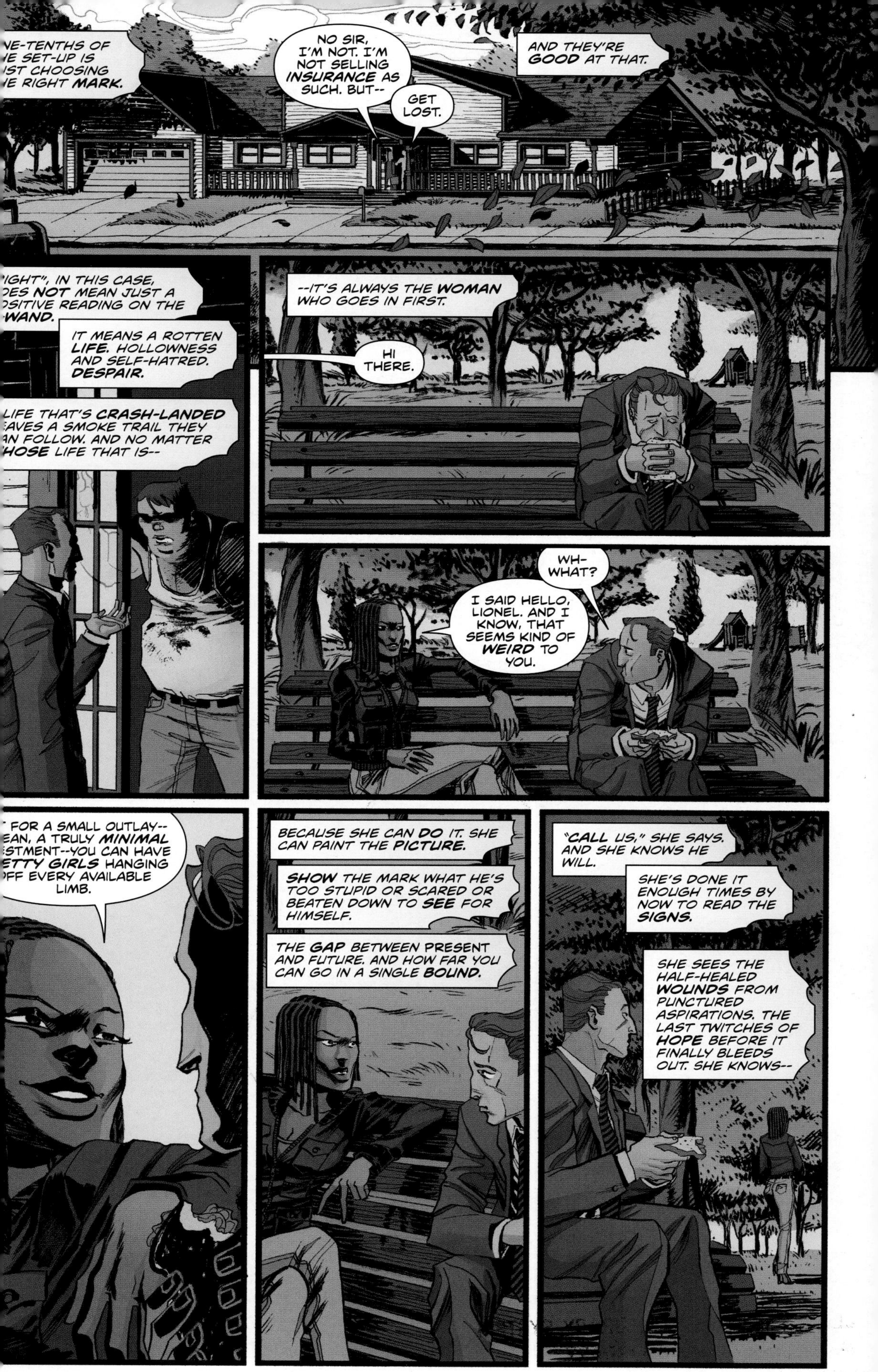
NE-TENTHS OF
IE SET-UP IS
IST CHOOSING
IE RIGHT MARK.
NO SIR, I'M NOT. I'M NOT SELLING INSURANCE AS SUCH. BUT--
GET LOST.
AND THEY'RE GOOD AT THAT.
IGHT", IN THIS CASE, DES NOT MEAN JUST A OSITIVE READING ON THE WAND.
IT MEANS A ROTTEN LIFE. HOLLOWNESS AND SELF-HATRED. DESPAIR.
LIFE THAT'S CRASH-LANDED EAVES A SMOKE TRAIL THEY AN FOLLOW. AND NO MATTER HOSE LIFE THAT IS--
--IT'S ALWAYS THE WOMAN WHO GOES IN FIRST.
HI THERE.
WH- WHAT?
I SAID HELLO, LIONEL. AND I KNOW, THAT SEEMS KIND OF WEIRD TO YOU.
FOR A SMALL OUTLAY-- EAN, A TRULY MINIMAL ESTMENT--YOU CAN HAVE ETTY GIRLS HANGING FF EVERY AVAILABLE LIMB.
BECAUSE SHE CAN DO IT. SHE CAN PAINT THE PICTURE.
SHOW THE MARK WHAT HE'S TOO STUPID OR SCARED OR BEATEN DOWN TO SEE FOR HIMSELF.
THE GAP BETWEEN PRESENT AND FUTURE. AND HOW FAR YOU CAN GO IN A SINGLE BOUND.
"CALL US," SHE SAYS. AND SHE KNOWS HE WILL.
SHE'S DONE IT ENOUGH TIMES BY NOW TO READ THE SIGNS.
SHE SEES THE HALF-HEALED WOUNDS FROM PUNCTURED ASPIRATIONS. THE LAST TWITCHES OF HOPE BEFORE IT FINALLY BLEEDS OUT. SHE KNOWS--

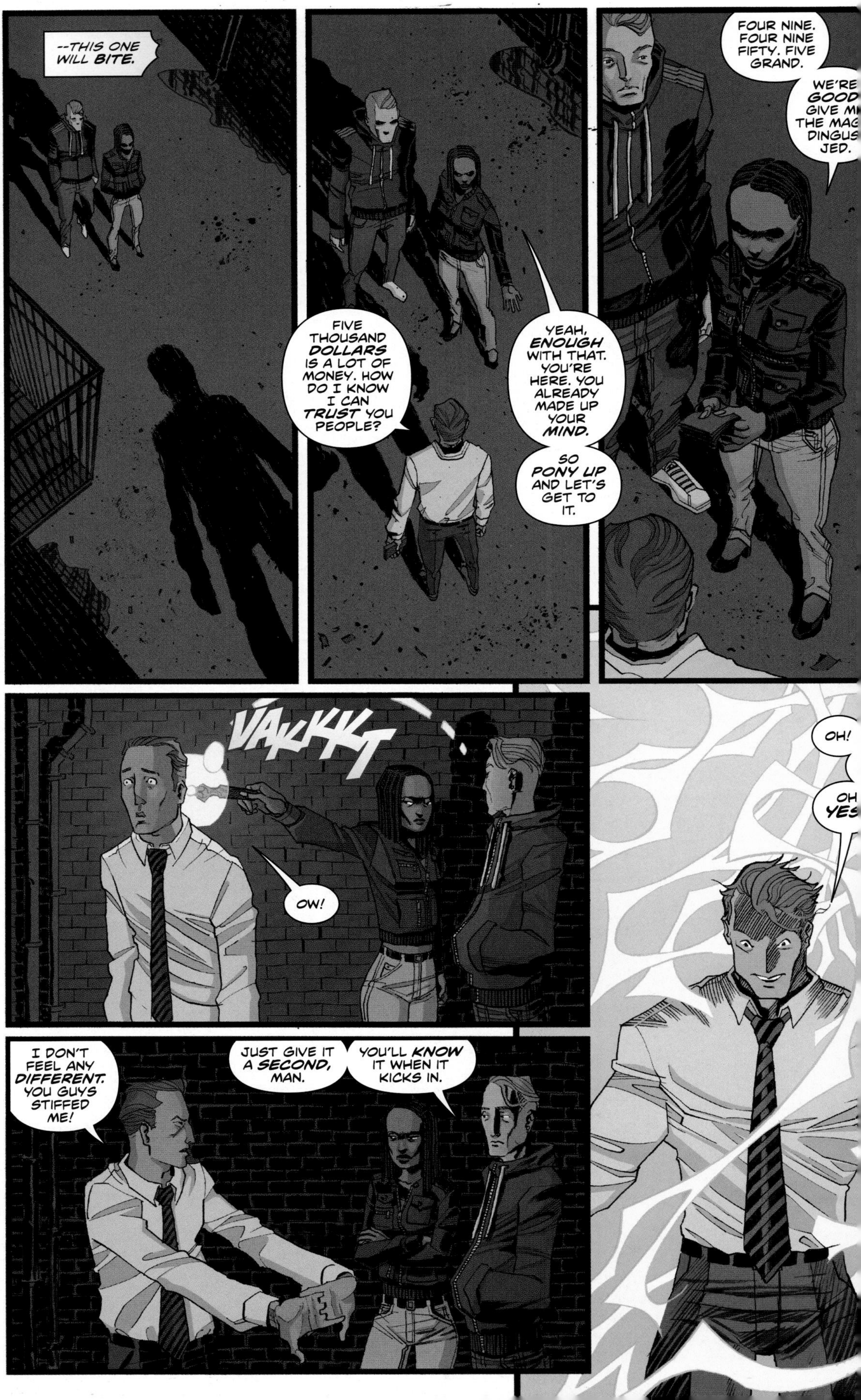
--THIS ONE WILL BITE.
FIVE THOUSAND DOLLARS IS A LOT OF MONEY. HOW DO I KNOW I CAN TRUST YOU PEOPLE?
YEAH, ENOUGH WITH THAT. YOU'RE HERE. YOU ALREADY MADE UP YOUR MIND.
SO PONY UP AND LET'S GET TO IT.
FOUR NINE. FOUR NINE FIFTY. FIVE GRAND.
VAKKKT
OW!
I DON'T FEEL ANY DIFFERENT. YOU GUYS STIFFED ME!
JUST GIVE IT A SECOND, MAN.
YOU'LL KNOW IT WHEN IT KICKS IN.
OH!

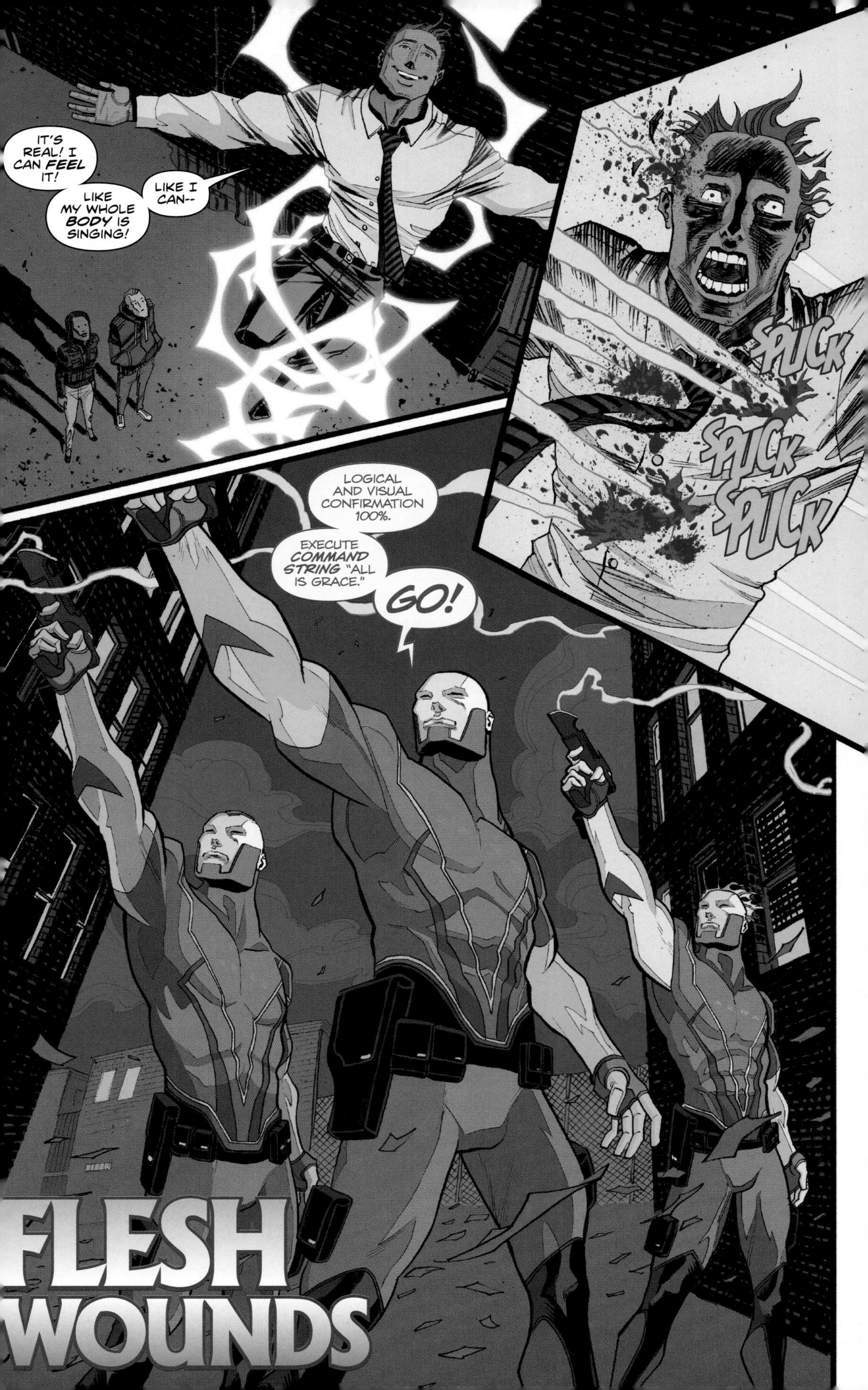
IT'S REAL! I CAN FEEL IT!
LIKE MY WHOLE BODY IS SINGING!
LIKE I CAN--
SPLUCK
SPLUCK
SPLUCK
LOGICAL AND VISUAL CONFIRMATION 100%.
EXECUTE COMMAND STRING "ALL IS GRACE."
GO!
FLESH WOUNDS

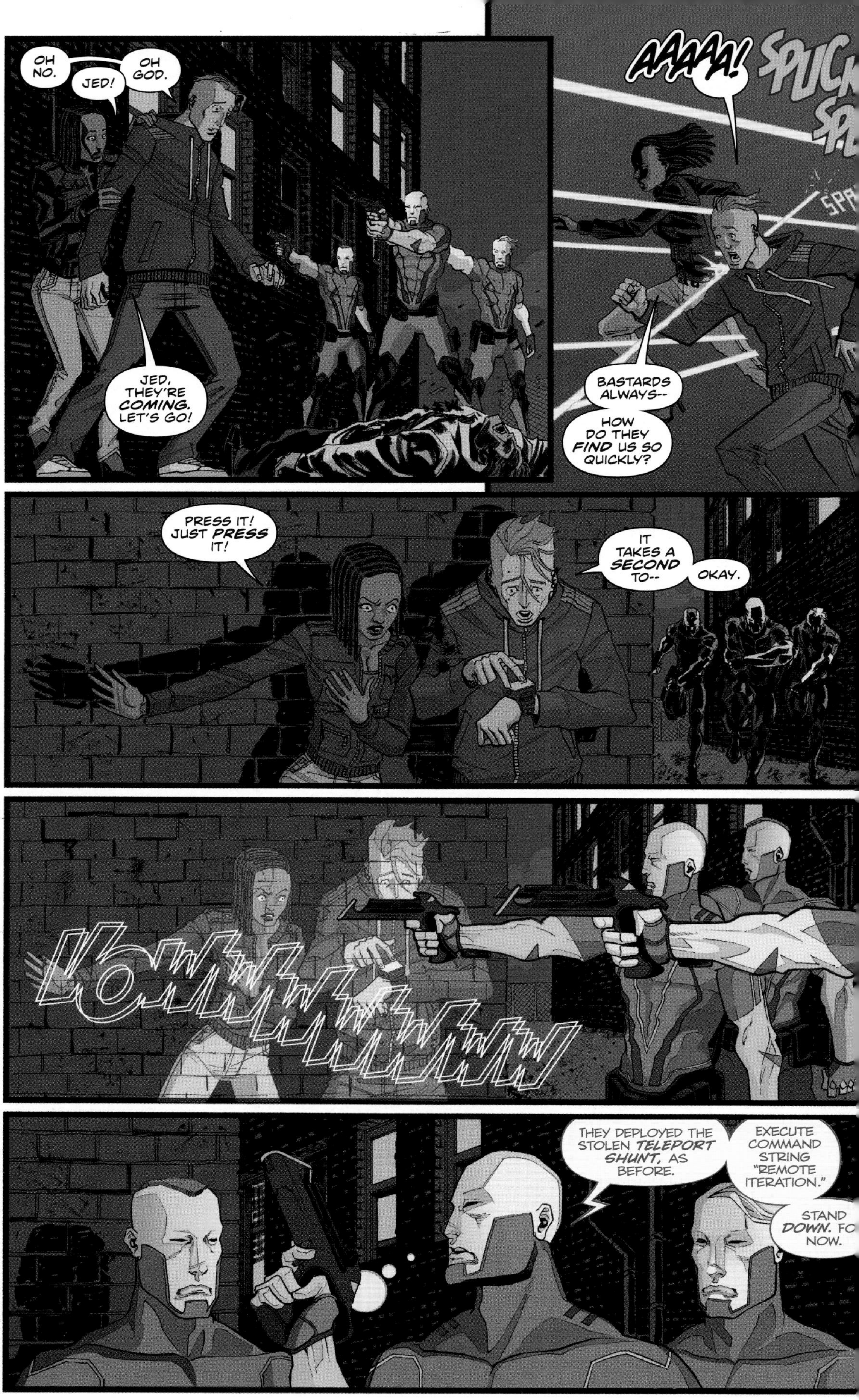

OH NO.
JED!
OH GOD.
JED, THEY'RE COMING. LET'S GO!
AAAAA!
SPUCK
SPL
SPA
BASTARDS ALWAYS--
HOW DO THEY FIND US SO QUICKLY?
PRESS IT! JUST PRESS IT!
IT TAKES A SECOND TO--
OKAY.
LOWWWWWWWWWWWWWW
THEY DEPLOYED THE STOLEN TELEPORT SHUNT, AS BEFORE.
EXECUTE COMMAND STRING "REMOTE ITERATION."
STAND DOWN. FO NOW.

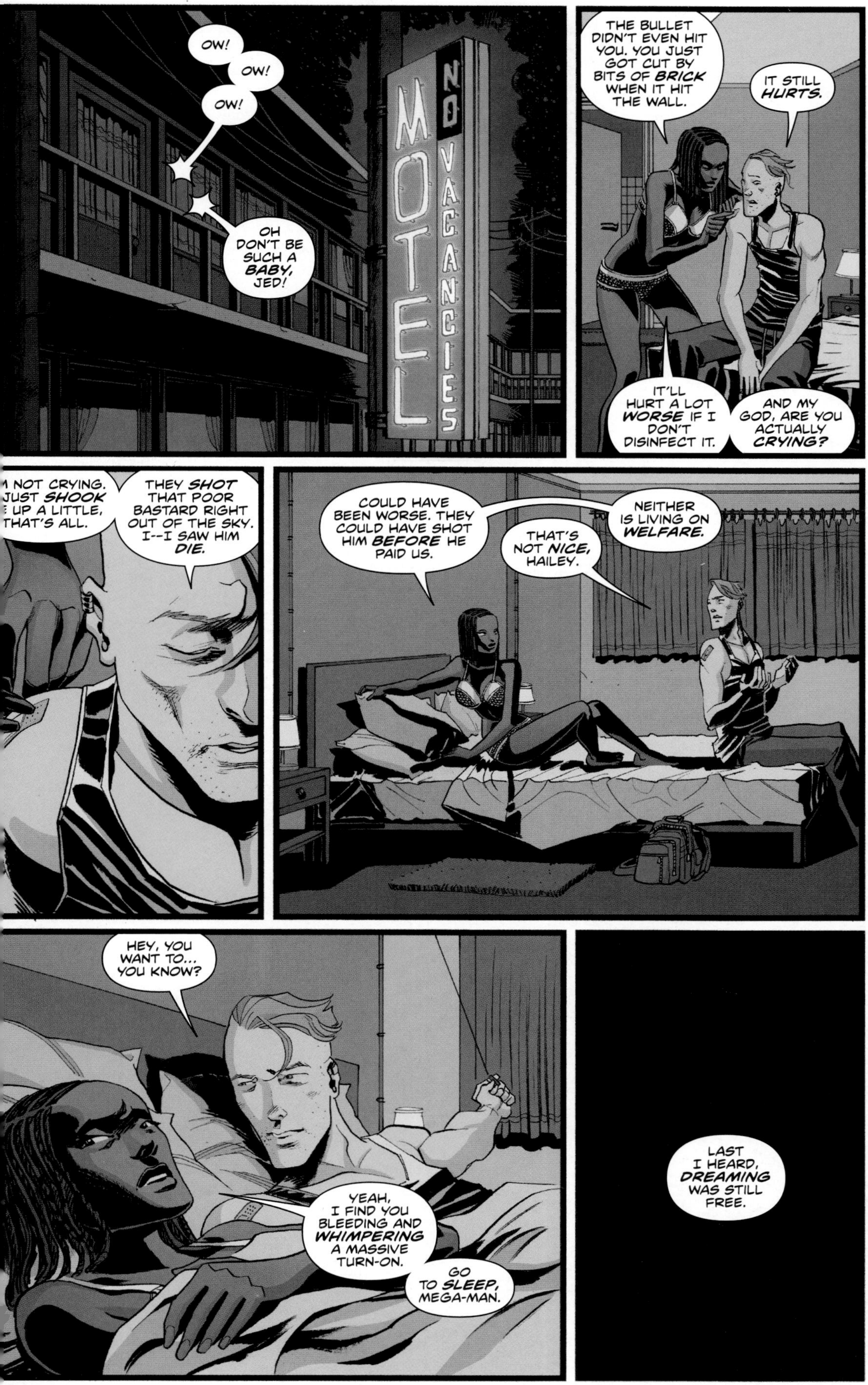
OW!
OW!
OW!
OH DON'T BE SUCH A BABY, JED!
MOTEL
NO VACANCIES
THE BULLET DIDN'T EVEN HIT YOU. YOU JUST GOT CUT BY BITS OF BRICK WHEN IT HIT THE WALL.
IT STILL HURTS.
IT'LL HURT A LOT WORSE IF I DON'T DISINFECT IT.
AND MY GOD, ARE YOU ACTUALLY CRYING?
M NOT CRYING. JUST SHOOK UP A LITTLE, THAT'S ALL.
THEY SHOT THAT POOR BASTARD RIGHT OUT OF THE SKY. I--I SAW HIM DIE.
COULD HAVE BEEN WORSE. THEY COULD HAVE SHOT HIM BEFORE HE PAID US.
THAT'S NOT NICE, HAILEY.
NEITHER IS LIVING ON WELFARE.
HEY, YOU WANT TO... YOU KNOW?
YEAH, I FIND YOU BLEEDING AND WHIMPERING A MASSIVE TURN-ON.
GO TO SLEEP, MEGA-MAN.
LAST I HEARD, DREAMING WAS STILL FREE.

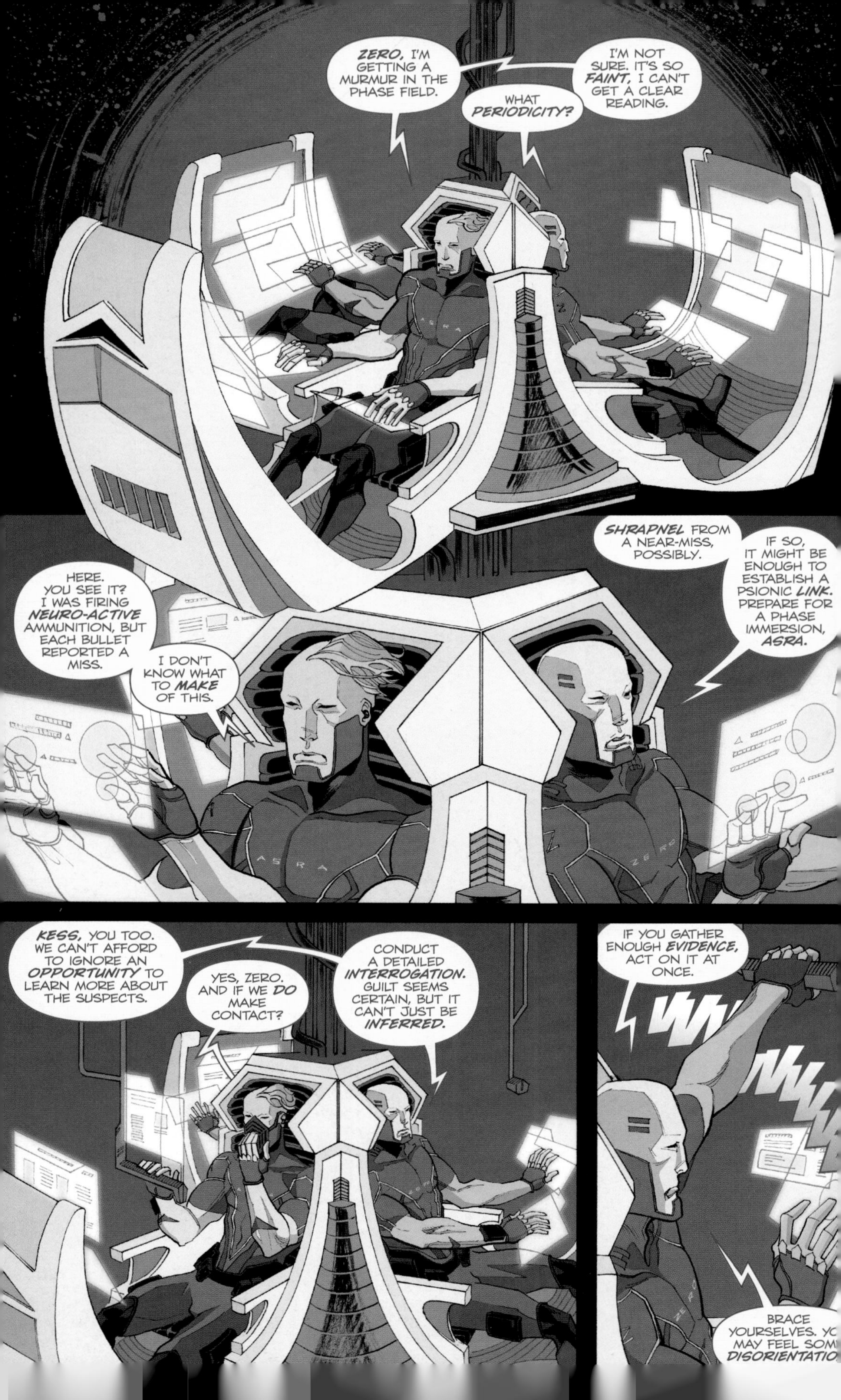
ZERO, I'M GETTING A MURMUR IN THE PHASE FIELD.
WHAT PERIODICITY?
I'M NOT SURE. IT'S SO FAINT, I CAN'T GET A CLEAR READING.
HERE. YOU SEE IT? I WAS FIRING NEURO-ACTIVE AMMUNITION, BUT EACH BULLET REPORTED A MISS.
I DON'T KNOW WHAT TO MAKE OF THIS.
SHRAPNEL FROM A NEAR-MISS, POSSIBLY.
IF SO, IT MIGHT BE ENOUGH TO ESTABLISH A PSIONIC LINK. PREPARE FOR A PHASE IMMERSION, ASRA.
KESS, YOU TOO. WE CAN'T AFFORD TO IGNORE AN OPPORTUNITY TO LEARN MORE ABOUT THE SUSPECTS.
YES, ZERO. AND IF WE DO MAKE CONTACT?
CONDUCT A DETAILED INTERROGATION. GUILT SEEMS CERTAIN, BUT IT CAN'T JUST BE INFERRED.
IF YOU GATHER ENOUGH EVIDENCE, ACT ON IT AT ONCE.
BRACE YOURSELVES. YO MAY FEEL SOM DISORIENTATIO

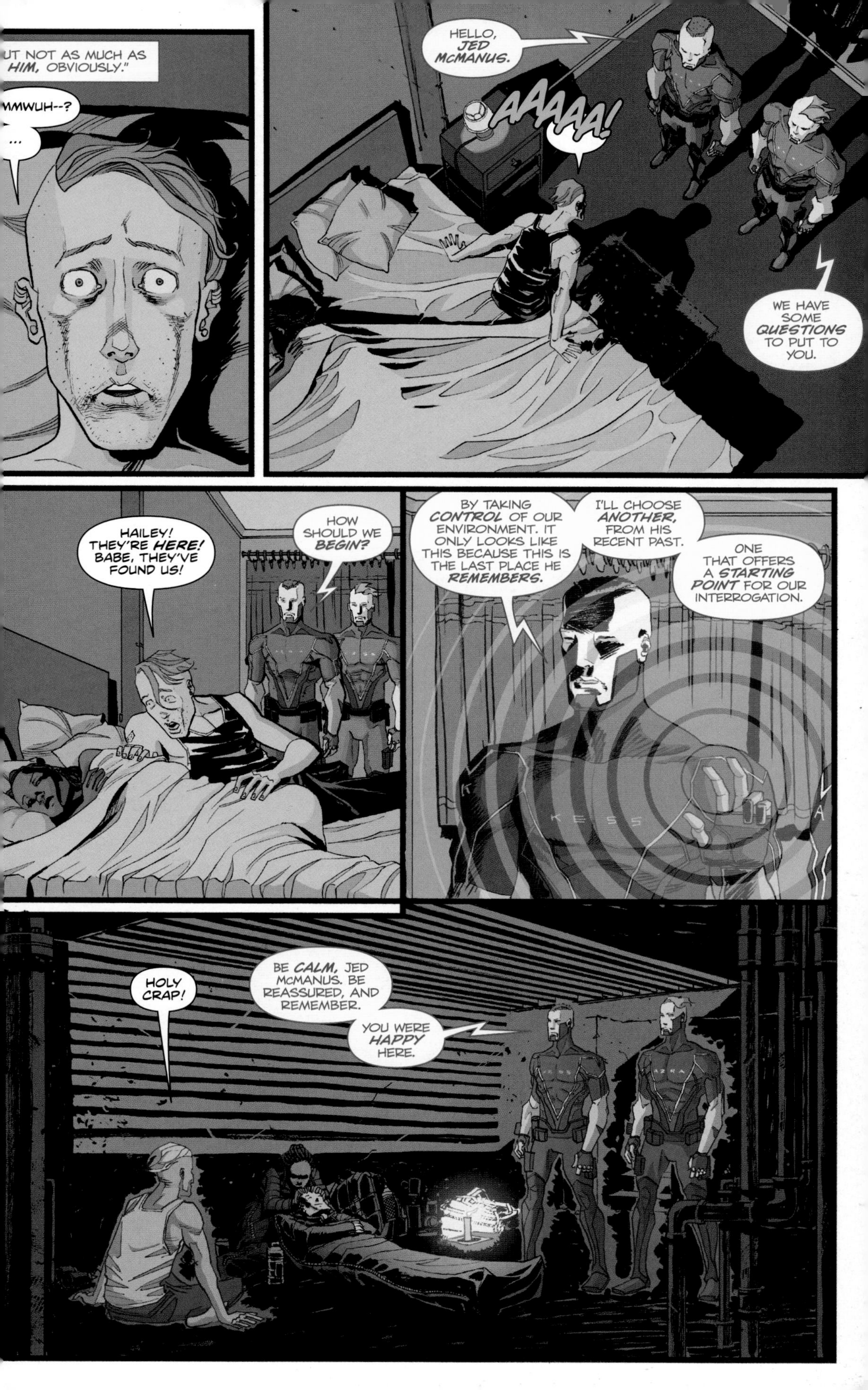
UT NOT AS MUCH AS HIM, OBVIOUSLY."
MMWUH--?
...
HELLO, JED McMANUS.
AAAAA!
WE HAVE SOME QUESTIONS TO PUT TO YOU.
HAILEY! THEY'RE HERE! BABE, THEY'VE FOUND US!
HOW SHOULD WE BEGIN?
BY TAKING CONTROL OF OUR ENVIRONMENT. IT ONLY LOOKS LIKE THIS BECAUSE THIS IS THE LAST PLACE HE REMEMBERS.
I'LL CHOOSE ANOTHER, FROM HIS RECENT PAST.
ONE THAT OFFERS A STARTING POINT FOR OUR INTERROGATION.
HOLY CRAP!
BE CALM, JED McMANUS. BE REASSURED, AND REMEMBER.
YOU WERE HAPPY HERE.

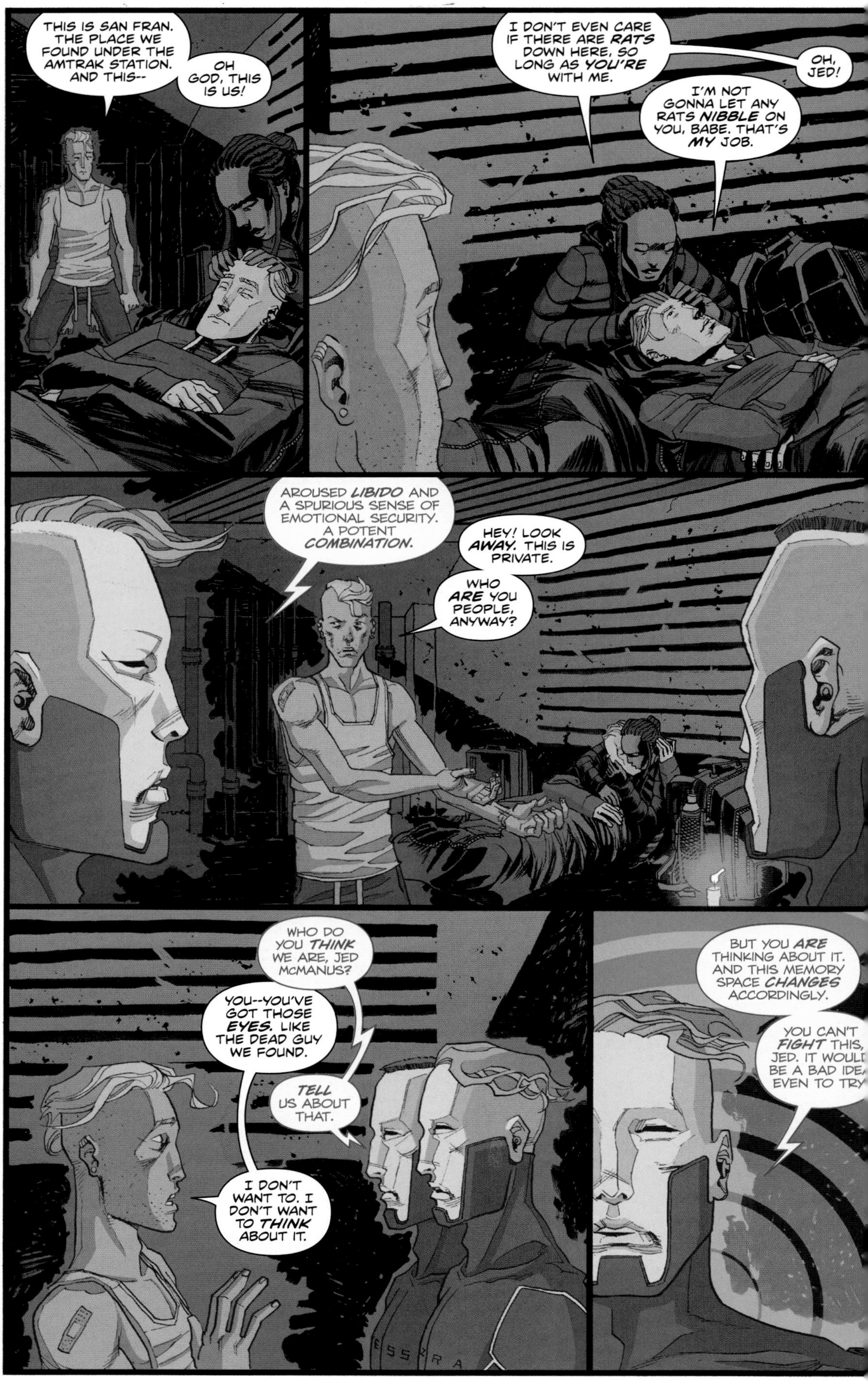
THIS IS SAN FRAN. THE PLACE WE FOUND UNDER THE AMTRAK STATION. AND THIS--
OH GOD, THIS IS US!
I DON'T EVEN CARE IF THERE ARE RATS DOWN HERE, SO LONG AS YOU'RE WITH ME.
OH, JED!
I'M NOT GONNA LET ANY RATS NIBBLE ON YOU, BABE. THAT'S MY JOB.
AROUSED LIBIDO AND A SPURIOUS SENSE OF EMOTIONAL SECURITY. A POTENT COMBINATION.
HEY! LOOK AWAY. THIS IS PRIVATE.
WHO ARE YOU PEOPLE, ANYWAY?
WHO DO YOU THINK WE ARE, JED McMANUS?
YOU--YOU'VE GOT THOSE EYES. LIKE THE DEAD GUY WE FOUND.
TELL US ABOUT THAT.
I DON'T WANT TO. I DON'T WANT TO THINK ABOUT IT.
BUT YOU ARE THINKING ABOUT IT. AND THIS MEMORY SPACE CHANGES ACCORDINGLY.
YOU CAN'T FIGHT THIS, JED. IT WOULI BE A BAD IDE, EVEN TO TRY
ESSZRA

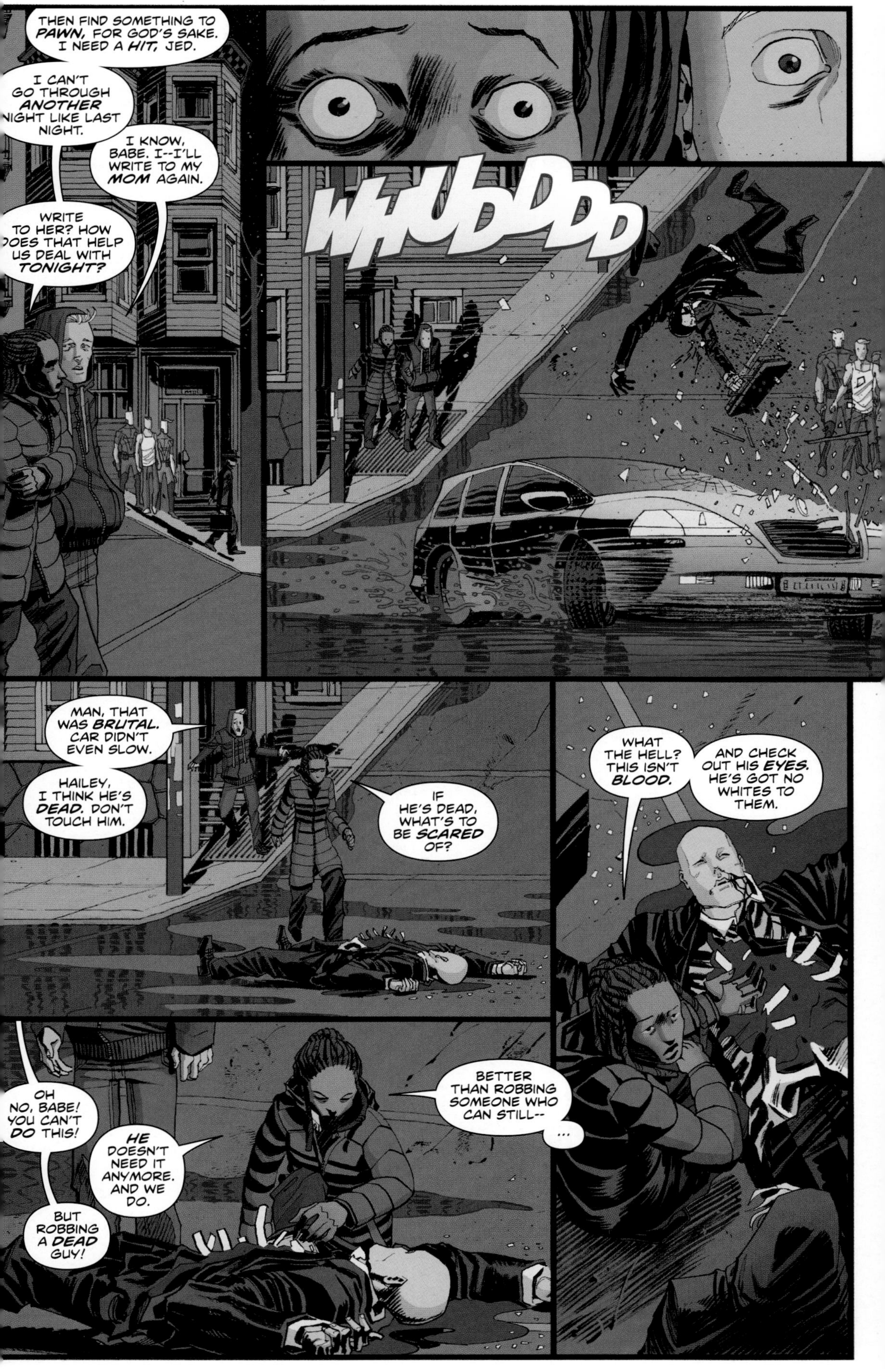

THEN FIND SOMETHING TO PAWN, FOR GOD'S SAKE. I NEED A HIT, JED.
I CAN'T GO THROUGH ANOTHER NIGHT LIKE LAST NIGHT.
I KNOW, BABE. I--I'LL WRITE TO MY MOM AGAIN.
WRITE TO HER? HOW DOES THAT HELP US DEAL WITH TONIGHT?
WHUDDDD
MAN, THAT WAS BRUTAL. CAR DIDN'T EVEN SLOW.
HAILEY, I THINK HE'S DEAD. DON'T TOUCH HIM.
IF HE'S DEAD, WHAT'S TO BE SCARED OF?
WHAT THE HELL? THIS ISN'T BLOOD.
AND CHECK OUT HIS EYES. HE'S GOT NO WHITES TO THEM.
OH NO, BABE! YOU CAN'T DO THIS!
HE DOESN'T NEED IT ANYMORE. AND WE DO.
BUT ROBBING A DEAD GUY!
BETTER THAN ROBBING SOMEONE WHO CAN STILL--
...

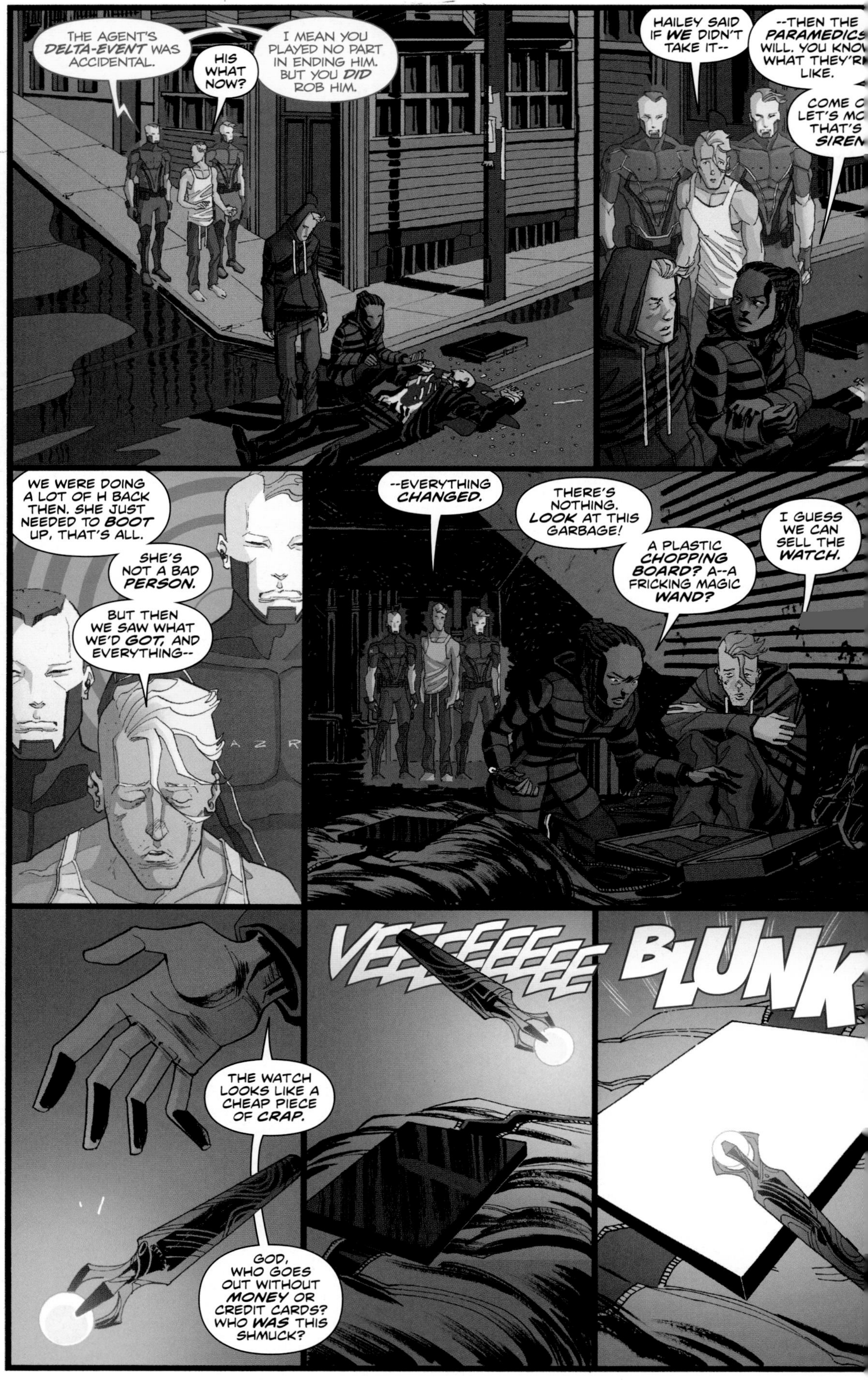

THE AGENT'S DELTA-EVENT WAS ACCIDENTAL.
HIS WHAT NOW?
I MEAN YOU PLAYED NO PART IN ENDING HIM. BUT YOU DID ROB HIM.
HAILEY SAID IF WE DIDN'T TAKE IT--
--THEN THE PARAMEDICS WILL. YOU KNOW WHAT THEY'RE LIKE.
WE WERE DOING A LOT OF H BACK THEN. SHE JUST NEEDED TO BOOT UP, THAT'S ALL.
SHE'S NOT A BAD PERSON.
BUT THEN WE SAW WHAT WE'D GOT, AND EVERYTHING--
--EVERYTHING CHANGED.
THERE'S NOTHING. LOOK AT THIS GARBAGE!
A PLASTIC CHOPPING BOARD? A--A FRICKING MAGIC WAND?
I GUESS WE CAN SELL THE WATCH.
THE WATCH LOOKS LIKE A CHEAP PIECE OF CRAP.
GOD, WHO GOES OUT WITHOUT MONEY OR CREDIT CARDS? WHO WAS THIS SHMUCK?
VEEEEEEEE
BLUNK

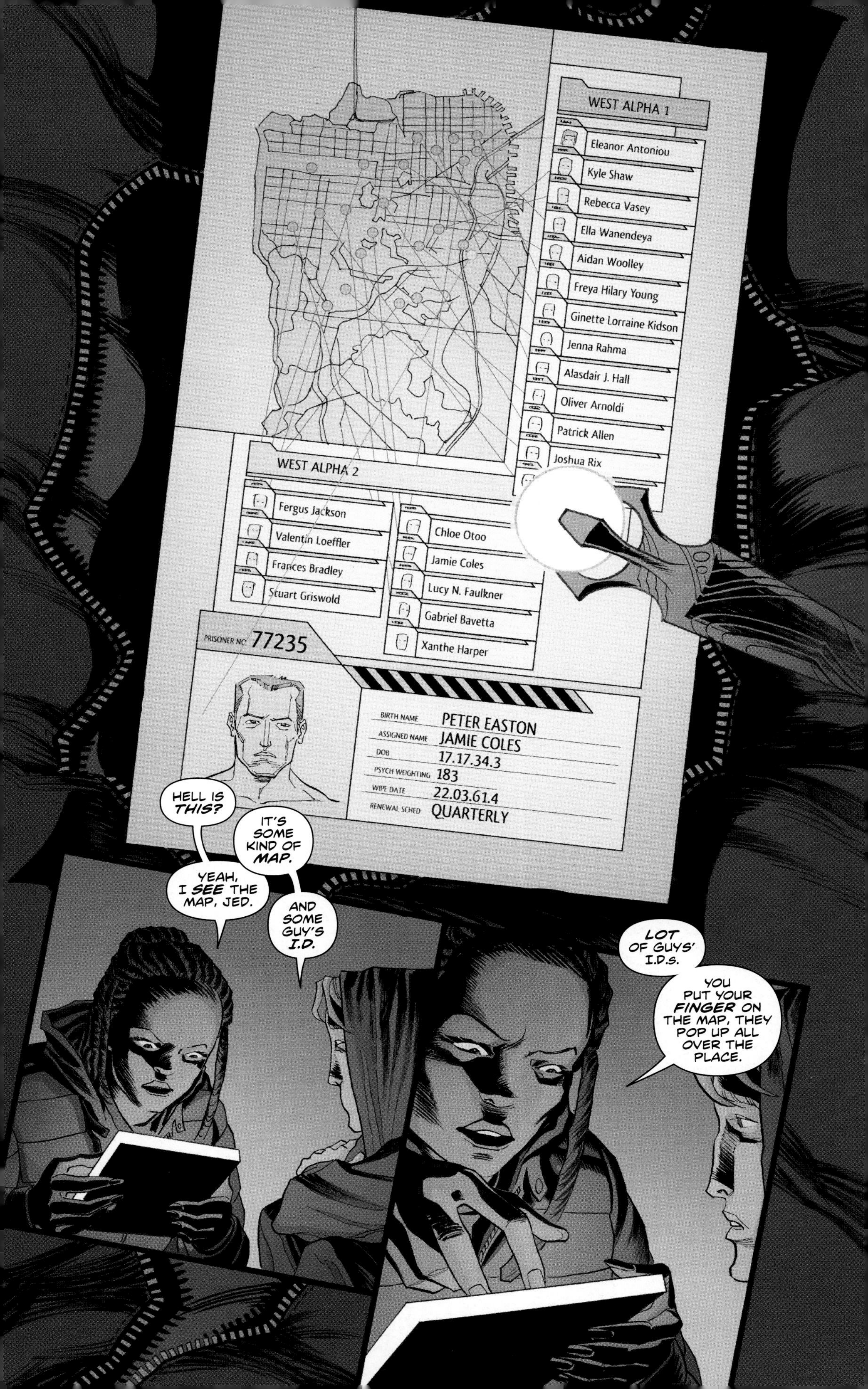

WEST ALPHA 1
Eleanor Antoniou
Kyle Shaw
Rebecca Vasey
Ella Wanendeya
Aidan Woolley
Freya Hilary Young
Ginette Lorraine Kidson
Jenna Rahma
Alasdair J. Hall
Oliver Arnoldi
Patrick Allen
Joshua Rix
WEST ALPHA 2
Fergus Jackson
Valentin Loeffler
Frances Bradley
Stuart Griswold
Chloe Otoo
Jamie Coles
Lucy N. Faulkner
Gabriel Bavetta
Xanthe Harper
PRISONER NO 77235
BIRTH NAME PETER EASTON
ASSIGNED NAME JAMIE COLES
DOB 17.17.34.3
PSYCH WEIGHTING 183
WIPE DATE 22.03.61.4
RENEWAL SCHED QUARTERLY
HELL IS THIS?
IT'S SOME KIND OF MAP.
YEAH, I SEE THE MAP, JED.
AND SOME GUY'S I.D.
LOT OF GUYS' I.D.s.
YOU PUT YOUR FINGER ON THE MAP, THEY POP UP ALL OVER THE PLACE.

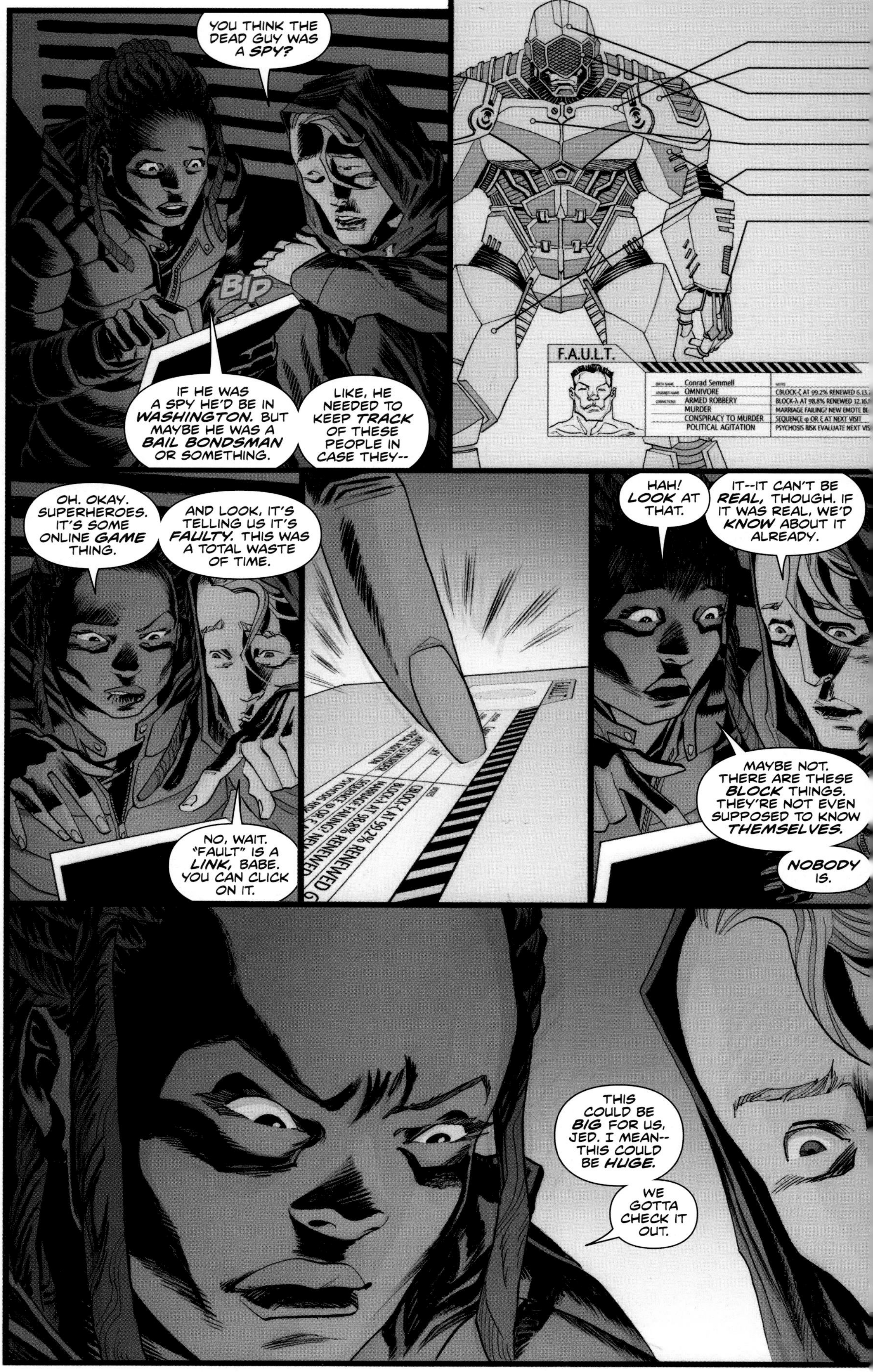
YOU THINK THE DEAD GUY WAS A *SPY?*
BIP
IF HE WAS A SPY HE'D BE IN *WASHINGTON.* BUT MAYBE HE WAS A *BAIL BONDSMAN* OR SOMETHING.
LIKE, HE NEEDED TO KEEP *TRACK* OF THESE PEOPLE IN CASE THEY--
F.A.U.L.T.
Conrad Semmell
OMNIVORE
ARMED ROBBERY
MURDER
CONSPIRACY TO MURDER
POLITICAL AGITATION
CBLOCK-ζ AT 99.2% RENEWED
BLOCK-λ AT 98.8% RENEWED
MARRIAGE FAILING? NEW EMOTE
SEQUENCE φ OR ζ AT NEXT VISIT
PSYCHOSIS RISK EVALUATE NEXT
OH. OKAY. SUPERHEROES. IT'S SOME ONLINE *GAME* THING.
AND LOOK, IT'S TELLING US IT'S *FAULTY.* THIS WAS A TOTAL WASTE OF TIME.
NO, WAIT. "FAULT" IS A *LINK,* BABE. YOU CAN CLICK ON IT.
HAH! *LOOK* AT THAT.
IT--IT CAN'T BE *REAL,* THOUGH. IF IT WAS REAL, WE'D *KNOW* ABOUT IT ALREADY.
MAYBE NOT. THERE ARE THESE *BLOCK* THINGS. THEY'RE NOT EVEN SUPPOSED TO KNOW *THEMSELVES.*
NOBODY IS.
THIS COULD BE *BIG* FOR US, JED. I MEAN-- THIS COULD BE *HUGE.*
WE GOTTA CHECK IT OUT.

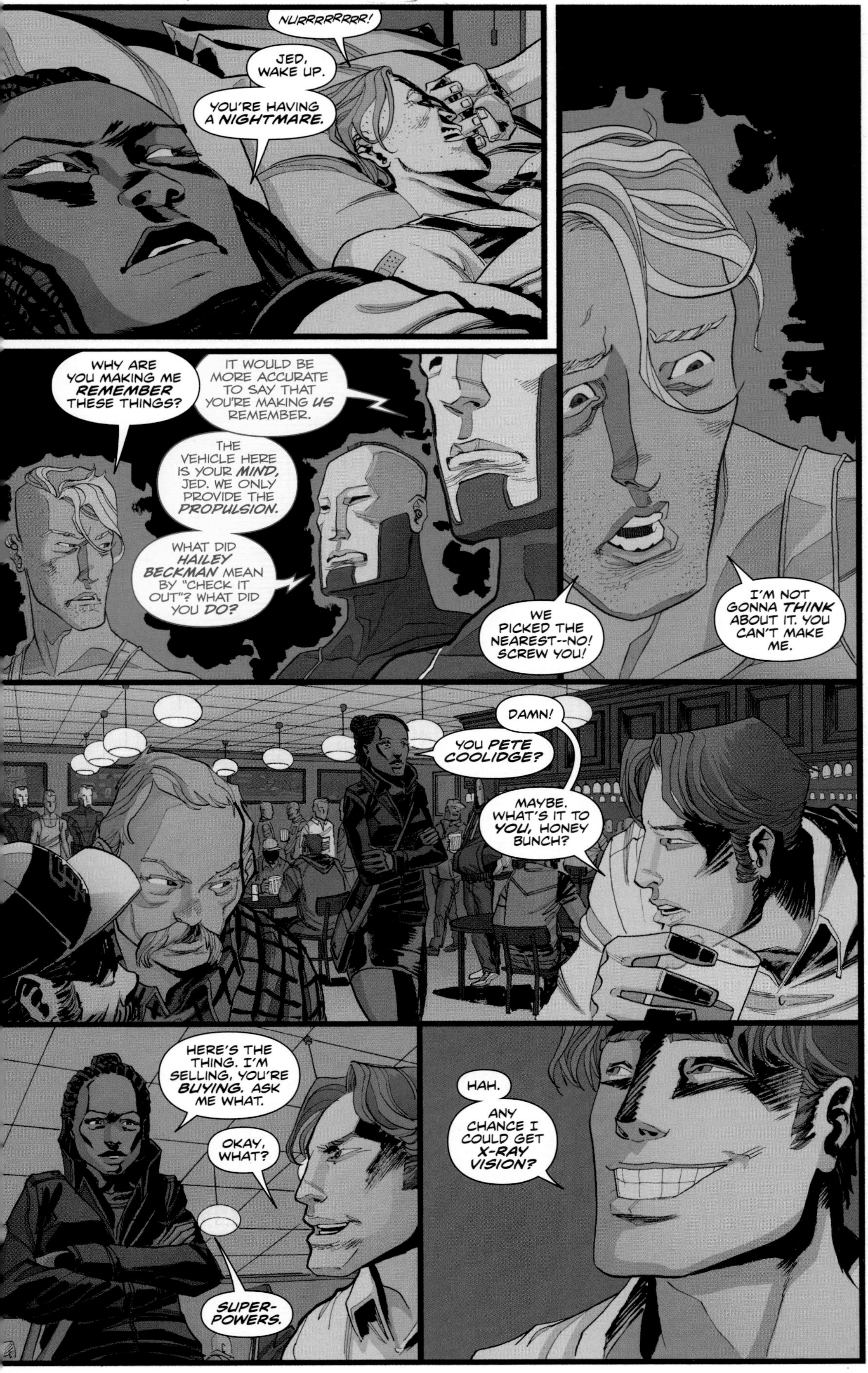
NURRRRRRRR!
JED, WAKE UP.
YOU'RE HAVING A NIGHTMARE.
WHY ARE YOU MAKING ME REMEMBER THESE THINGS?
IT WOULD BE MORE ACCURATE TO SAY THAT YOU'RE MAKING US REMEMBER.
THE VEHICLE HERE IS YOUR MIND, JED. WE ONLY PROVIDE THE PROPULSION.
WHAT DID HAILEY BECKMAN MEAN BY "CHECK IT OUT"? WHAT DID YOU DO?
WE PICKED THE NEAREST--NO! SCREW YOU!
I'M NOT GONNA THINK ABOUT IT. YOU CAN'T MAKE ME.
DAMN!
YOU PETE COOLIDGE?
MAYBE. WHAT'S IT TO YOU, HONEY BUNCH?
HERE'S THE THING. I'M SELLING, YOU'RE BUYING. ASK ME WHAT.
OKAY, WHAT?
SUPER-POWERS.
HAH.
ANY CHANCE I COULD GET X-RAY VISION?

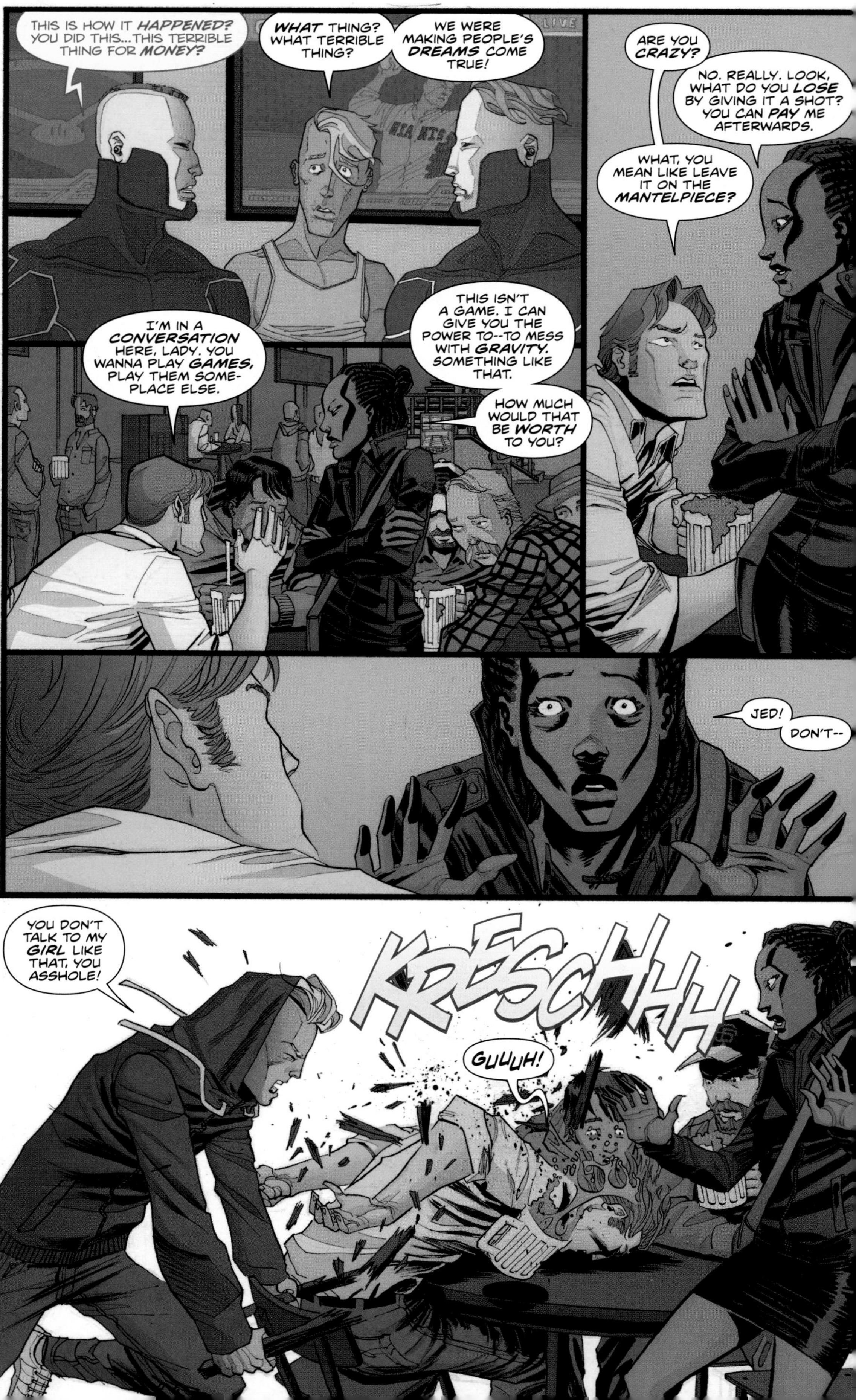
THIS IS HOW IT HAPPENED? YOU DID THIS...THIS TERRIBLE THING FOR MONEY?
WHAT THING? WHAT TERRIBLE THING?
WE WERE MAKING PEOPLE'S DREAMS COME TRUE!
LIVE
ARE YOU CRAZY?
NO. REALLY. LOOK, WHAT DO YOU LOSE BY GIVING IT A SHOT? YOU CAN PAY ME AFTERWARDS.
WHAT, YOU MEAN LIKE LEAVE IT ON THE MANTELPIECE?
I'M IN A CONVERSATION HERE, LADY. YOU WANNA PLAY GAMES, PLAY THEM SOME-PLACE ELSE.
THIS ISN'T A GAME. I CAN GIVE YOU THE POWER TO--TO MESS WITH GRAVITY. SOMETHING LIKE THAT.
HOW MUCH WOULD THAT BE WORTH TO YOU?
JED!
DON'T--
YOU DON'T TALK TO MY GIRL LIKE THAT, YOU ASSHOLE!
KRESCHHH
GUUUH!

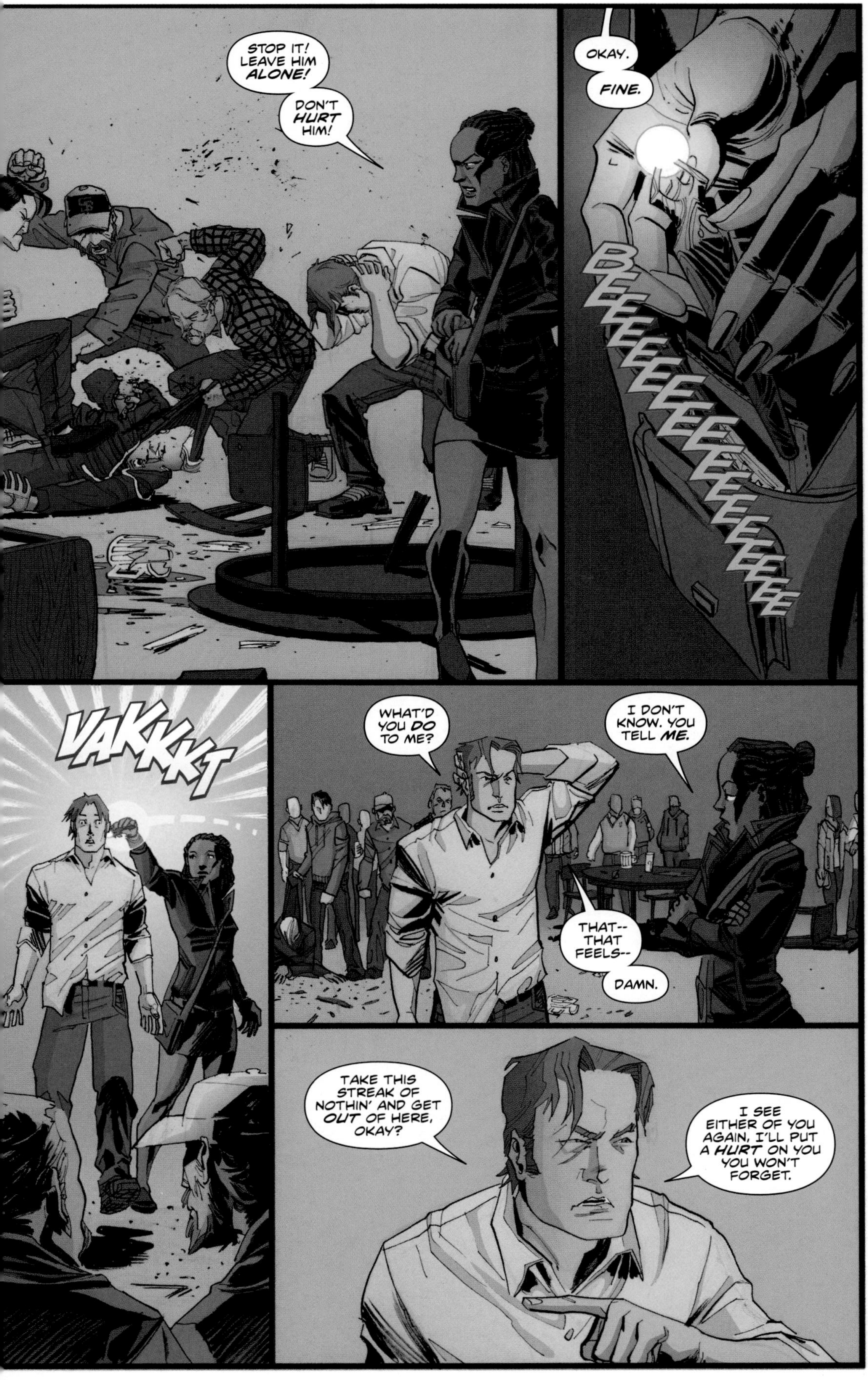
STOP IT! LEAVE HIM ALONE!
DON'T HURT HIM!
OKAY.
FINE.
BEEEEEEEEEEEEEEEE
VAKKKT
WHAT'D YOU DO TO ME?
I DON'T KNOW. YOU TELL ME.
THAT-- THAT FEELS--
DAMN.
TAKE THIS STREAK OF NOTHIN' AND GET OUT OF HERE, OKAY?
I SEE EITHER OF YOU AGAIN, I'LL PUT A HURT ON YOU YOU WON'T FORGET.

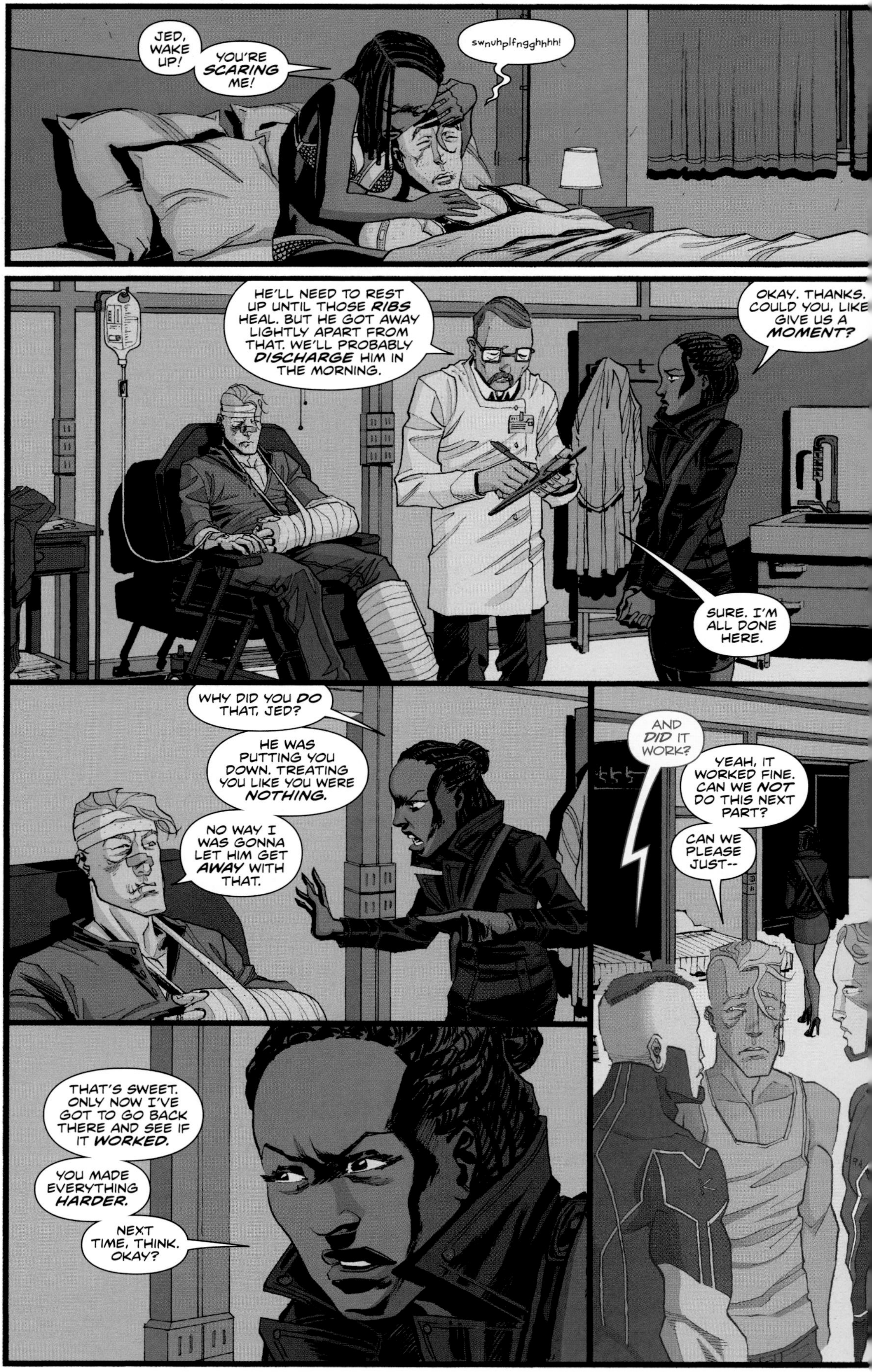

JED, WAKE UP!
YOU'RE SCARING ME!
swnuhplfngghhhh!
HE'LL NEED TO REST UP UNTIL THOSE RIBS HEAL. BUT HE GOT AWAY LIGHTLY APART FROM THAT. WE'LL PROBABLY DISCHARGE HIM IN THE MORNING.
OKAY. THANKS. COULD YOU, LIKE GIVE US A MOMENT?
SURE. I'M ALL DONE HERE.
WHY DID YOU DO THAT, JED?
HE WAS PUTTING YOU DOWN. TREATING YOU LIKE YOU WERE NOTHING.
NO WAY I WAS GONNA LET HIM GET AWAY WITH THAT.
THAT'S SWEET. ONLY NOW I'VE GOT TO GO BACK THERE AND SEE IF IT WORKED.
YOU MADE EVERYTHING HARDER.
NEXT TIME, THINK. OKAY?
AND DID IT WORK?
YEAH, IT WORKED FINE. CAN WE NOT DO THIS NEXT PART?
CAN WE PLEASE JUST--

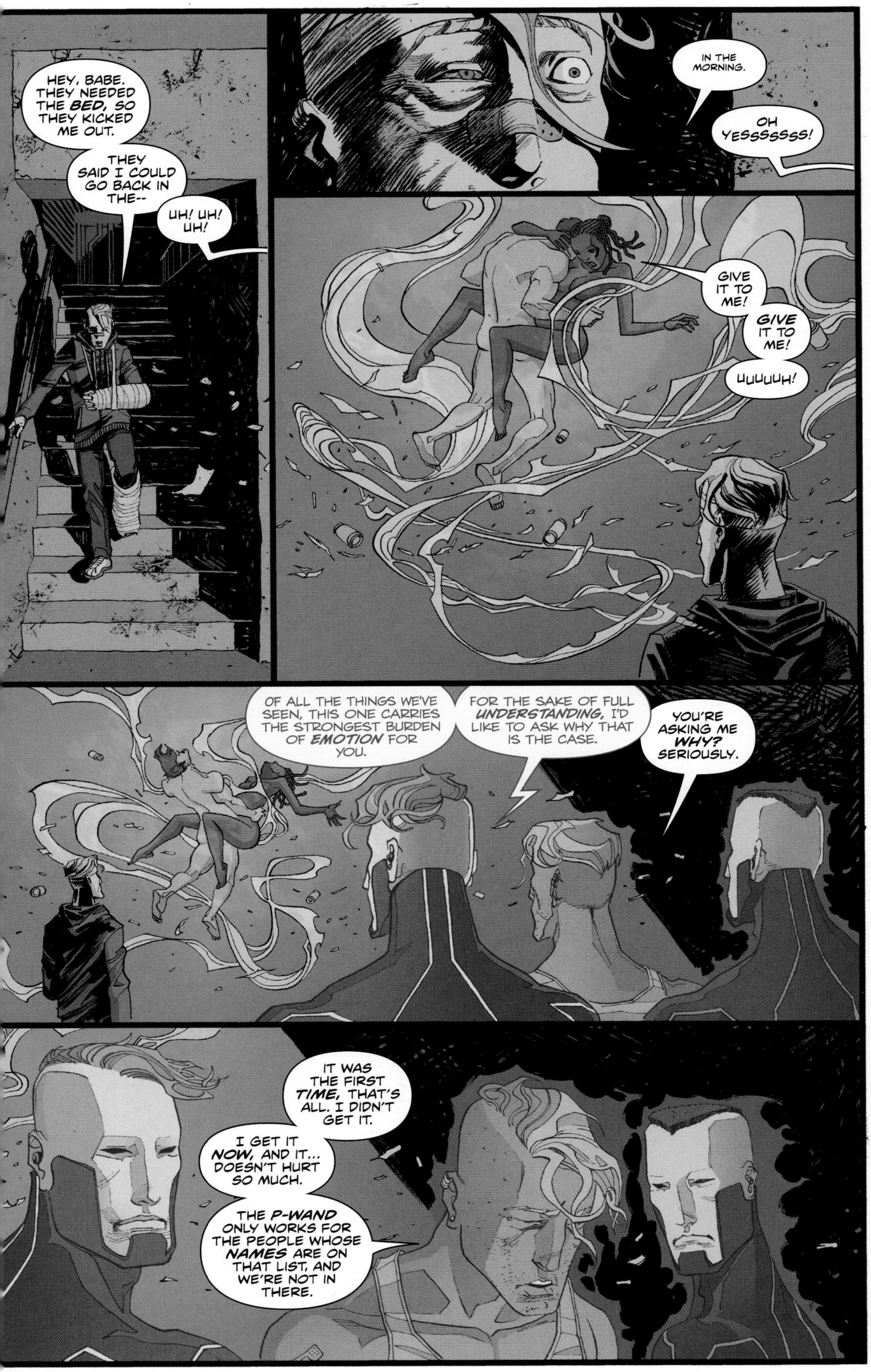
HEY, BABE. THEY NEEDED THE BED, SO THEY KICKED ME OUT.
THEY SAID I COULD GO BACK IN THE--
UH! UH! UH!
IN THE MORNING.
OH YESSSSSSS!
GIVE IT TO ME!
GIVE IT TO ME!
UUUUUH!
OF ALL THE THINGS WE'VE SEEN, THIS ONE CARRIES THE STRONGEST BURDEN OF EMOTION FOR YOU.
FOR THE SAKE OF FULL UNDERSTANDING, I'D LIKE TO ASK WHY THAT IS THE CASE.
YOU'RE ASKING ME WHY? SERIOUSLY.
IT WAS THE FIRST TIME, THAT'S ALL. I DIDN'T GET IT.
I GET IT NOW, AND IT... DOESN'T HURT SO MUCH.
THE P-WAND ONLY WORKS FOR THE PEOPLE WHOSE NAMES ARE ON THAT LIST, AND WE'RE NOT IN THERE.

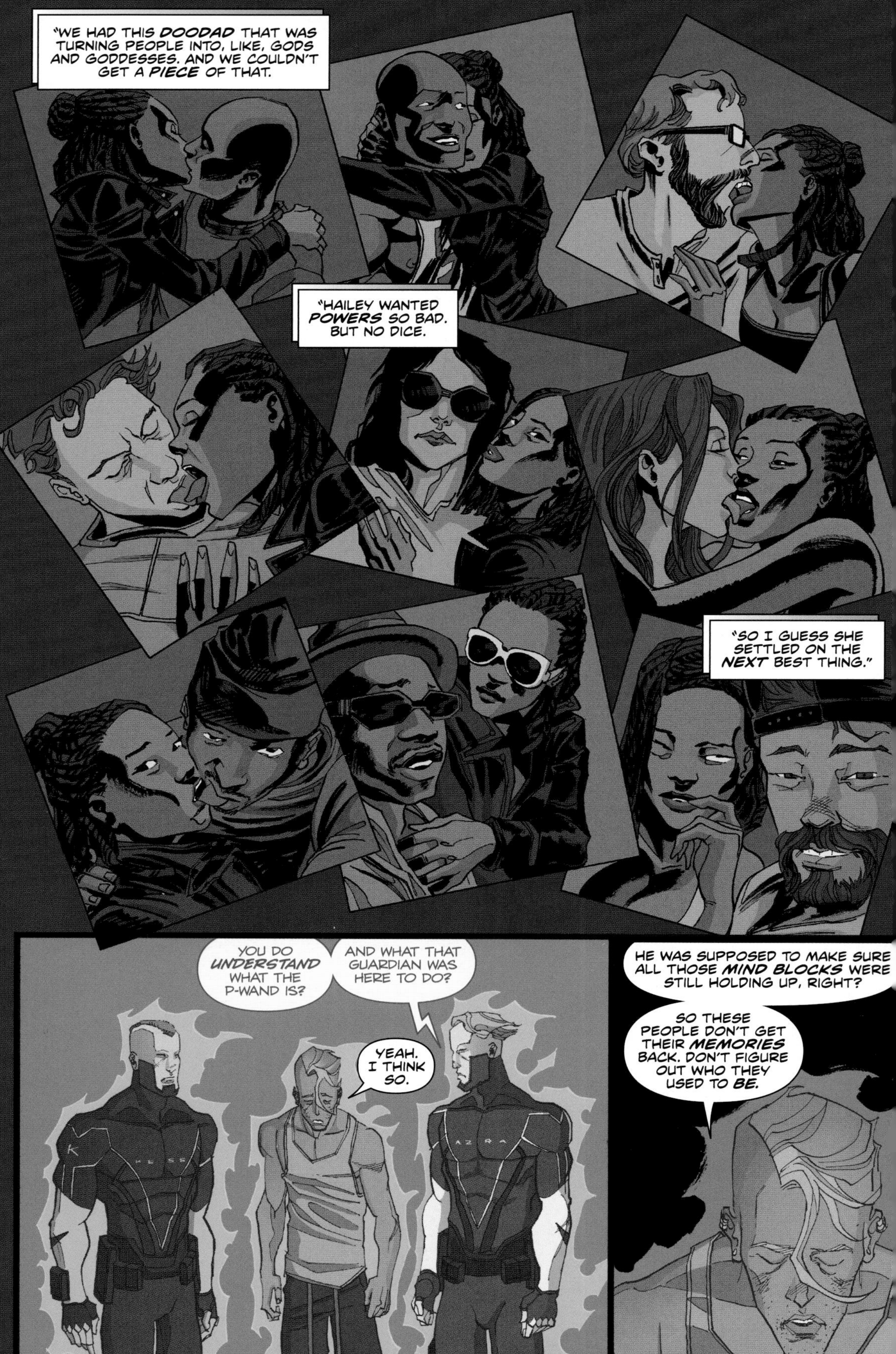
"WE HAD THIS DOODAD THAT WAS TURNING PEOPLE INTO, LIKE, GODS AND GODDESSES. AND WE COULDN'T GET A PIECE OF THAT.
"HAILEY WANTED POWERS SO BAD. BUT NO DICE.
"SO I GUESS SHE SETTLED ON THE NEXT BEST THING."
YOU DO UNDERSTAND WHAT THE P-WAND IS?
AND WHAT THAT GUARDIAN WAS HERE TO DO?
YEAH. I THINK SO.
HE WAS SUPPOSED TO MAKE SURE ALL THOSE MIND BLOCKS WERE STILL HOLDING UP, RIGHT?
SO THESE PEOPLE DON'T GET THEIR MEMORIES BACK. DON'T FIGURE OUT WHO THEY USED TO BE.

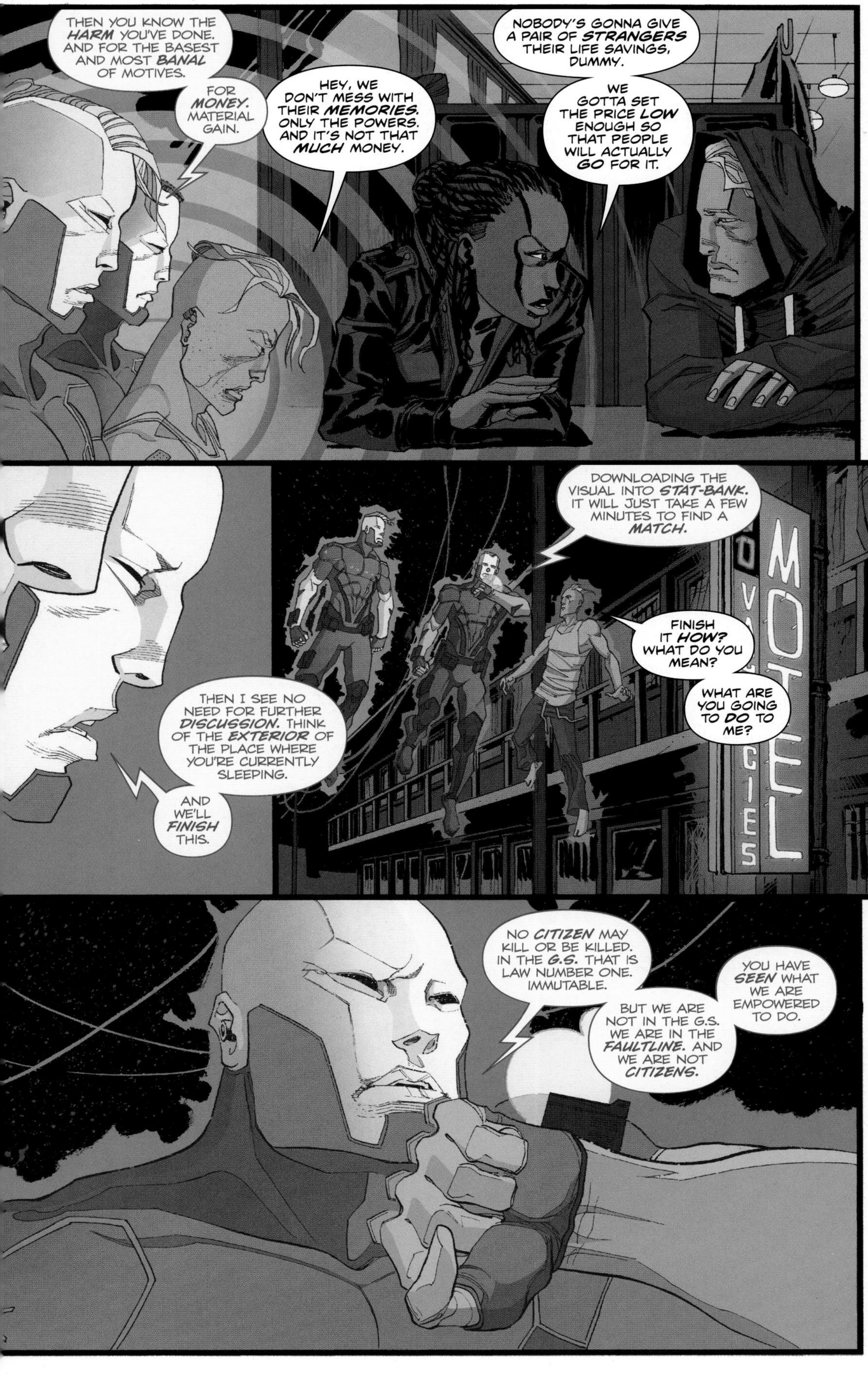
THEN YOU KNOW THE HARM YOU'VE DONE. AND FOR THE BASEST AND MOST BANAL OF MOTIVES.
FOR MONEY. MATERIAL GAIN.
HEY, WE DON'T MESS WITH THEIR MEMORIES. ONLY THE POWERS. AND IT'S NOT THAT MUCH MONEY.
NOBODY'S GONNA GIVE A PAIR OF STRANGERS THEIR LIFE SAVINGS, DUMMY.
WE GOTTA SET THE PRICE LOW ENOUGH SO THAT PEOPLE WILL ACTUALLY GO FOR IT.
THEN I SEE NO NEED FOR FURTHER DISCUSSION. THINK OF THE EXTERIOR OF THE PLACE WHERE YOU'RE CURRENTLY SLEEPING.
AND WE'LL FINISH THIS.
DOWNLOADING THE VISUAL INTO STAT-BANK. IT WILL JUST TAKE A FEW MINUTES TO FIND A MATCH.
FINISH IT HOW? WHAT DO YOU MEAN?
WHAT ARE YOU GOING TO DO TO ME?
MOTEL
NO CITIZEN MAY KILL OR BE KILLED. IN THE G.S. THAT IS LAW NUMBER ONE. IMMUTABLE.
BUT WE ARE NOT IN THE G.S. WE ARE IN THE FAULTLINE. AND WE ARE NOT CITIZENS.
YOU HAVE SEEN WHAT WE ARE EMPOWERED TO DO.

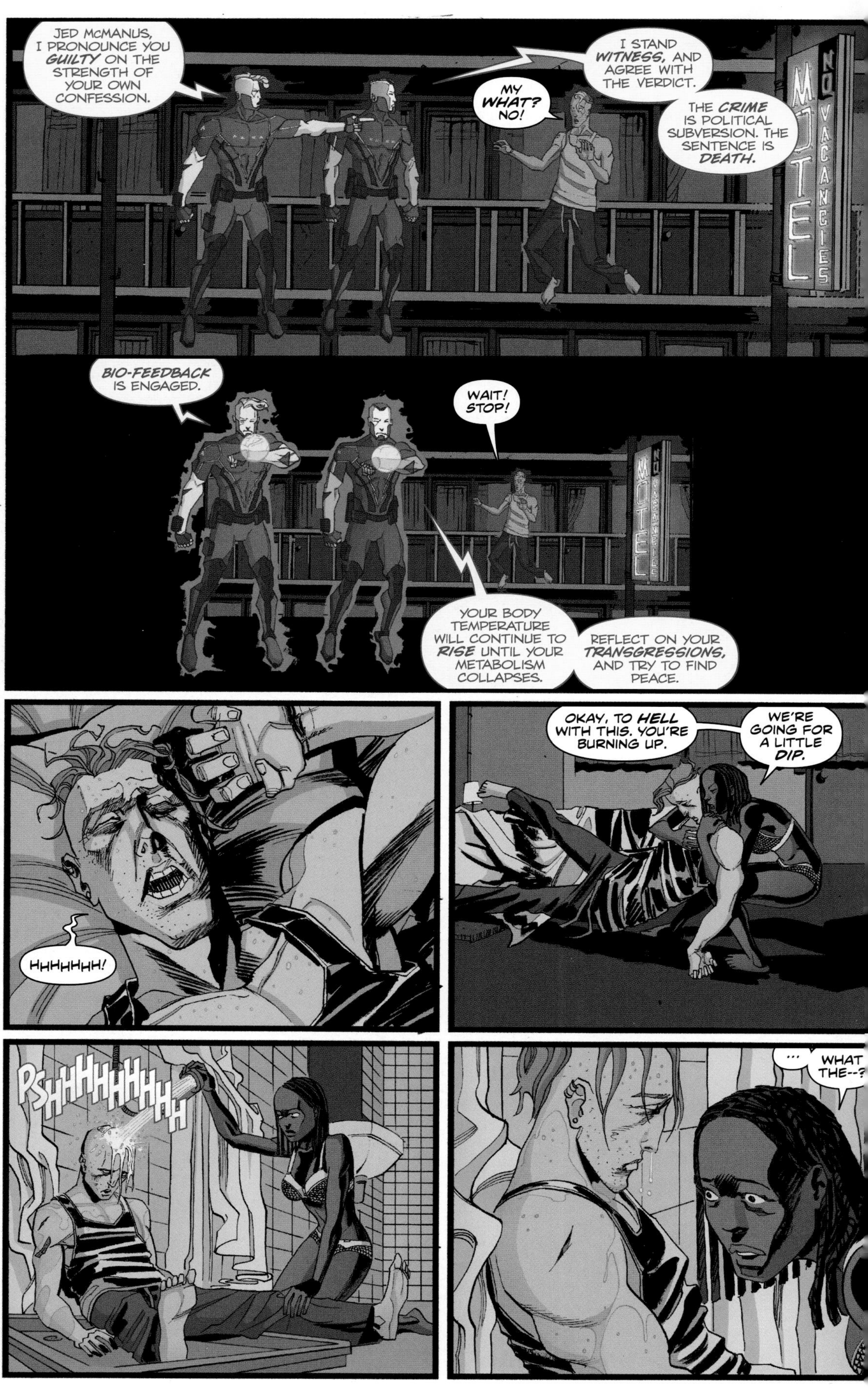
JED McMANUS, I PRONOUNCE YOU GUILTY ON THE STRENGTH OF YOUR OWN CONFESSION.
MY WHAT? NO!
I STAND WITNESS, AND AGREE WITH THE VERDICT.
THE CRIME IS POLITICAL SUBVERSION. THE SENTENCE IS DEATH.
NO VACANCIES
MOTEL
BIO-FEEDBACK IS ENGAGED.
WAIT! STOP!
YOUR BODY TEMPERATURE WILL CONTINUE TO RISE UNTIL YOUR METABOLISM COLLAPSES.
REFLECT ON YOUR TRANSGRESSIONS, AND TRY TO FIND PEACE.
HHHHHHH!
OKAY, TO HELL WITH THIS. YOU'RE BURNING UP.
WE'RE GOING FOR A LITTLE DIP.
PSHHHHHHHHHH
...
WHAT THE--?

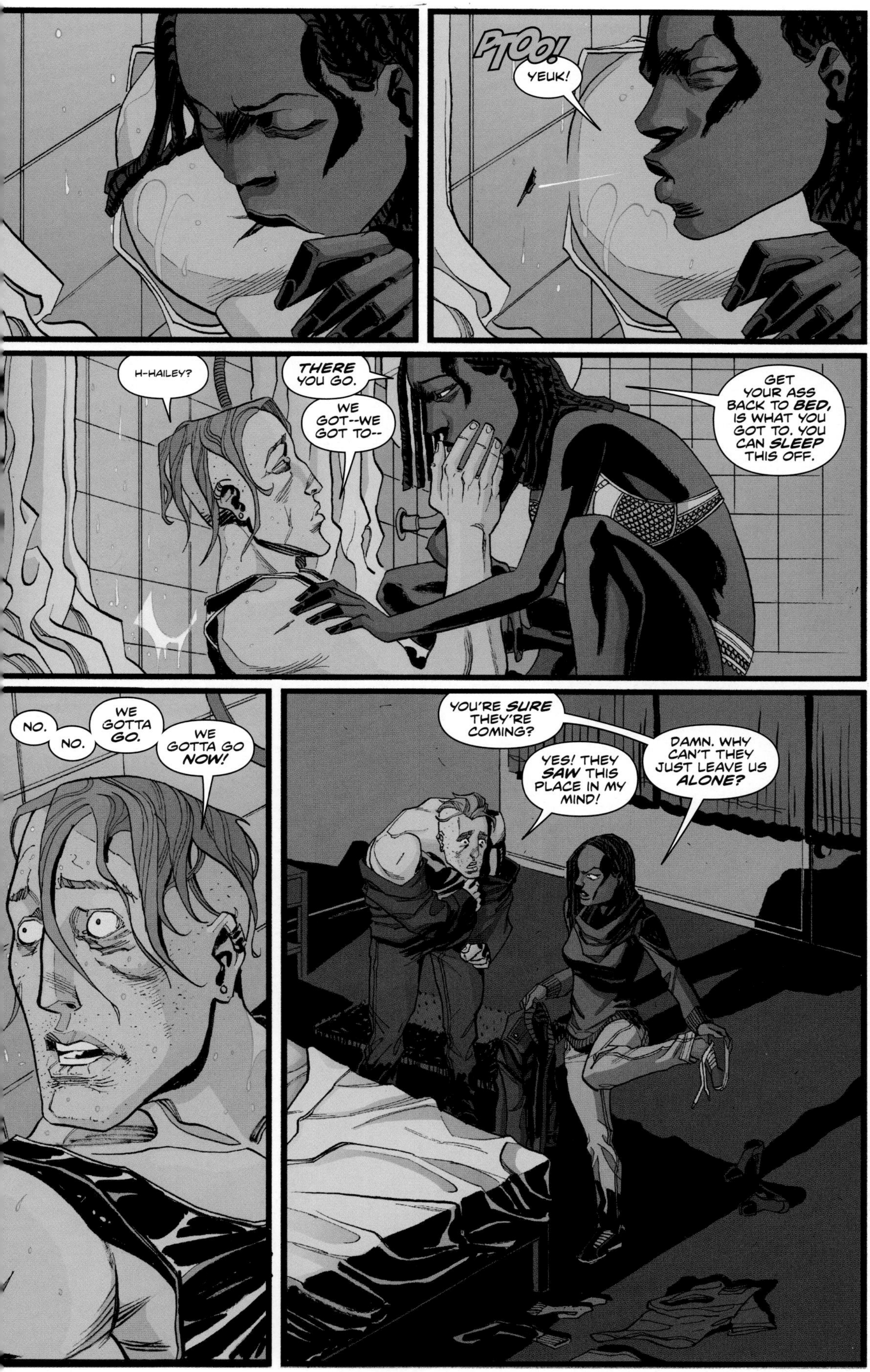
PTOO!
YEUK!
H-HAILEY?
THERE YOU GO.
WE GOT--WE GOT TO--
GET YOUR ASS BACK TO BED, IS WHAT YOU GOT TO. YOU CAN SLEEP THIS OFF.
NO.
NO.
WE GOTTA GO.
WE GOTTA GO NOW!
YOU'RE SURE THEY'RE COMING?
YES! THEY SAW THIS PLACE IN MY MIND!
DAMN. WHY CAN'T THEY JUST LEAVE US ALONE?

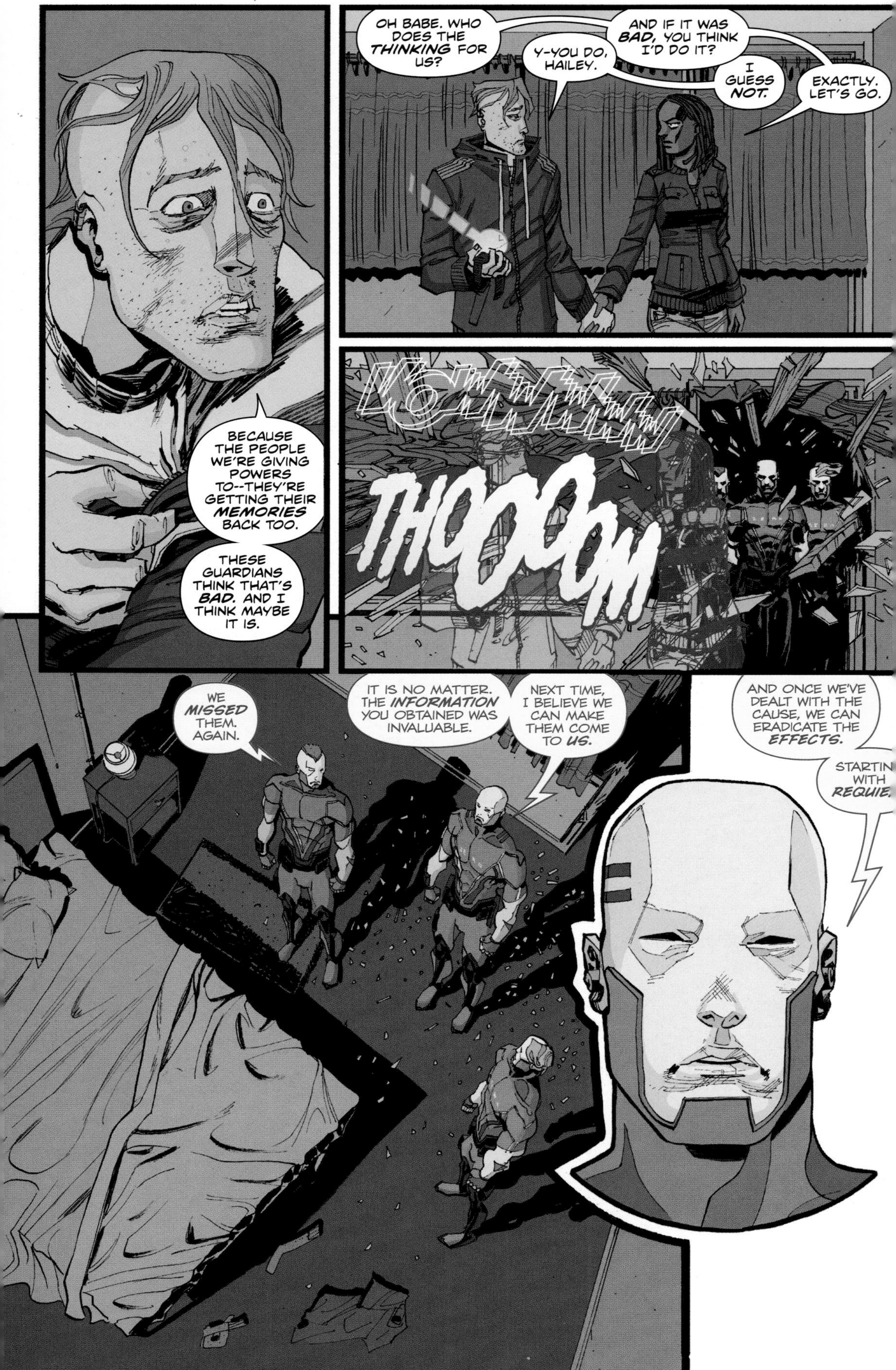

OH BABE. WHO DOES THE THINKING FOR US?
Y-YOU DO, HAILEY.
AND IF IT WAS BAD, YOU THINK I'D DO IT?
I GUESS NOT.
EXACTLY. LET'S GO.
BECAUSE THE PEOPLE WE'RE GIVING POWERS TO--THEY'RE GETTING THEIR MEMORIES BACK TOO.
THESE GUARDIANS THINK THAT'S BAD. AND I THINK MAYBE IT IS.
THOOOOM
WE MISSED THEM. AGAIN.
IT IS NO MATTER. THE INFORMATION YOU OBTAINED WAS INVALUABLE.
NEXT TIME, I BELIEVE WE CAN MAKE THEM COME TO US.
AND ONCE WE'VE DEALT WITH THE CAUSE, WE CAN ERADICATE THE EFFECTS.
STARTIN WITH REQUIE

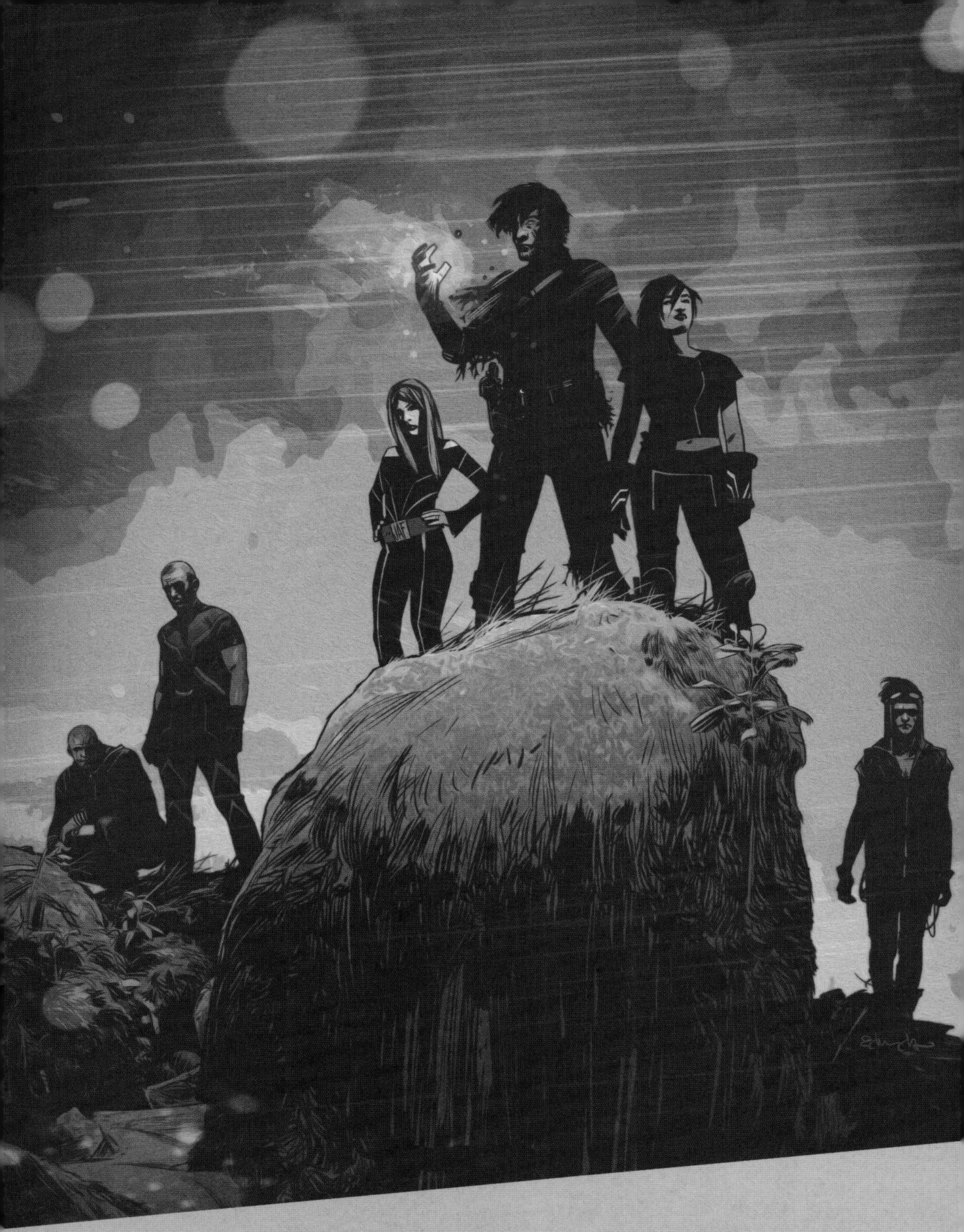

"NOTHING IN THIS **WRETCHED** PLACE IS FAMILIAR TO ME."

Chapter 11

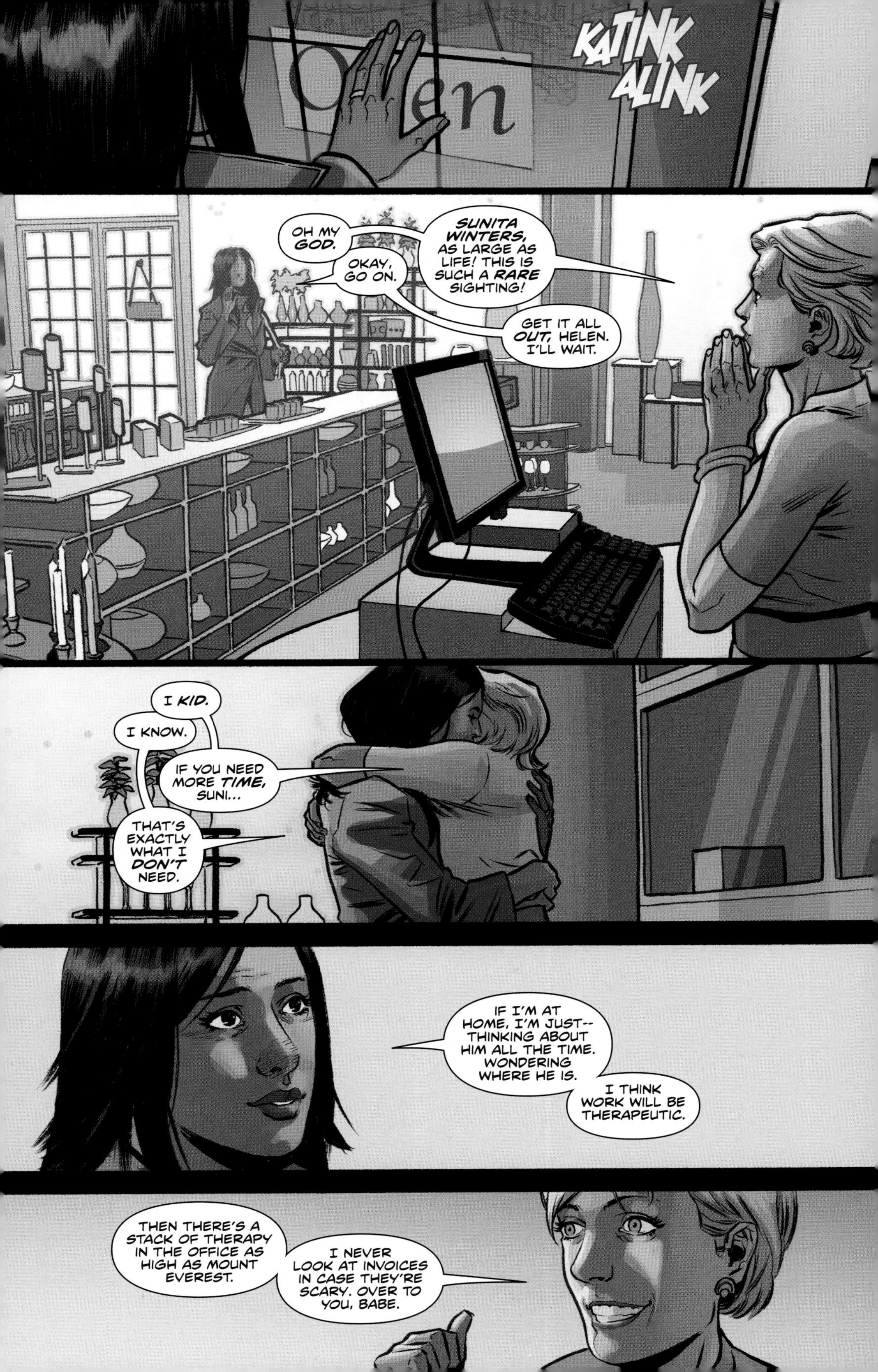
Open
KATINK ALINK
OH MY GOD.
SUNITA WINTERS, AS LARGE AS LIFE! THIS IS SUCH A RARE SIGHTING!
OKAY, GO ON.
GET IT ALL OUT, HELEN. I'LL WAIT.
I KID.
I KNOW.
IF YOU NEED MORE TIME, SUNI...
THAT'S EXACTLY WHAT I DON'T NEED.
IF I'M AT HOME, I'M JUST-- THINKING ABOUT HIM ALL THE TIME. WONDERING WHERE HE IS.
I THINK WORK WILL BE THERAPEUTIC.
THEN THERE'S A STACK OF THERAPY IN THE OFFICE AS HIGH AS MOUNT EVEREST.
I NEVER LOOK AT INVOICES IN CASE THEY'RE SCARY. OVER TO YOU, BABE.

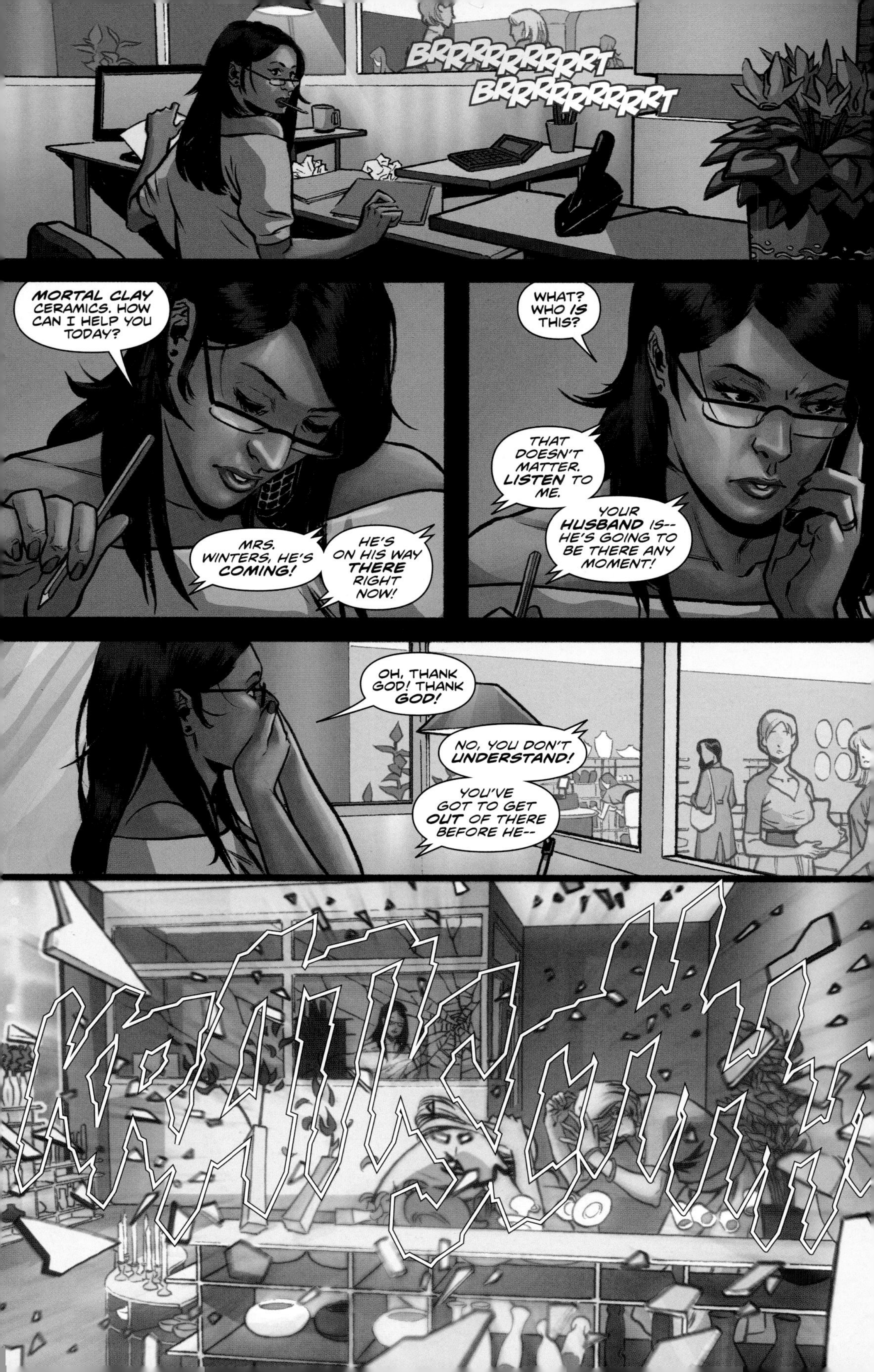
BRRRRRRRRRT
BRRRRRRRRRT
MORTAL CLAY CERAMICS. HOW CAN I HELP YOU TODAY?
MRS. WINTERS, HE'S COMING!
HE'S ON HIS WAY THERE RIGHT NOW!
WHAT? WHO IS THIS?
THAT DOESN'T MATTER. LISTEN TO ME.
YOUR HUSBAND IS-- HE'S GOING TO BE THERE ANY MOMENT!
OH, THANK GOD! THANK GOD!
NO, YOU DON'T UNDERSTAND!
YOU'VE GOT TO GET OUT OF THERE BEFORE HE--

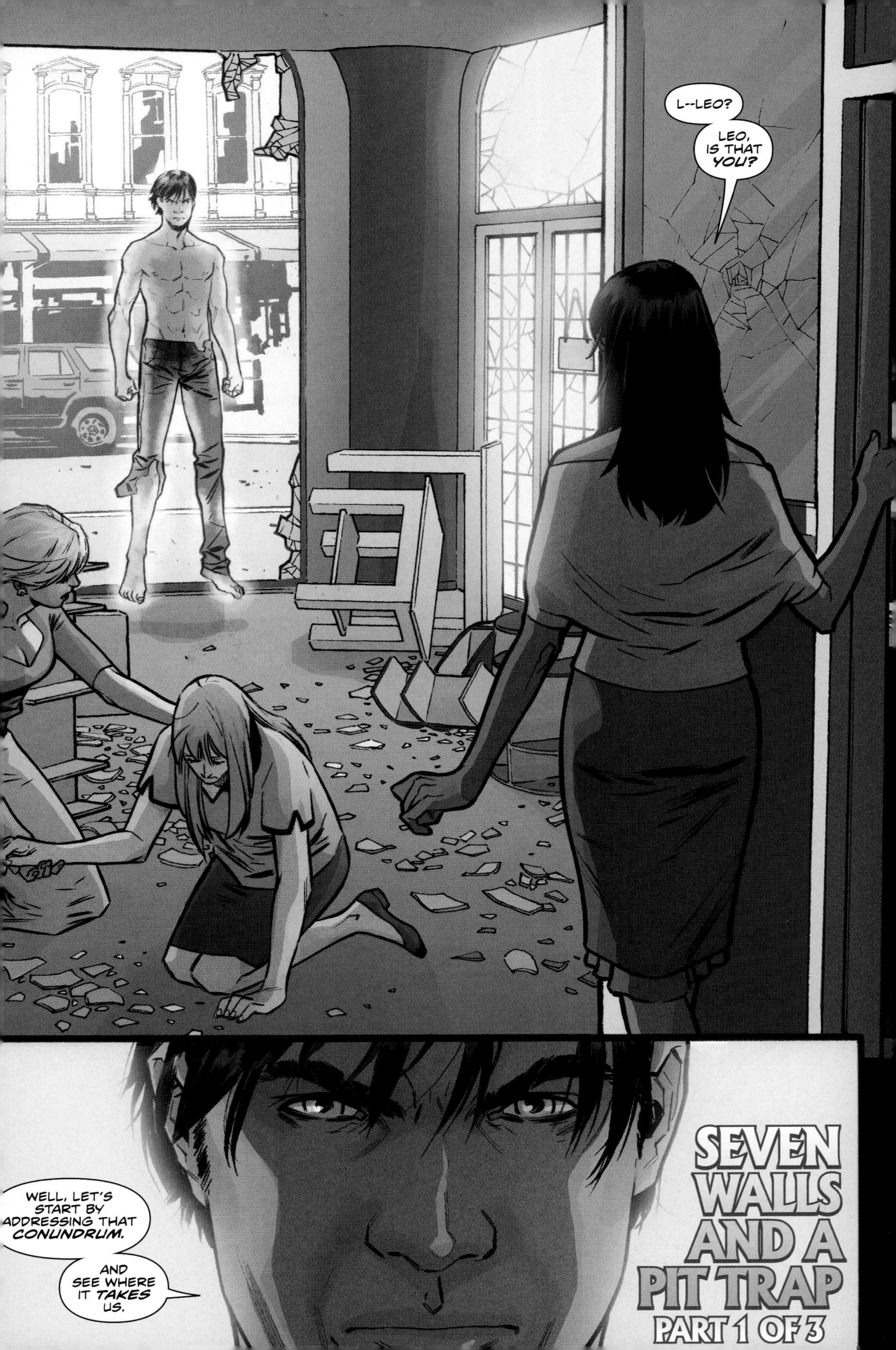

L--LEO?
LEO, IS THAT YOU?
WELL, LET'S START BY ADDRESSING THAT CONUNDRUM.
AND SEE WHERE IT TAKES US.
SEVEN WALLS AND A PIT TRAP
PART 1 OF 3

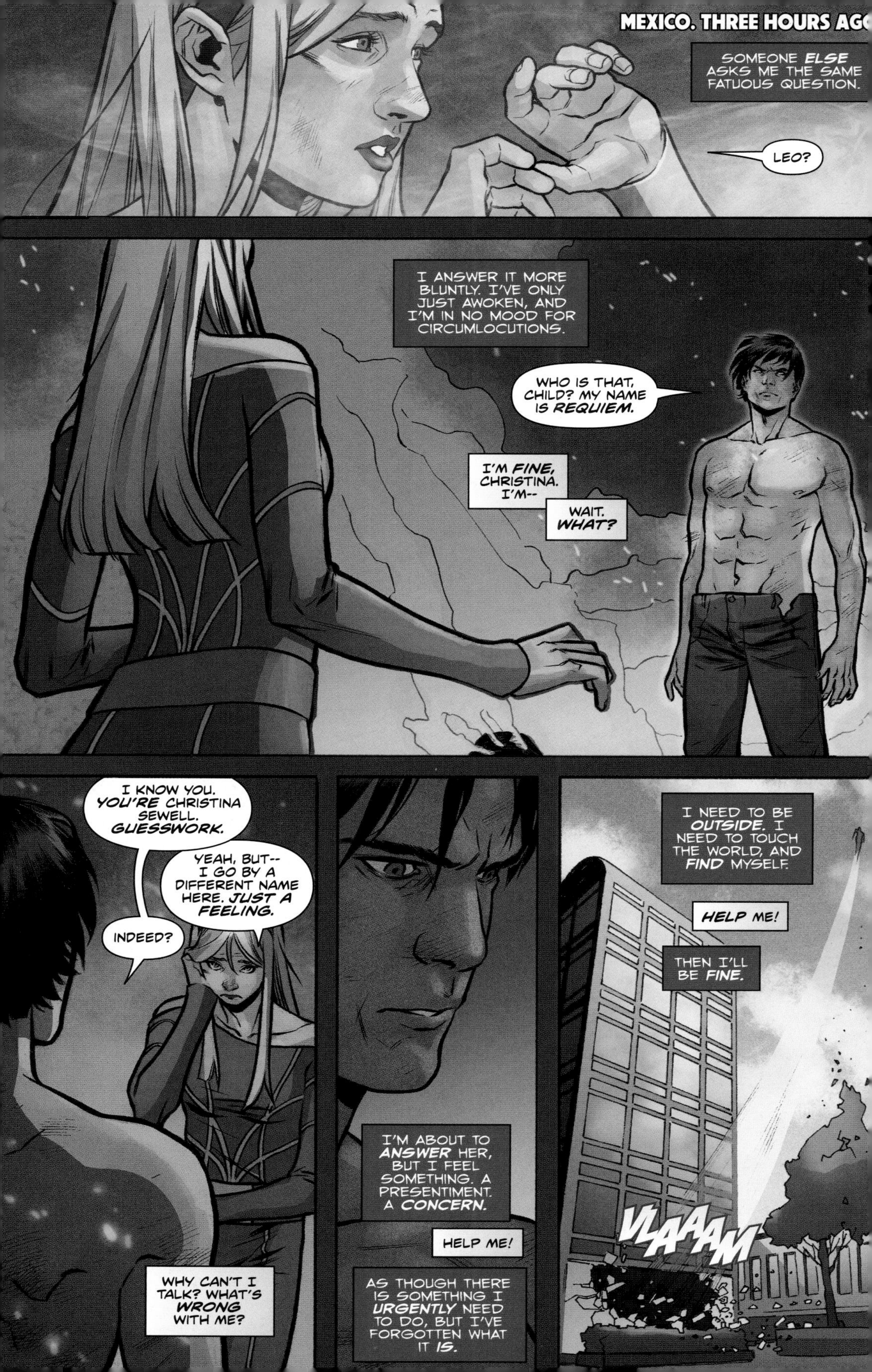
MEXICO. THREE HOURS AGO
SOMEONE ELSE ASKS ME THE SAME FATUOUS QUESTION.
LEO?
I ANSWER IT MORE BLUNTLY. I'VE ONLY JUST AWOKEN, AND I'M IN NO MOOD FOR CIRCUMLOCUTIONS.
WHO IS THAT, CHILD? MY NAME IS REQUIEM.
I'M FINE, CHRISTINA. I'M--
WAIT. WHAT?
I KNOW YOU. YOU'RE CHRISTINA SEWELL. GUESSWORK.
YEAH, BUT-- I GO BY A DIFFERENT NAME HERE. JUST A FEELING.
INDEED?
WHY CAN'T I TALK? WHAT'S WRONG WITH ME?
I'M ABOUT TO ANSWER HER, BUT I FEEL SOMETHING. A PRESENTIMENT. A CONCERN.
HELP ME!
AS THOUGH THERE IS SOMETHING I URGENTLY NEED TO DO, BUT I'VE FORGOTTEN WHAT IT IS.
I NEED TO BE OUTSIDE. I NEED TO TOUCH THE WORLD, AND FIND MYSELF.
HELP ME!
THEN I'LL BE FINE.
VLAAAM

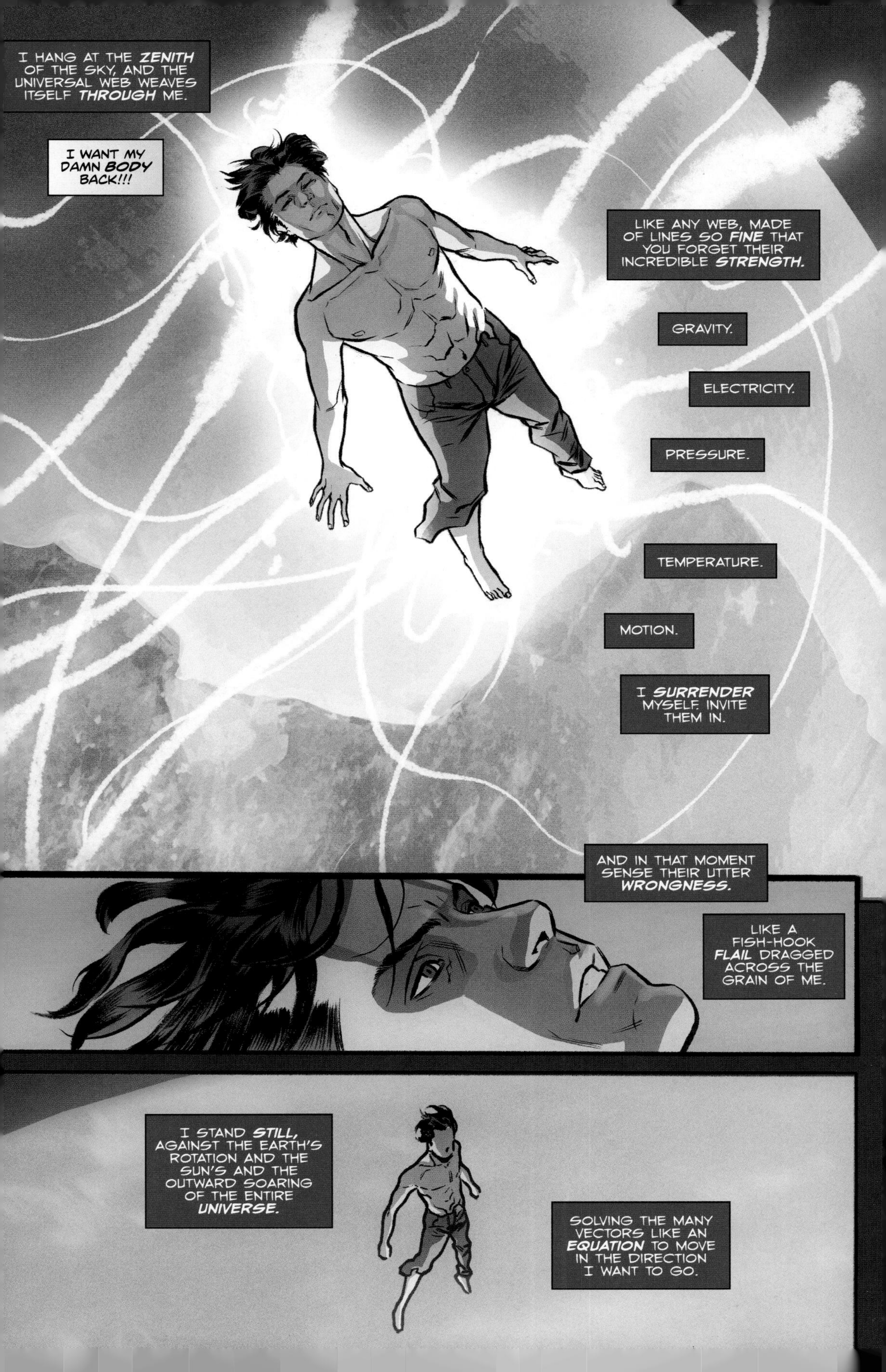
I HANG AT THE ZENITH OF THE SKY, AND THE UNIVERSAL WEB WEAVES ITSELF THROUGH ME.
I WANT MY DAMN BODY BACK!!!
LIKE ANY WEB, MADE OF LINES SO FINE THAT YOU FORGET THEIR INCREDIBLE STRENGTH.
GRAVITY.
ELECTRICITY.
PRESSURE.
TEMPERATURE.
MOTION.
I SURRENDER MYSELF. INVITE THEM IN.
AND IN THAT MOMENT SENSE THEIR UTTER WRONGNESS.
LIKE A FISH-HOOK FLAIL DRAGGED ACROSS THE GRAIN OF ME.
I STAND STILL, AGAINST THE EARTH'S ROTATION AND THE SUN'S AND THE OUTWARD SOARING OF THE ENTIRE UNIVERSE.
SOLVING THE MANY VECTORS LIKE AN EQUATION TO MOVE IN THE DIRECTION I WANT TO GO.

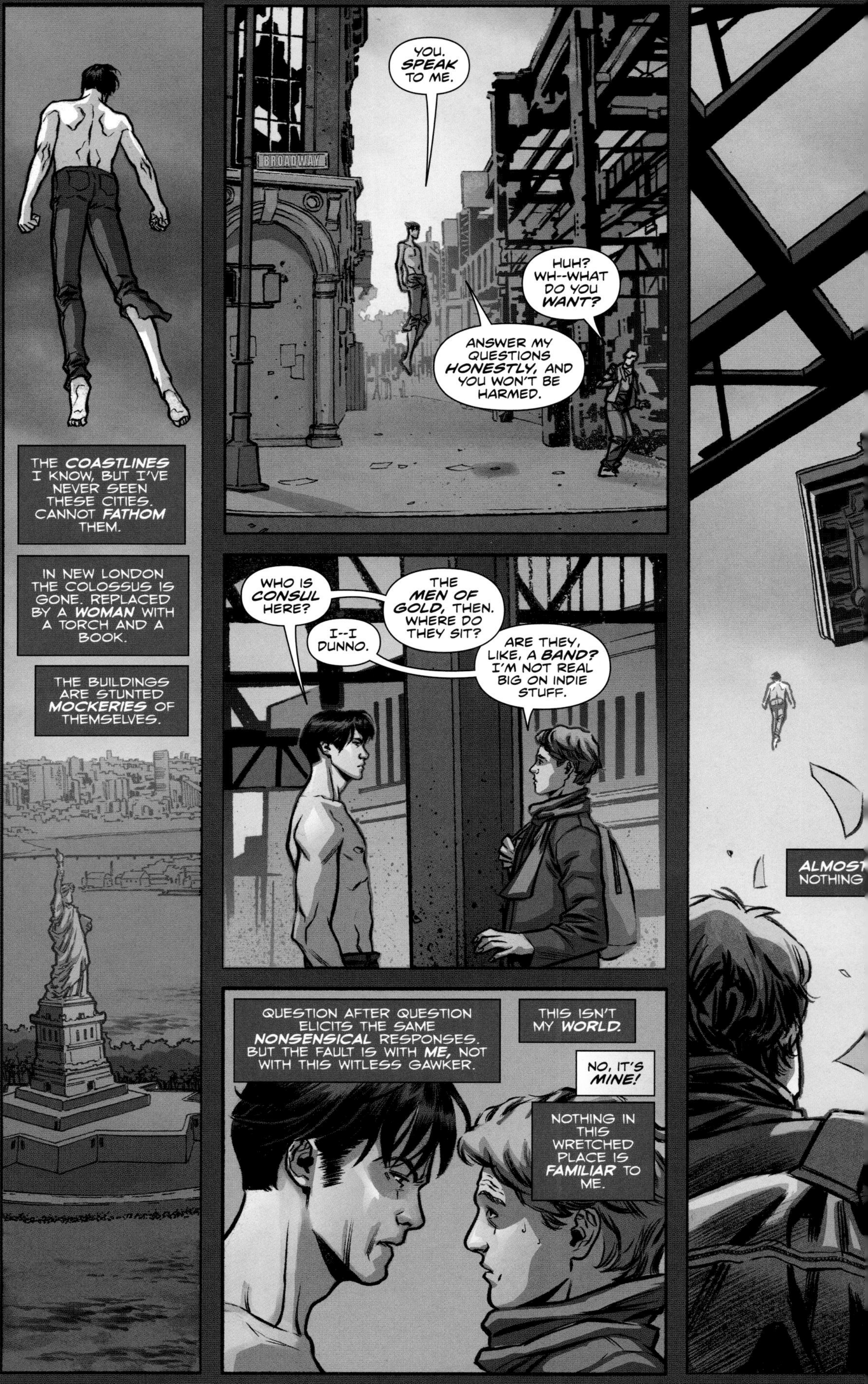
THE COASTLINES I KNOW, BUT I'VE NEVER SEEN THESE CITIES. CANNOT FATHOM THEM.
IN NEW LONDON THE COLOSSUS IS GONE. REPLACED BY A WOMAN WITH A TORCH AND A BOOK.
THE BUILDINGS ARE STUNTED MOCKERIES OF THEMSELVES.
BROADWAY
YOU. SPEAK TO ME.
HUH? WH--WHAT DO YOU WANT?
ANSWER MY QUESTIONS HONESTLY, AND YOU WON'T BE HARMED.
WHO IS CONSUL HERE?
I--I DUNNO.
THE MEN OF GOLD, THEN. WHERE DO THEY SIT?
ARE THEY, LIKE, A BAND? I'M NOT REAL BIG ON INDIE STUFF.
QUESTION AFTER QUESTION ELICITS THE SAME NONSENSICAL RESPONSES. BUT THE FAULT IS WITH ME, NOT WITH THIS WITLESS GAWKER.
THIS ISN'T MY WORLD.
NO, IT'S MINE!
NOTHING IN THIS WRETCHED PLACE IS FAMILIAR TO ME.
ALMOST NOTHING

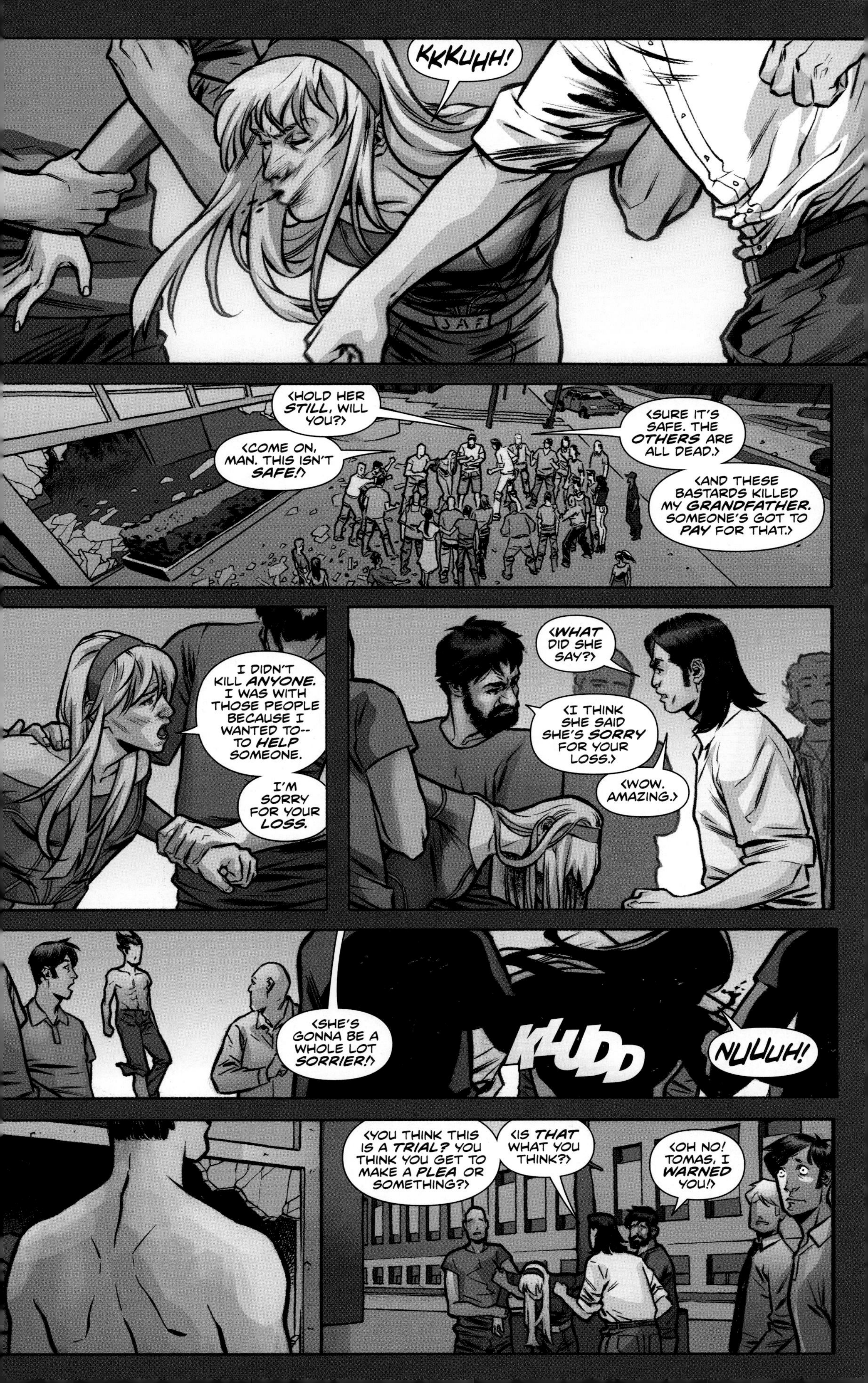
KKKUHH!
‹HOLD HER STILL, WILL YOU?›
‹COME ON, MAN. THIS ISN'T SAFE!›
‹SURE IT'S SAFE. THE OTHERS ARE ALL DEAD.›
‹AND THESE BASTARDS KILLED MY GRANDFATHER. SOMEONE'S GOT TO PAY FOR THAT.›
I DIDN'T KILL ANYONE. I WAS WITH THOSE PEOPLE BECAUSE I WANTED TO-- TO HELP SOMEONE.
I'M SORRY FOR YOUR LOSS.
‹WHAT DID SHE SAY?›
‹I THINK SHE SAID SHE'S SORRY FOR YOUR LOSS.›
‹WOW. AMAZING.›
‹SHE'S GONNA BE A WHOLE LOT SORRIER!›
KLUDD
NUUUH!
‹YOU THINK THIS IS A TRIAL? YOU THINK YOU GET TO MAKE A PLEA OR SOMETHING?›
‹IS THAT WHAT YOU THINK?›
‹OH NO! TOMAS, I WARNED YOU!›

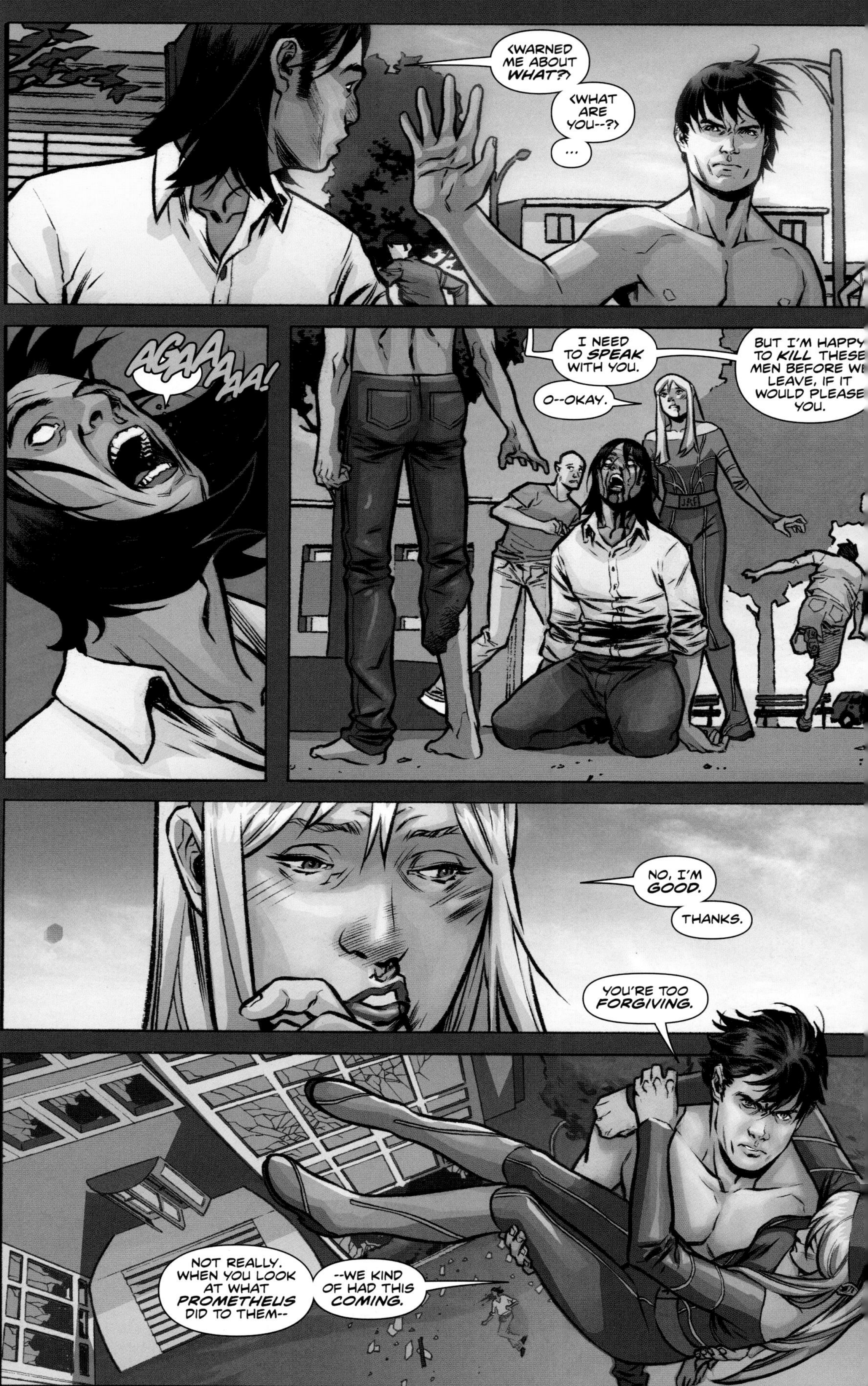
<WARNED ME ABOUT WHAT?>
<WHAT ARE YOU--?>
...
AGAAAAAA!
I NEED TO SPEAK WITH YOU.
O--OKAY.
BUT I'M HAPPY TO KILL THESE MEN BEFORE WE LEAVE, IF IT WOULD PLEASE YOU.
NO, I'M GOOD.
THANKS.
YOU'RE TOO FORGIVING.
NOT REALLY. WHEN YOU LOOK AT WHAT PROMETHEUS DID TO THEM--
--WE KIND OF HAD THIS COMING.

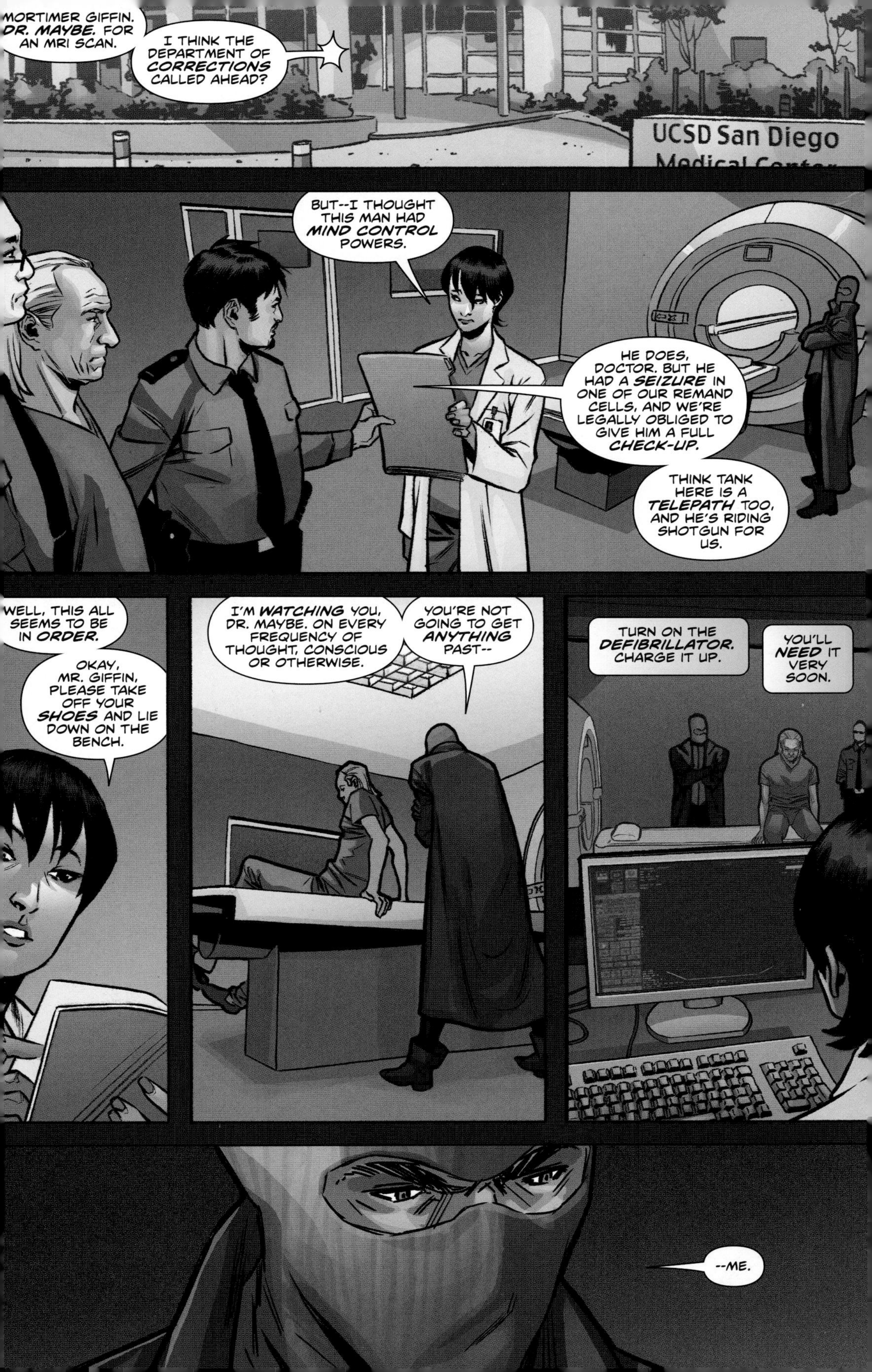
MORTIMER GIFFIN. DR. MAYBE. FOR AN MRI SCAN.
I THINK THE DEPARTMENT OF CORRECTIONS CALLED AHEAD?
UCSD San Diego
BUT--I THOUGHT THIS MAN HAD MIND CONTROL POWERS.
HE DOES, DOCTOR. BUT HE HAD A SEIZURE IN ONE OF OUR REMAND CELLS, AND WE'RE LEGALLY OBLIGED TO GIVE HIM A FULL CHECK-UP.
THINK TANK HERE IS A TELEPATH TOO, AND HE'S RIDING SHOTGUN FOR US.
WELL, THIS ALL SEEMS TO BE IN ORDER.
OKAY, MR. GIFFIN, PLEASE TAKE OFF YOUR SHOES AND LIE DOWN ON THE BENCH.
I'M WATCHING YOU, DR. MAYBE. ON EVERY FREQUENCY OF THOUGHT, CONSCIOUS OR OTHERWISE.
YOU'RE NOT GOING TO GET ANYTHING PAST--
TURN ON THE DEFIBRILLATOR. CHARGE IT UP.
YOU'LL NEED IT VERY SOON.
--ME.

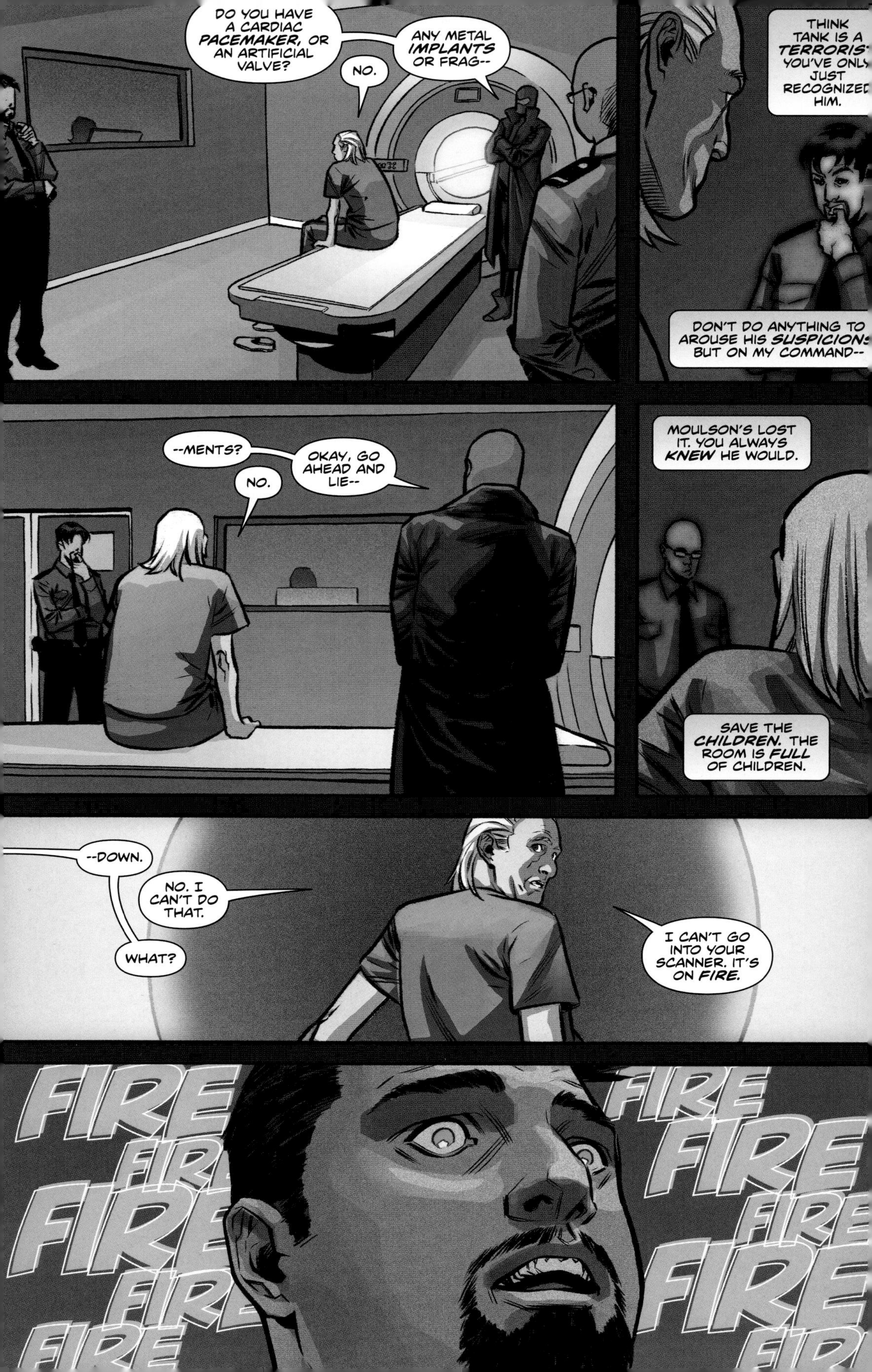
DO YOU HAVE A CARDIAC PACEMAKER, OR AN ARTIFICIAL VALVE?
NO.
ANY METAL IMPLANTS OR FRAG--
THINK TANK IS A TERRORIST YOU'VE ONLY JUST RECOGNIZED HIM.
DON'T DO ANYTHING TO AROUSE HIS SUSPICIONS BUT ON MY COMMAND--
--MENTS?
NO.
OKAY, GO AHEAD AND LIE--
MOULSON'S LOST IT. YOU ALWAYS KNEW HE WOULD.
SAVE THE CHILDREN. THE ROOM IS FULL OF CHILDREN.
--DOWN.
NO. I CAN'T DO THAT.
WHAT?
I CAN'T GO INTO YOUR SCANNER. IT'S ON FIRE.
FIRE
FIRE
FIRE
FIRE
FIRE
FIRE
FIRE
FIRE
FIRE

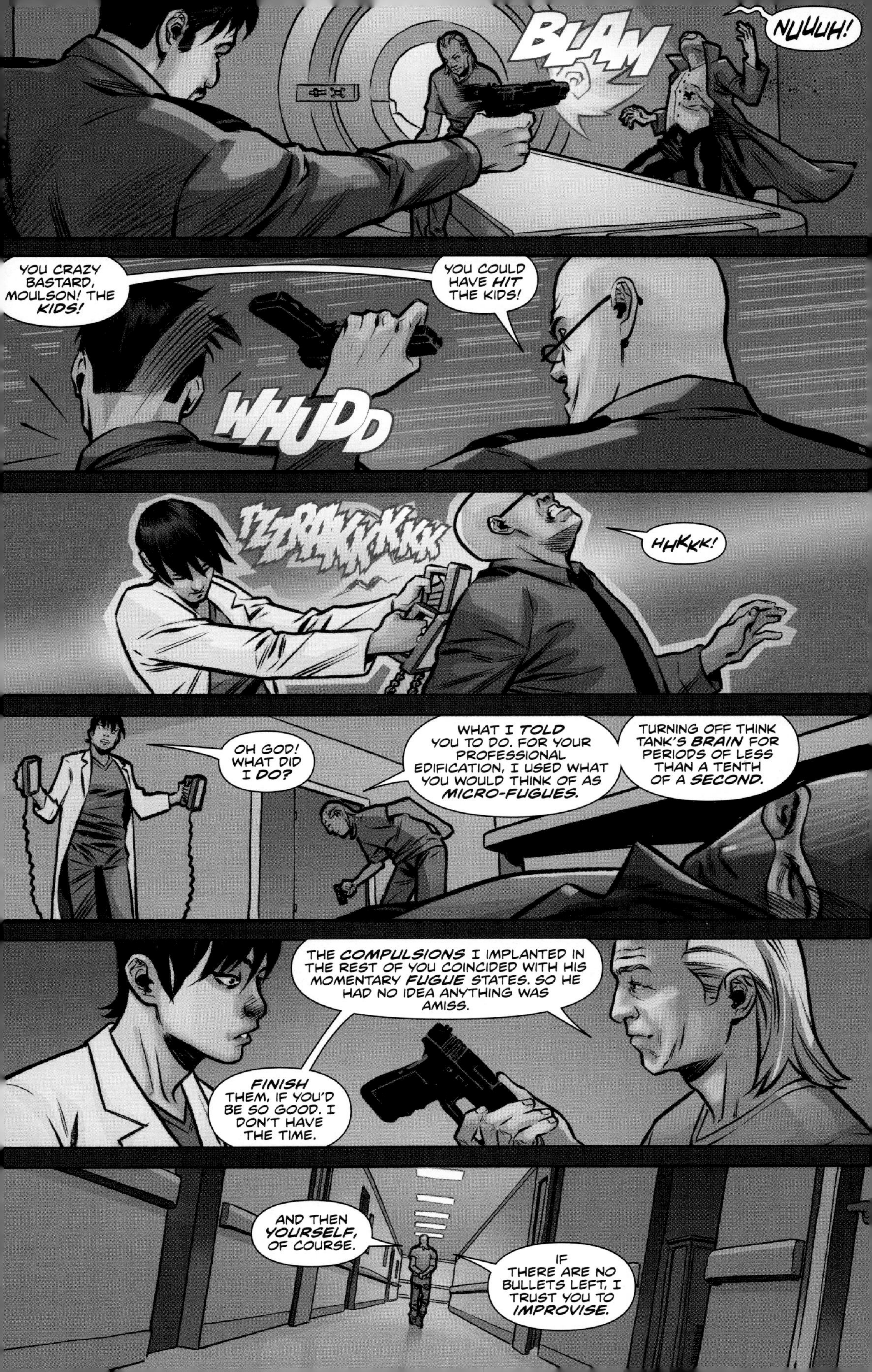
BLAM
NUUUH!
YOU CRAZY BASTARD, MOULSON! THE KIDS!
YOU COULD HAVE HIT THE KIDS!
WHUDD
TZZZRAKKKKKK
HHKKK!
OH GOD! WHAT DID I DO?
WHAT I TOLD YOU TO DO. FOR YOUR PROFESSIONAL EDIFICATION, I USED WHAT YOU WOULD THINK OF AS MICRO-FUGUES.
TURNING OFF THINK TANK'S BRAIN FOR PERIODS OF LESS THAN A TENTH OF A SECOND.
THE COMPULSIONS I IMPLANTED IN THE REST OF YOU COINCIDED WITH HIS MOMENTARY FUGUE STATES. SO HE HAD NO IDEA ANYTHING WAS AMISS.
FINISH THEM, IF YOU'D BE SO GOOD. I DON'T HAVE THE TIME.
AND THEN YOURSELF, OF COURSE.
IF THERE ARE NO BULLETS LEFT, I TRUST YOU TO IMPROVISE.

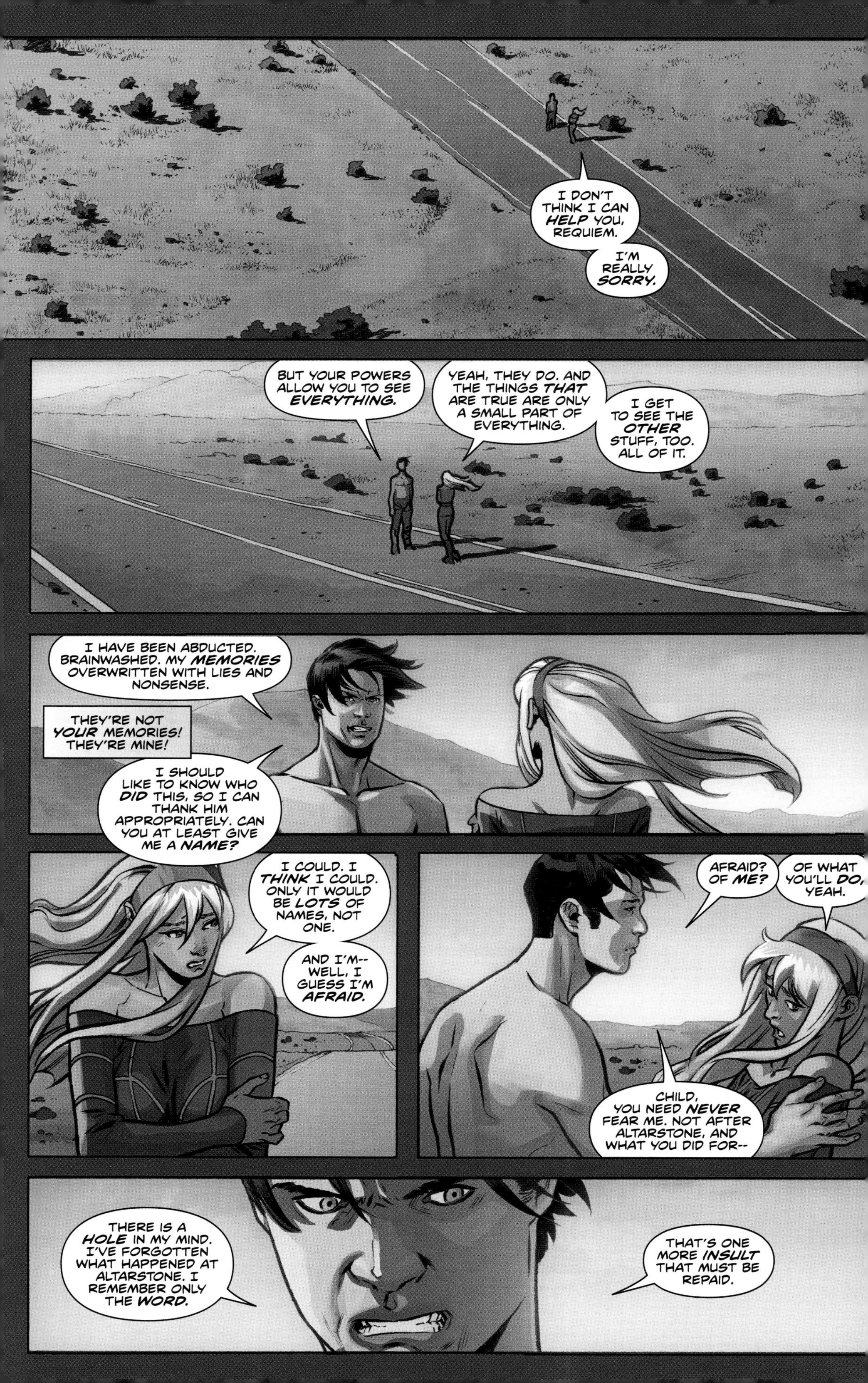
I DON'T THINK I CAN HELP YOU, REQUIEM.
I'M REALLY SORRY.
BUT YOUR POWERS ALLOW YOU TO SEE EVERYTHING.
YEAH, THEY DO. AND THE THINGS THAT ARE TRUE ARE ONLY A SMALL PART OF EVERYTHING.
I GET TO SEE THE OTHER STUFF, TOO. ALL OF IT.
I HAVE BEEN ABDUCTED. BRAINWASHED. MY MEMORIES OVERWRITTEN WITH LIES AND NONSENSE.
THEY'RE NOT YOUR MEMORIES! THEY'RE MINE!
I SHOULD LIKE TO KNOW WHO DID THIS, SO I CAN THANK HIM APPROPRIATELY. CAN YOU AT LEAST GIVE ME A NAME?
I COULD. I THINK I COULD. ONLY IT WOULD BE LOTS OF NAMES, NOT ONE.
AND I'M-- WELL, I GUESS I'M AFRAID.
AFRAID? OF ME?
OF WHAT YOU'LL DO, YEAH.
CHILD, YOU NEED NEVER FEAR ME. NOT AFTER ALTARSTONE, AND WHAT YOU DID FOR--
THERE IS A HOLE IN MY MIND. I'VE FORGOTTEN WHAT HAPPENED AT ALTARSTONE. I REMEMBER ONLY THE WORD.
THAT'S ONE MORE INSULT THAT MUST BE REPAID.

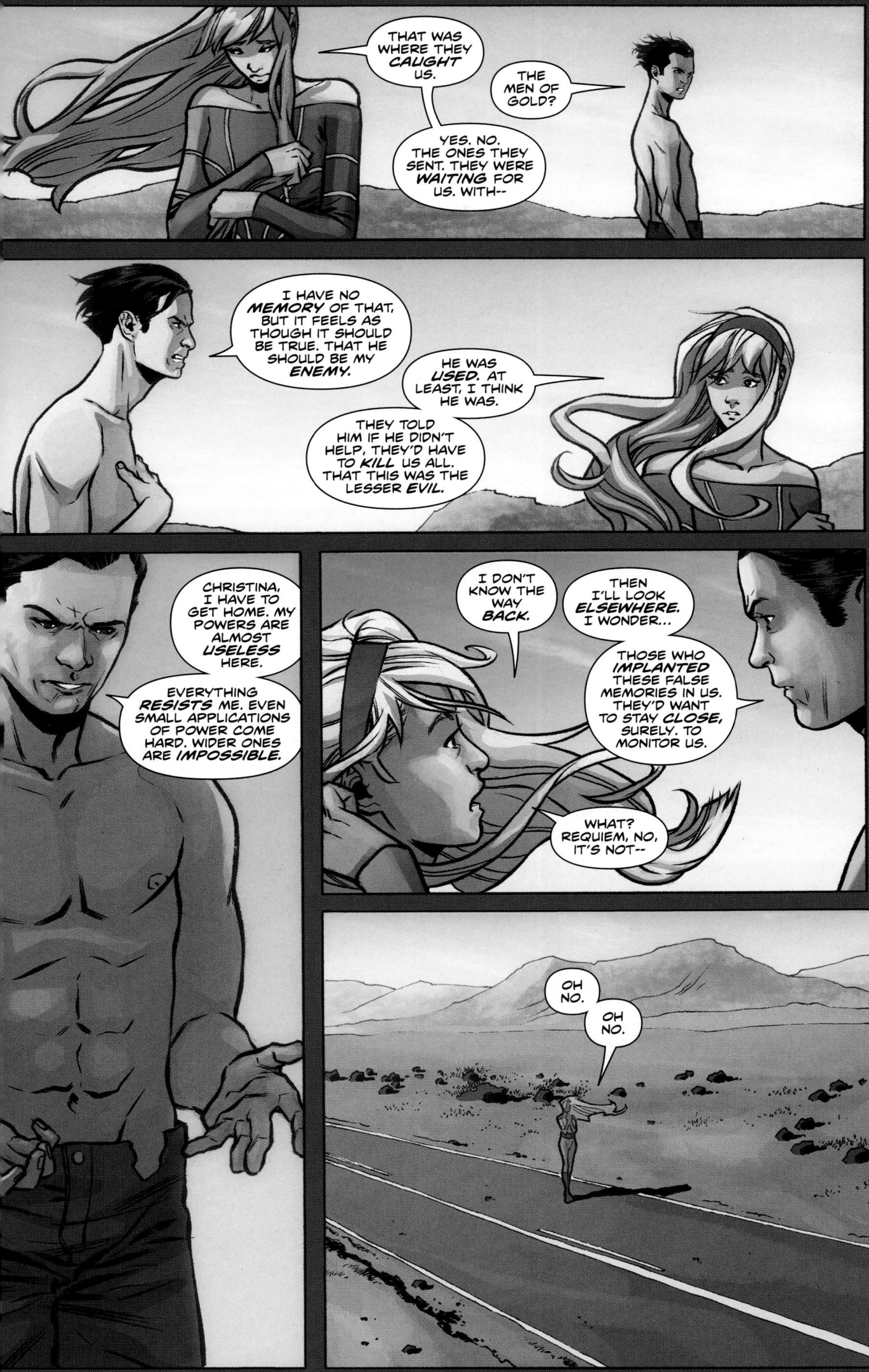
THAT WAS WHERE THEY *CAUGHT* US.
THE MEN OF GOLD?
YES. NO. THE ONES THEY SENT. THEY WERE *WAITING* FOR US. WITH--
I HAVE NO *MEMORY* OF THAT, BUT IT FEELS AS THOUGH IT SHOULD BE TRUE. THAT HE SHOULD BE MY *ENEMY.*
HE WAS *USED.* AT LEAST, I THINK HE WAS.
THEY TOLD HIM IF HE DIDN'T HELP, THEY'D HAVE TO *KILL* US ALL. THAT THIS WAS THE LESSER *EVIL.*
CHRISTINA, I HAVE TO GET HOME. MY POWERS ARE ALMOST *USELESS* HERE.
EVERYTHING *RESISTS* ME. EVEN SMALL APPLICATIONS OF POWER COME HARD. WIDER ONES ARE *IMPOSSIBLE.*
I DON'T KNOW THE WAY *BACK.*
THEN I'LL LOOK *ELSEWHERE.* I WONDER...
THOSE WHO *IMPLANTED* THESE FALSE MEMORIES IN US. THEY'D WANT TO STAY *CLOSE,* SURELY. TO MONITOR US.
WHAT? REQUIEM, NO, IT'S NOT--
OH NO.
OH NO.

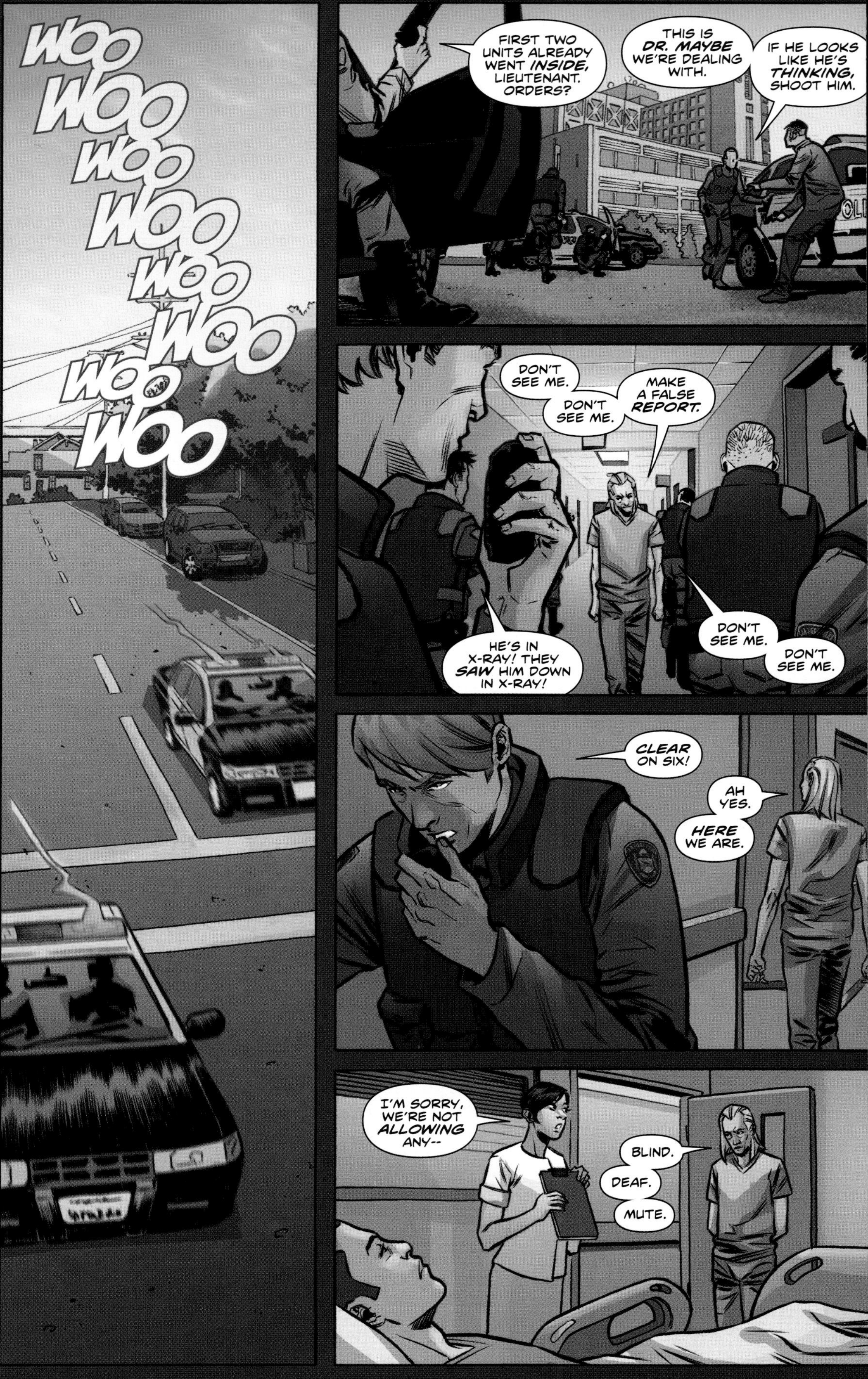
WOO WOO WOO WOO WOO WOO WOO WOO
FIRST TWO UNITS ALREADY WENT INSIDE, LIEUTENANT. ORDERS?
THIS IS DR. MAYBE WE'RE DEALING WITH.
IF HE LOOKS LIKE HE'S THINKING, SHOOT HIM.
DON'T SEE ME.
DON'T SEE ME.
MAKE A FALSE REPORT.
HE'S IN X-RAY! THEY SAW HIM DOWN IN X-RAY!
DON'T SEE ME.
DON'T SEE ME.
CLEAR ON SIX!
AH YES.
HERE WE ARE.
I'M SORRY, WE'RE NOT ALLOWING ANY--
BLIND.
DEAF.
MUTE.

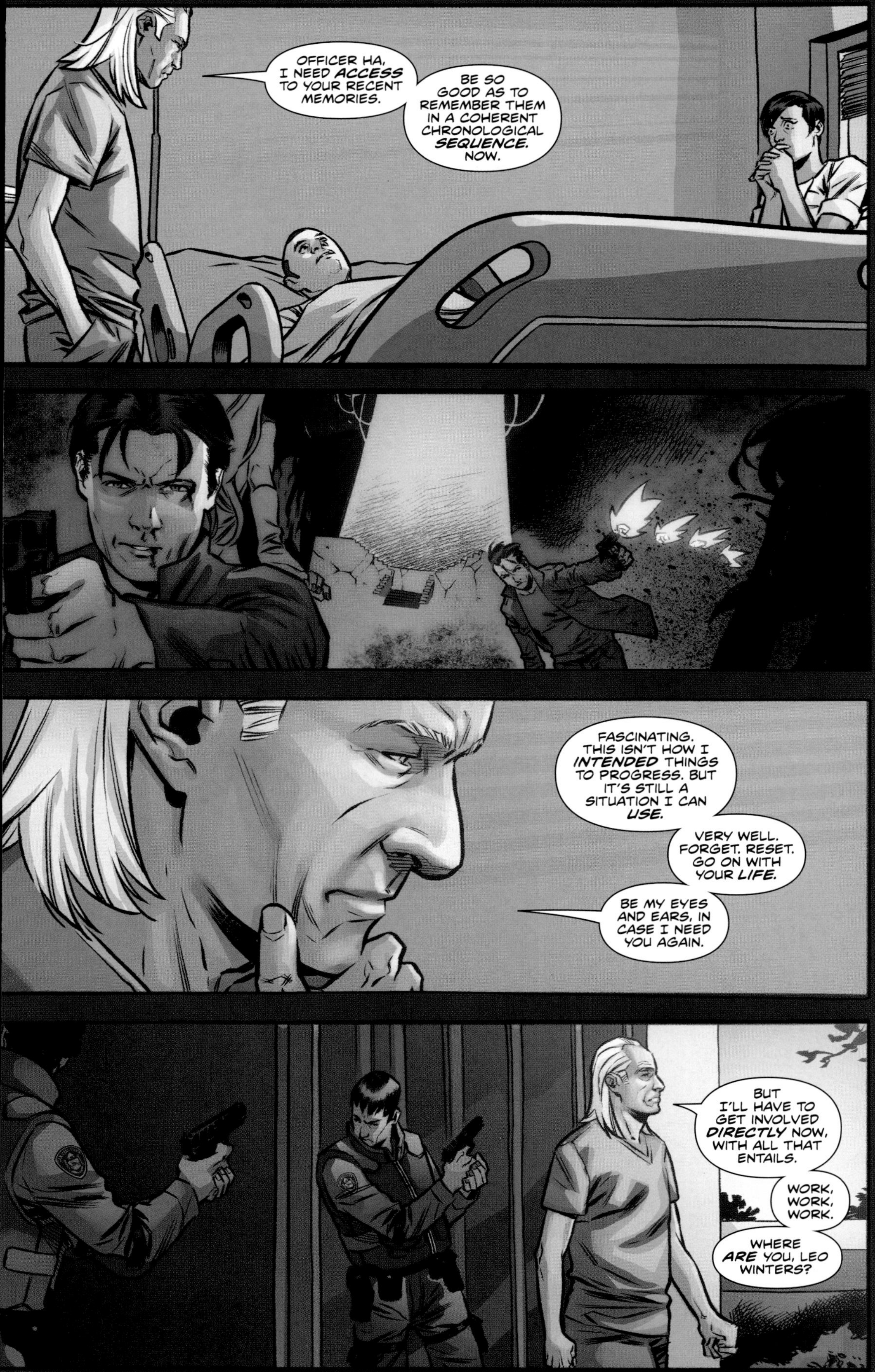
OFFICER HA, I NEED ACCESS TO YOUR RECENT MEMORIES.
BE SO GOOD AS TO REMEMBER THEM IN A COHERENT CHRONOLOGICAL SEQUENCE. NOW.
FASCINATING. THIS ISN'T HOW I INTENDED THINGS TO PROGRESS. BUT IT'S STILL A SITUATION I CAN USE.
VERY WELL. FORGET. RESET. GO ON WITH YOUR LIFE.
BE MY EYES AND EARS, IN CASE I NEED YOU AGAIN.
BUT I'LL HAVE TO GET INVOLVED DIRECTLY NOW, WITH ALL THAT ENTAILS.
WORK, WORK, WORK.
WHERE ARE YOU, LEO WINTERS?

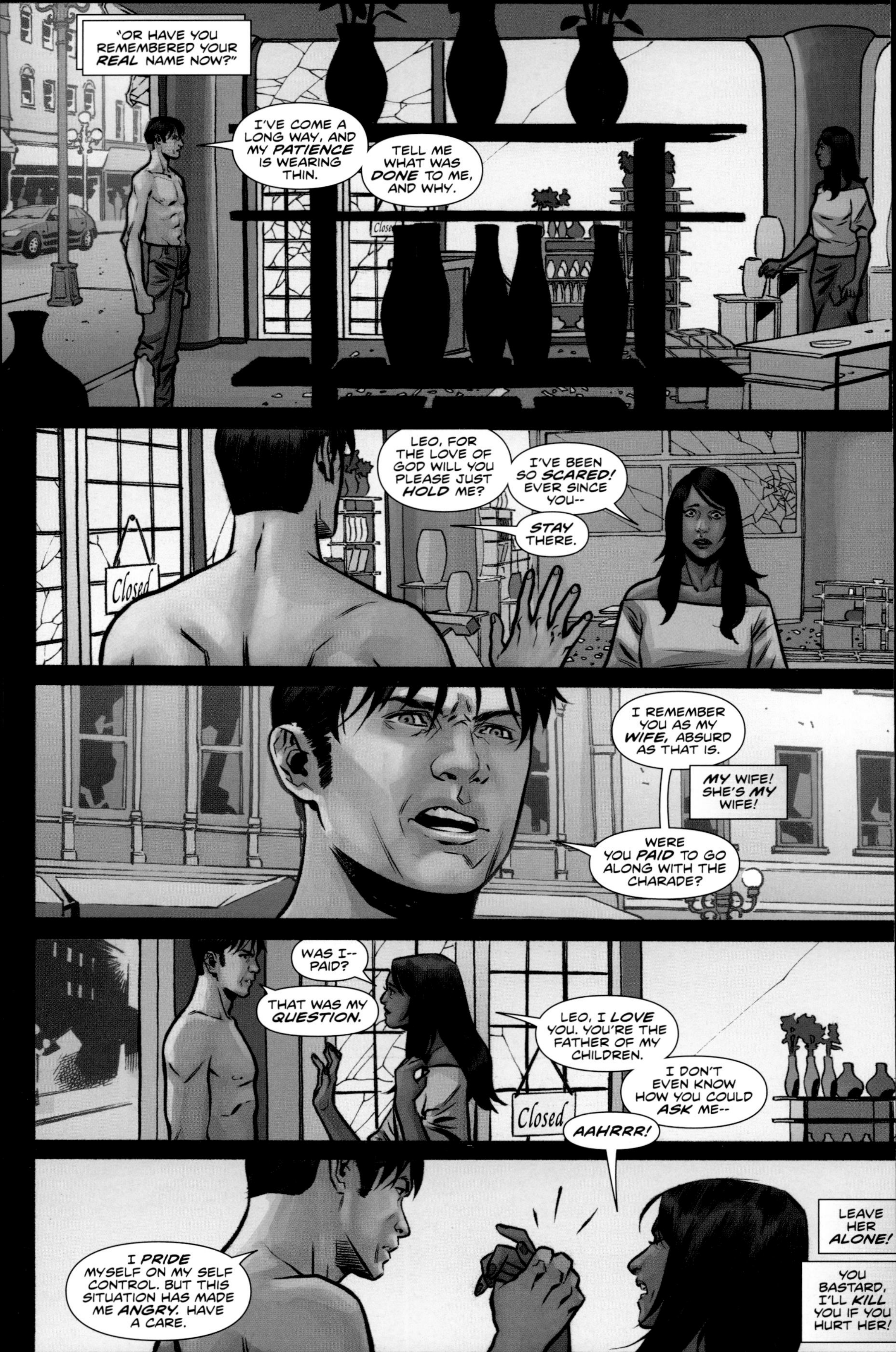
"OR HAVE YOU REMEMBERED YOUR REAL NAME NOW?"
I'VE COME A LONG WAY, AND MY PATIENCE IS WEARING THIN.
TELL ME WHAT WAS DONE TO ME, AND WHY.
Closed
LEO, FOR THE LOVE OF GOD WILL YOU PLEASE JUST HOLD ME?
I'VE BEEN SO SCARED! EVER SINCE YOU--
STAY THERE.
Closed
I REMEMBER YOU AS MY WIFE, ABSURD AS THAT IS.
MY WIFE! SHE'S MY WIFE!
WERE YOU PAID TO GO ALONG WITH THE CHARADE?
WAS I-- PAID?
THAT WAS MY QUESTION.
LEO, I LOVE YOU. YOU'RE THE FATHER OF MY CHILDREN.
I DON'T EVEN KNOW HOW YOU COULD ASK ME--
Closed
AAHRRR!
I PRIDE MYSELF ON MY SELF CONTROL. BUT THIS SITUATION HAS MADE ME ANGRY. HAVE A CARE.
LEAVE HER ALONE!
YOU BASTARD, I'LL KILL YOU IF YOU HURT HER!

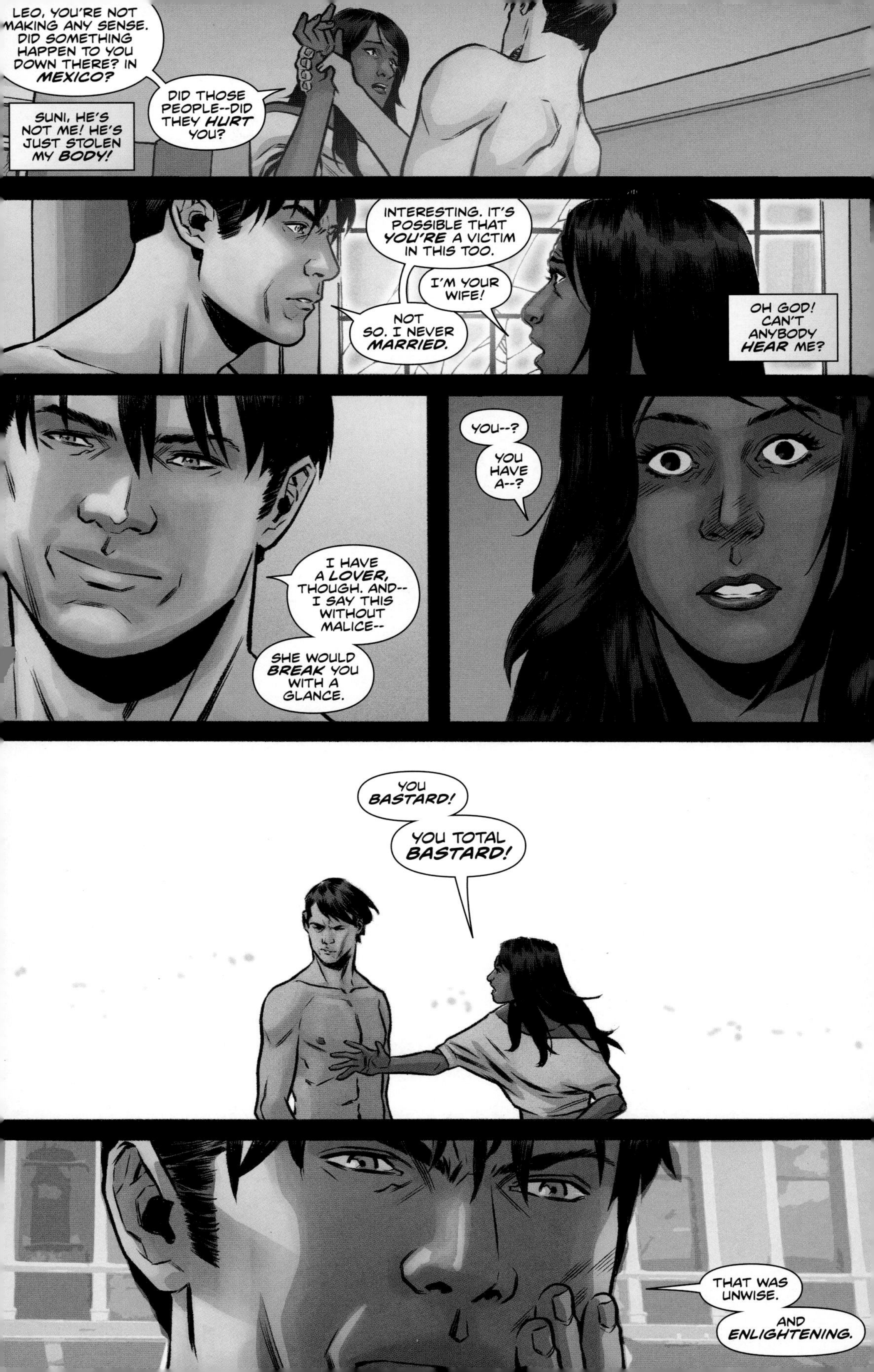
LEO, YOU'RE NOT MAKING ANY SENSE. DID SOMETHING HAPPEN TO YOU DOWN THERE? IN MEXICO?
DID THOSE PEOPLE--DID THEY HURT YOU?
SUNI, HE'S NOT ME! HE'S JUST STOLEN MY BODY!
INTERESTING. IT'S POSSIBLE THAT YOU'RE A VICTIM IN THIS TOO.
I'M YOUR WIFE!
NOT SO. I NEVER MARRIED.
OH GOD! CAN'T ANYBODY HEAR ME?
YOU--?
YOU HAVE A--?
I HAVE A LOVER, THOUGH. AND-- I SAY THIS WITHOUT MALICE--
SHE WOULD BREAK YOU WITH A GLANCE.
YOU BASTARD!
YOU TOTAL BASTARD!
THAT WAS UNWISE.
AND ENLIGHTENING.

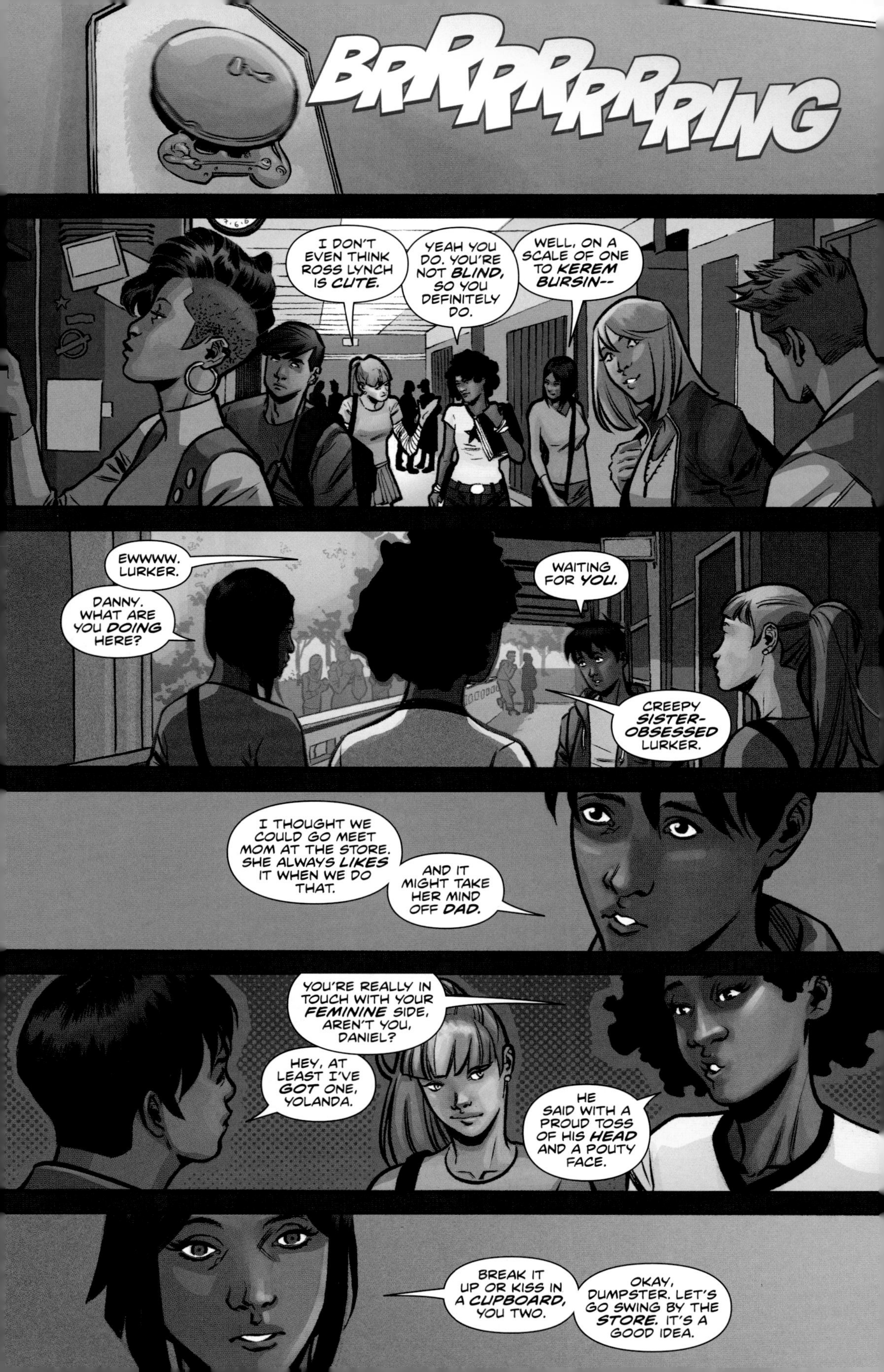
BRRRRRRRRING
I DON'T EVEN THINK ROSS LYNCH IS CUTE.
YEAH YOU DO. YOU'RE NOT BLIND, SO YOU DEFINITELY DO.
WELL, ON A SCALE OF ONE TO KEREM BURSIN--
EWWWW. LURKER.
DANNY. WHAT ARE YOU DOING HERE?
WAITING FOR YOU.
CREEPY SISTER-OBSESSED LURKER.
I THOUGHT WE COULD GO MEET MOM AT THE STORE. SHE ALWAYS LIKES IT WHEN WE DO THAT.
AND IT MIGHT TAKE HER MIND OFF DAD.
YOU'RE REALLY IN TOUCH WITH YOUR FEMININE SIDE, AREN'T YOU, DANIEL?
HEY, AT LEAST I'VE GOT ONE, YOLANDA.
HE SAID WITH A PROUD TOSS OF HIS HEAD AND A POUTY FACE.
BREAK IT UP OR KISS IN A CUPBOARD, YOU TWO.
OKAY, DUMPSTER. LET'S GO SWING BY THE STORE. IT'S A GOOD IDEA.

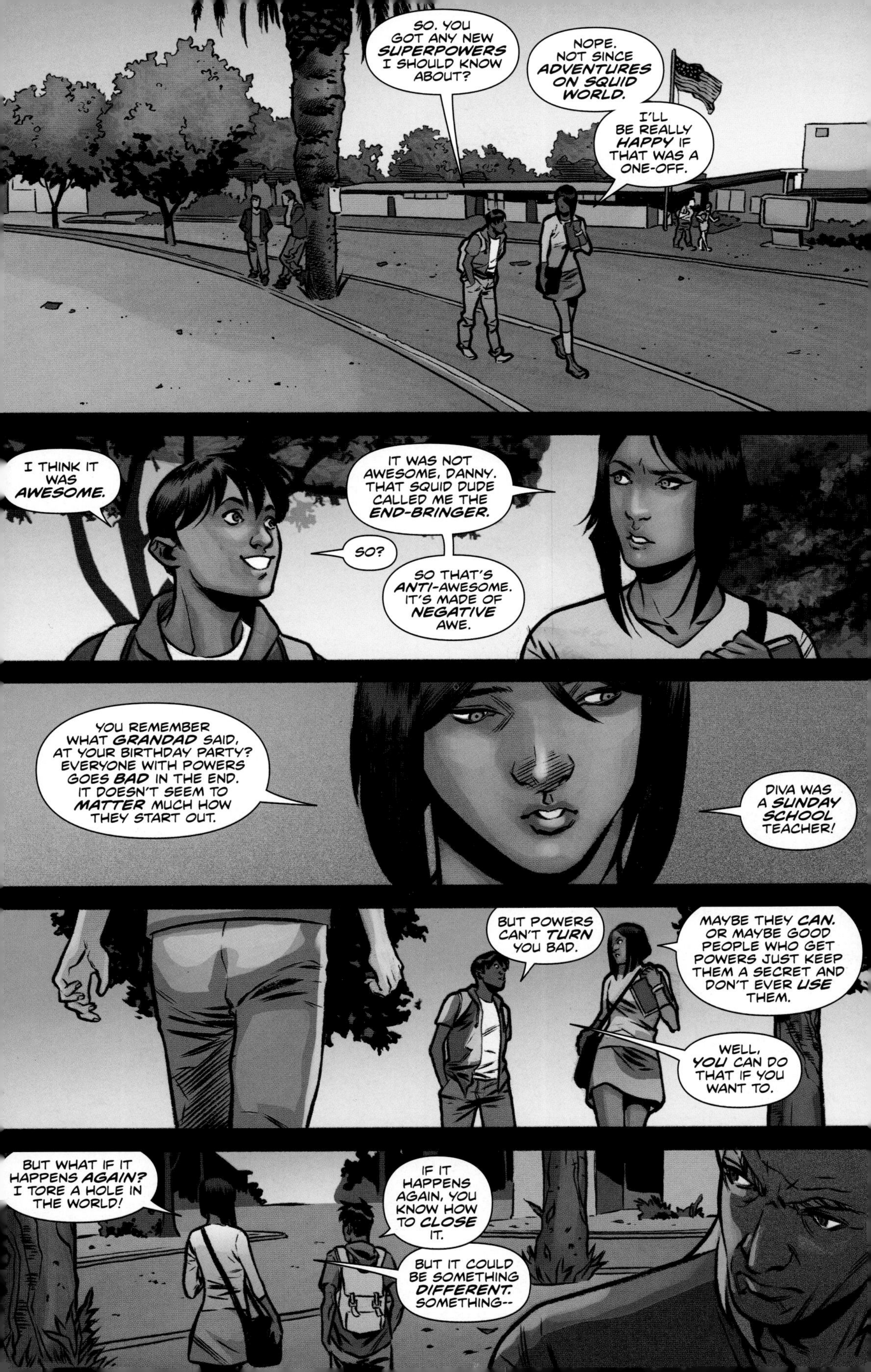
SO. YOU GOT ANY NEW SUPERPOWERS I SHOULD KNOW ABOUT?
NOPE. NOT SINCE ADVENTURES ON SQUID WORLD.
I'LL BE REALLY HAPPY IF THAT WAS A ONE-OFF.
I THINK IT WAS AWESOME.
IT WAS NOT AWESOME, DANNY. THAT SQUID DUDE CALLED ME THE END-BRINGER.
SO?
SO THAT'S ANTI-AWESOME. IT'S MADE OF NEGATIVE AWE.
YOU REMEMBER WHAT GRANDAD SAID, AT YOUR BIRTHDAY PARTY? EVERYONE WITH POWERS GOES BAD IN THE END. IT DOESN'T SEEM TO MATTER MUCH HOW THEY START OUT.
DIVA WAS A SUNDAY SCHOOL TEACHER!
BUT POWERS CAN'T TURN YOU BAD.
MAYBE THEY CAN. OR MAYBE GOOD PEOPLE WHO GET POWERS JUST KEEP THEM A SECRET AND DON'T EVER USE THEM.
WELL, YOU CAN DO THAT IF YOU WANT TO.
BUT WHAT IF IT HAPPENS AGAIN? I TORE A HOLE IN THE WORLD!
IF IT HAPPENS AGAIN, YOU KNOW HOW TO CLOSE IT.
BUT IT COULD BE SOMETHING DIFFERENT. SOMETHING--

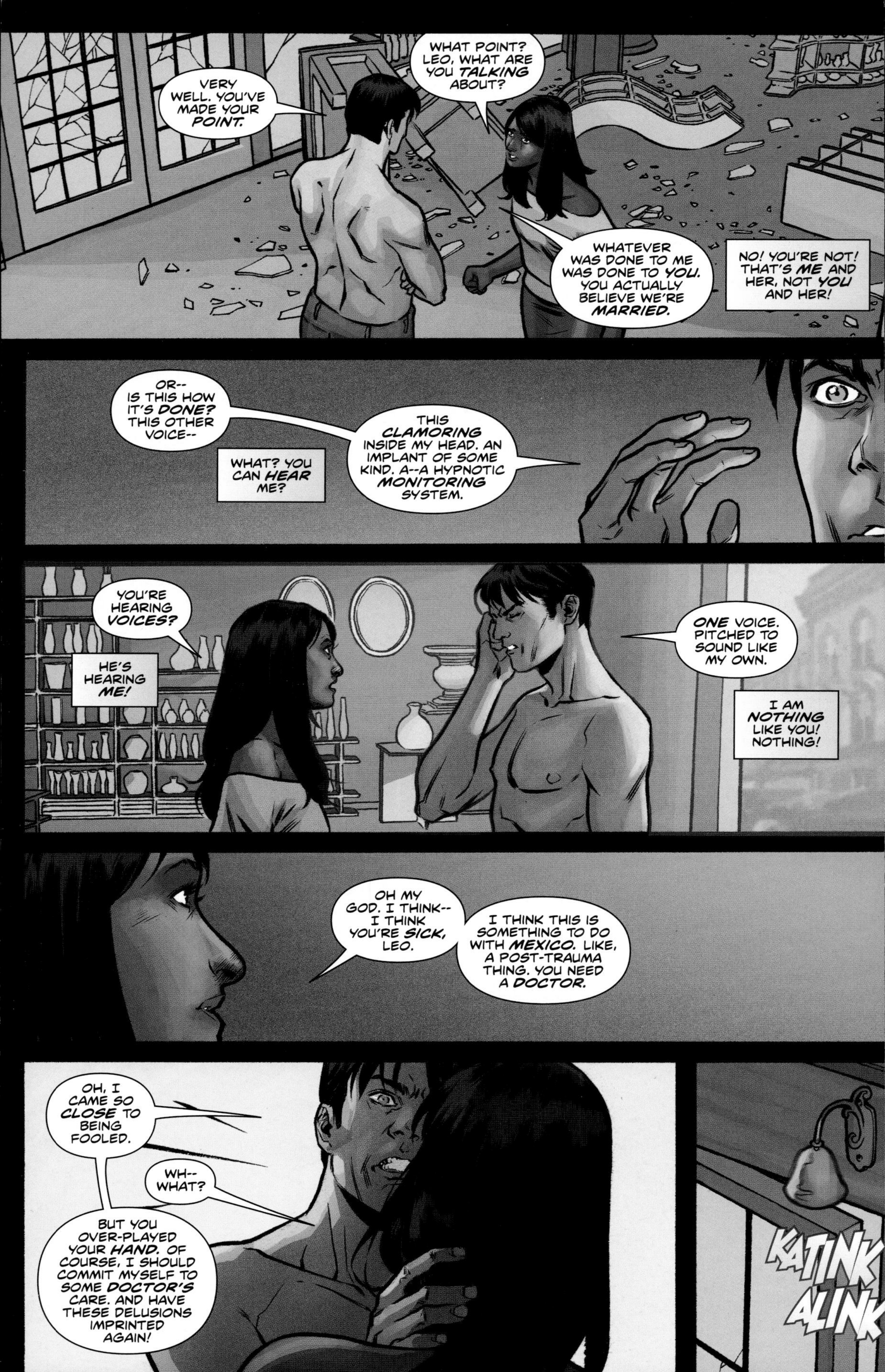
VERY WELL. YOU'VE MADE YOUR POINT.
WHAT POINT? LEO, WHAT ARE YOU TALKING ABOUT?
WHATEVER WAS DONE TO ME WAS DONE TO YOU. YOU ACTUALLY BELIEVE WE'RE MARRIED.
NO! YOU'RE NOT! THAT'S ME AND HER, NOT YOU AND HER!
OR-- IS THIS HOW IT'S DONE? THIS OTHER VOICE--
WHAT? YOU CAN HEAR ME?
THIS CLAMORING INSIDE MY HEAD. AN IMPLANT OF SOME KIND. A--A HYPNOTIC MONITORING SYSTEM.
YOU'RE HEARING VOICES?
HE'S HEARING ME!
ONE VOICE. PITCHED TO SOUND LIKE MY OWN.
I AM NOTHING LIKE YOU! NOTHING!
OH MY GOD. I THINK-- I THINK YOU'RE SICK, LEO.
I THINK THIS IS SOMETHING TO DO WITH MEXICO. LIKE, A POST-TRAUMA THING. YOU NEED A DOCTOR.
OH, I CAME SO CLOSE TO BEING FOOLED.
WH-- WHAT?
BUT YOU OVER-PLAYED YOUR HAND. OF COURSE, I SHOULD COMMIT MYSELF TO SOME DOCTOR'S CARE. AND HAVE THESE DELUSIONS IMPRINTED AGAIN!
KATINK ALINK

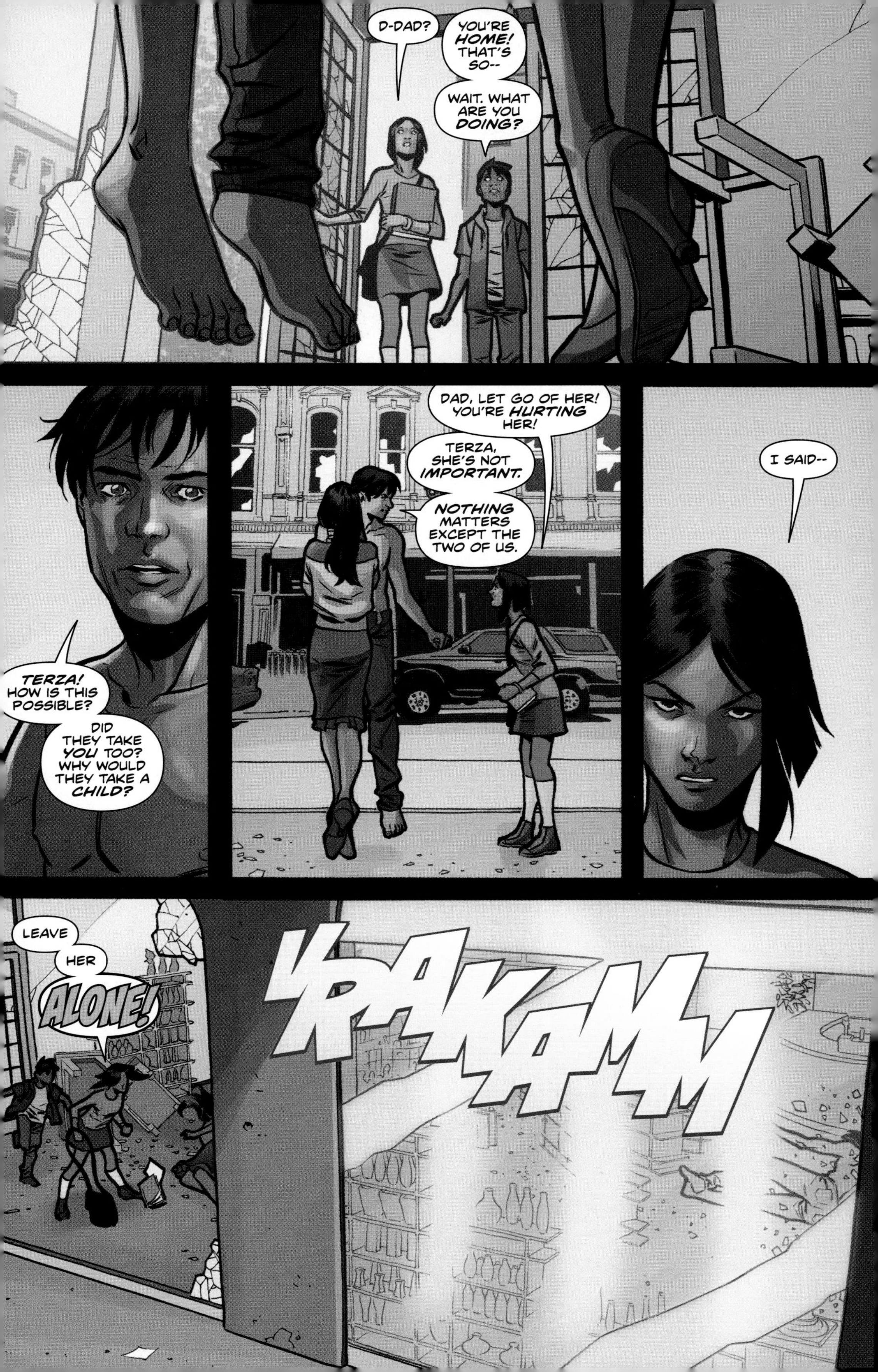

D-DAD?
YOU'RE HOME! THAT'S SO--
WAIT. WHAT ARE YOU DOING?
TERZA! HOW IS THIS POSSIBLE?
DID THEY TAKE YOU TOO? WHY WOULD THEY TAKE A CHILD?
DAD, LET GO OF HER! YOU'RE HURTING HER!
TERZA, SHE'S NOT IMPORTANT.
NOTHING MATTERS EXCEPT THE TWO OF US.
I SAID--
LEAVE
HER
ALONE!
KRAKAMM

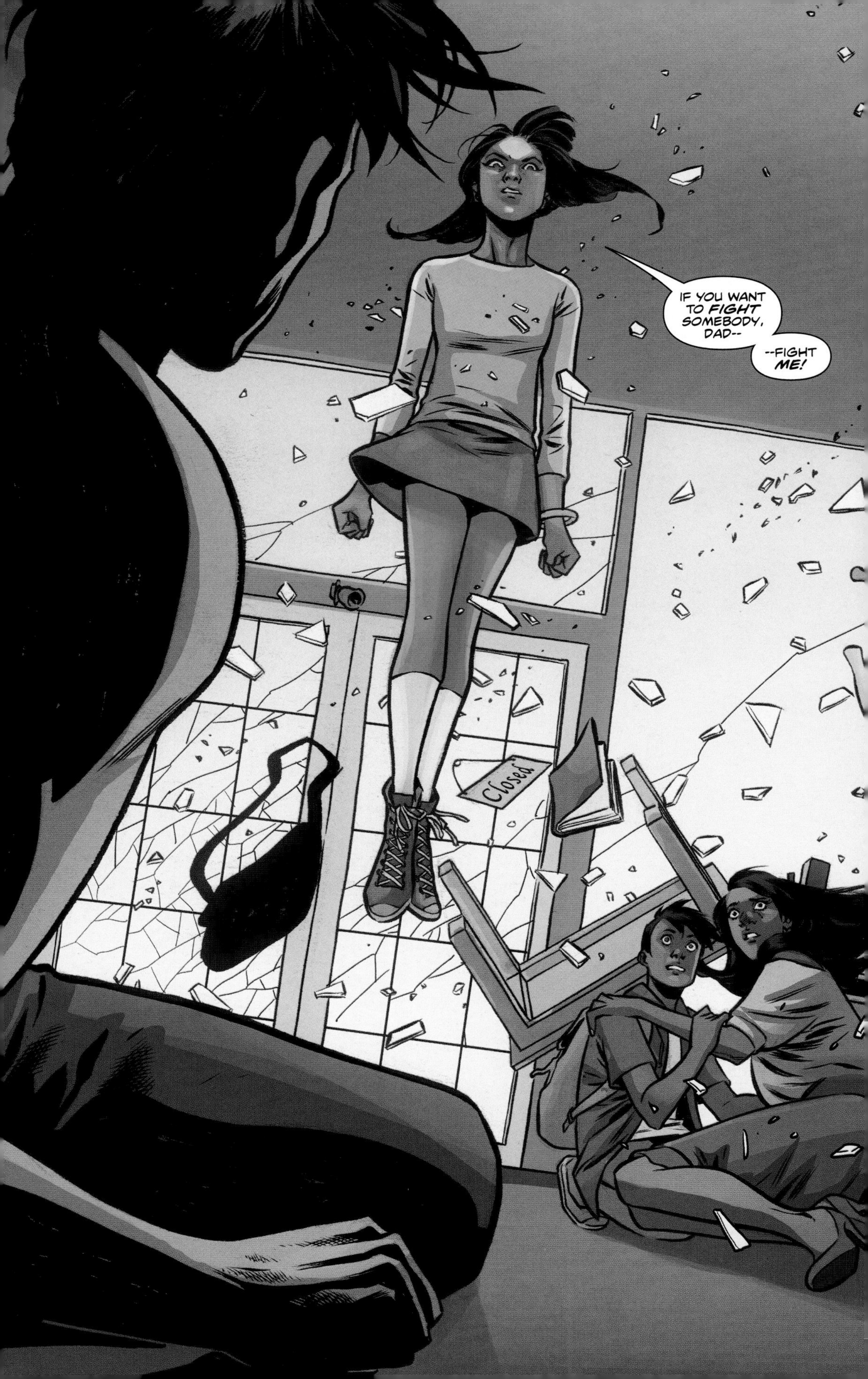
IF YOU WANT TO FIGHT SOMEBODY, DAD--
--FIGHT ME!
Closed

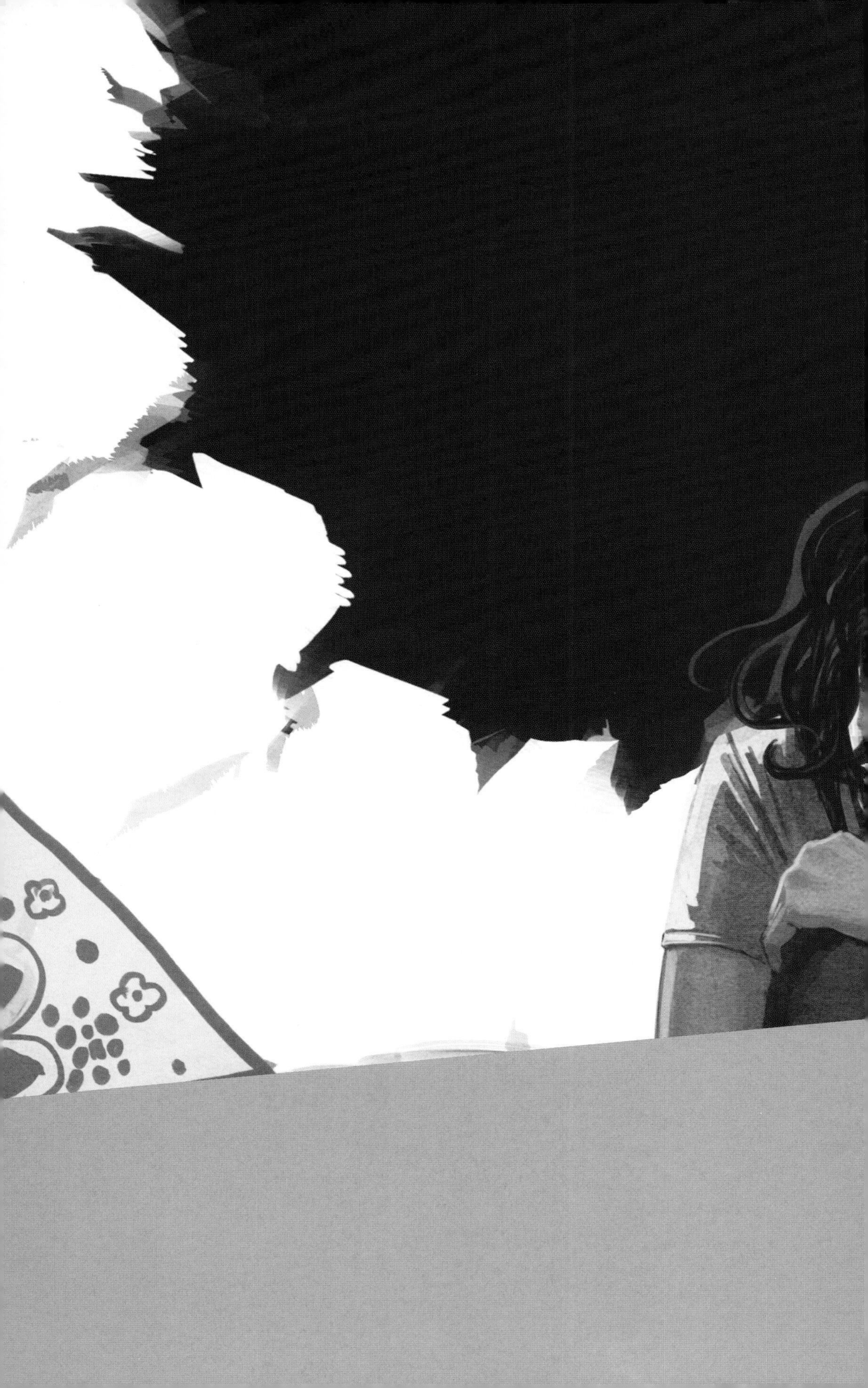

"I SWALLOW **BLOOD** AND HEAR HER VOICE AGAIN."
Chapter 12

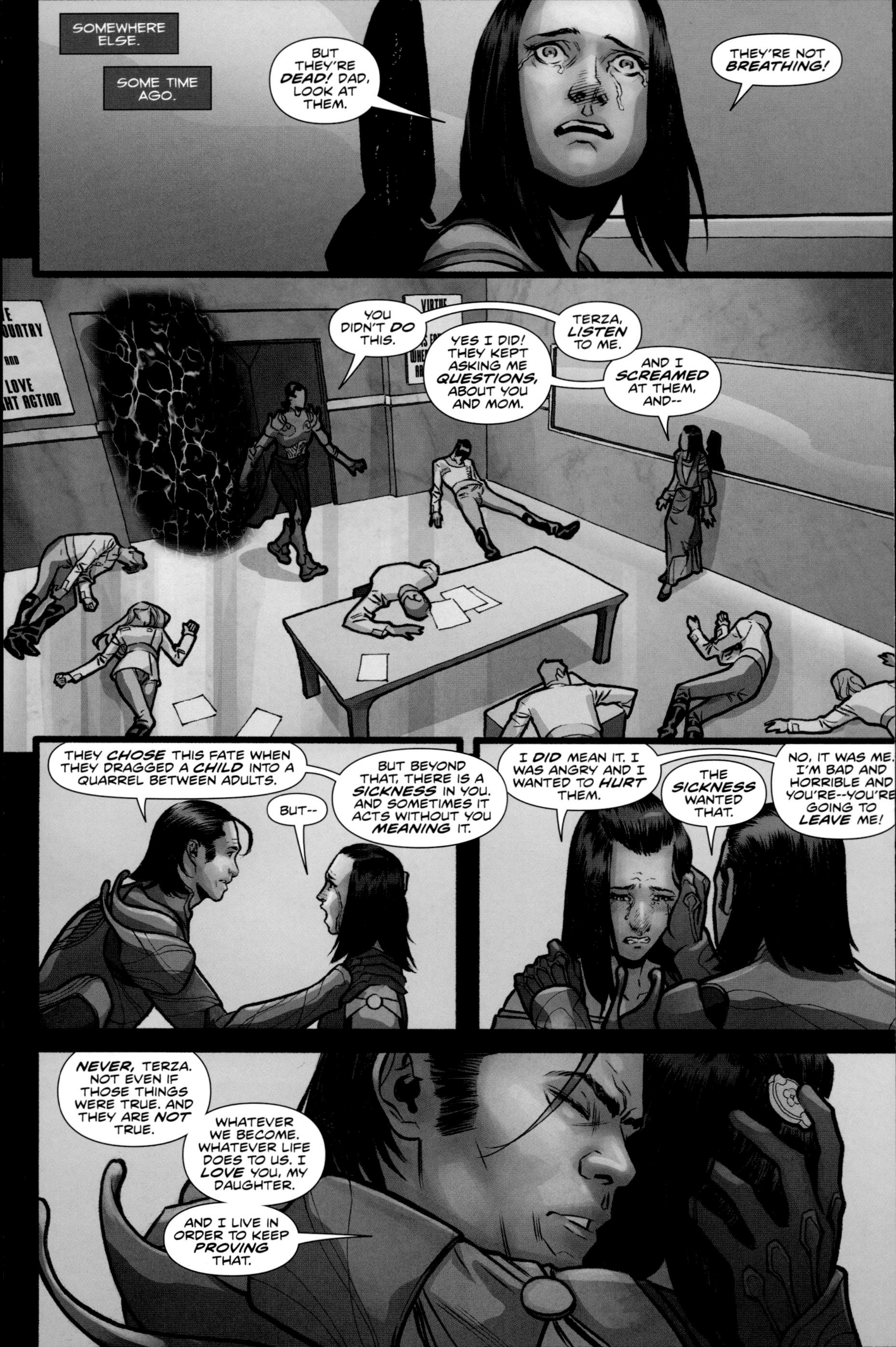
SOMEWHERE ELSE.
SOME TIME AGO.
BUT THEY'RE *DEAD!* DAD, LOOK AT THEM.
THEY'RE NOT *BREATHING!*
YOU DIDN'T *DO* THIS.
TERZA, *LISTEN* TO ME.
YES I DID! THEY KEPT ASKING ME *QUESTIONS,* ABOUT YOU AND MOM.
AND I *SCREAMED* AT THEM, AND--
THEY *CHOSE* THIS FATE WHEN THEY DRAGGED A *CHILD* INTO A QUARREL BETWEEN ADULTS.
BUT--
BUT BEYOND THAT, THERE IS A *SICKNESS* IN YOU. AND SOMETIMES IT ACTS WITHOUT YOU *MEANING* IT.
I *DID* MEAN IT. I WAS ANGRY AND I WANTED TO *HURT* THEM.
THE *SICKNESS* WANTED THAT.
NO, IT WAS ME. I'M BAD AND HORRIBLE AND YOU'RE--YOU'RE GOING TO *LEAVE* ME!
NEVER, TERZA. NOT EVEN IF THOSE THINGS WERE TRUE. AND THEY ARE *NOT* TRUE.
WHATEVER WE BECOME. WHATEVER LIFE DOES TO US. I *LOVE* YOU, MY DAUGHTER.
AND I LIVE IN ORDER TO KEEP *PROVING* THAT.

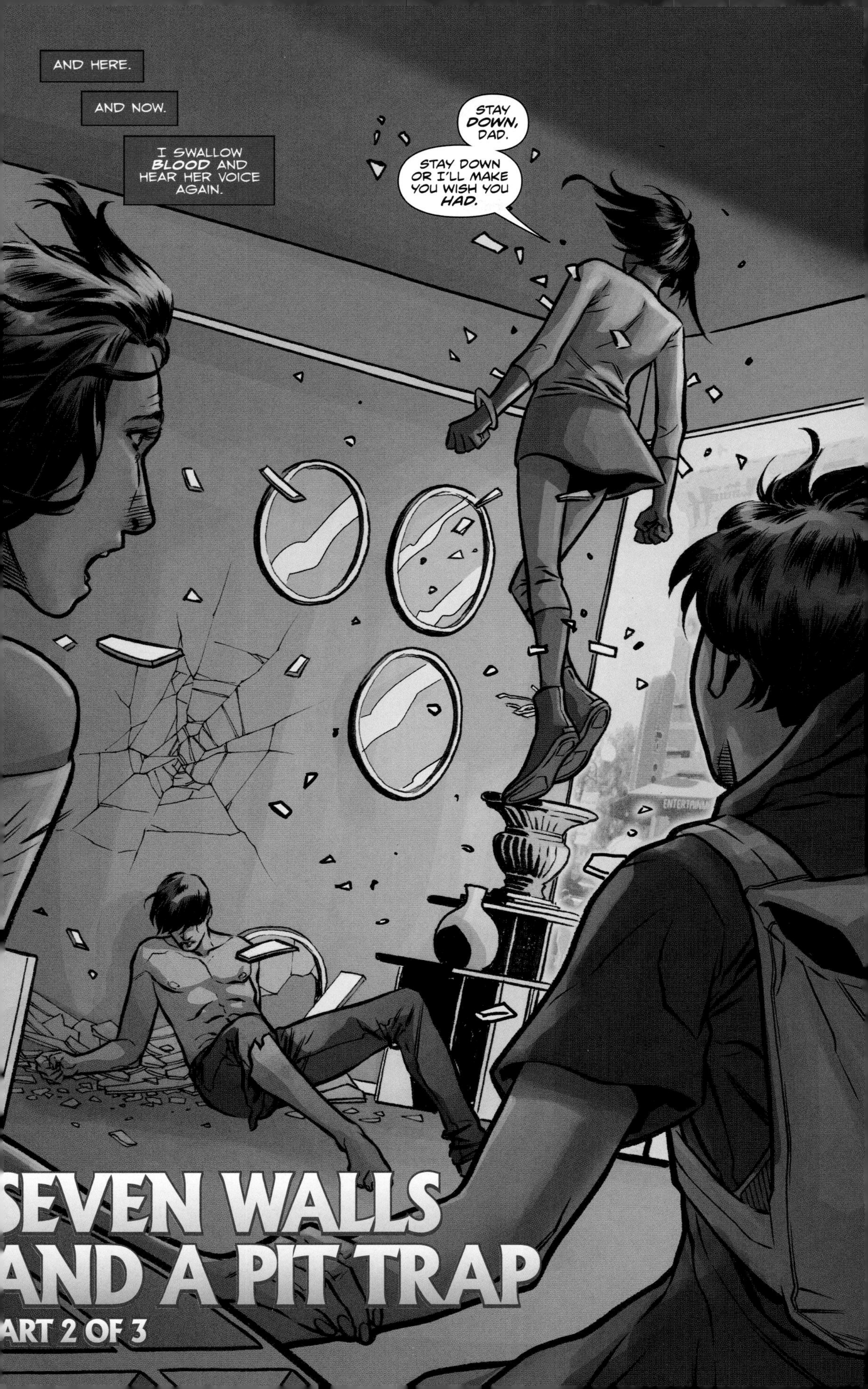
AND HERE.
AND NOW.
I SWALLOW BLOOD AND HEAR HER VOICE AGAIN.
STAY DOWN, DAD.
STAY DOWN OR I'LL MAKE YOU WISH YOU HAD.
SEVEN WALLS AND A PIT TRAP
PART 2 OF 3

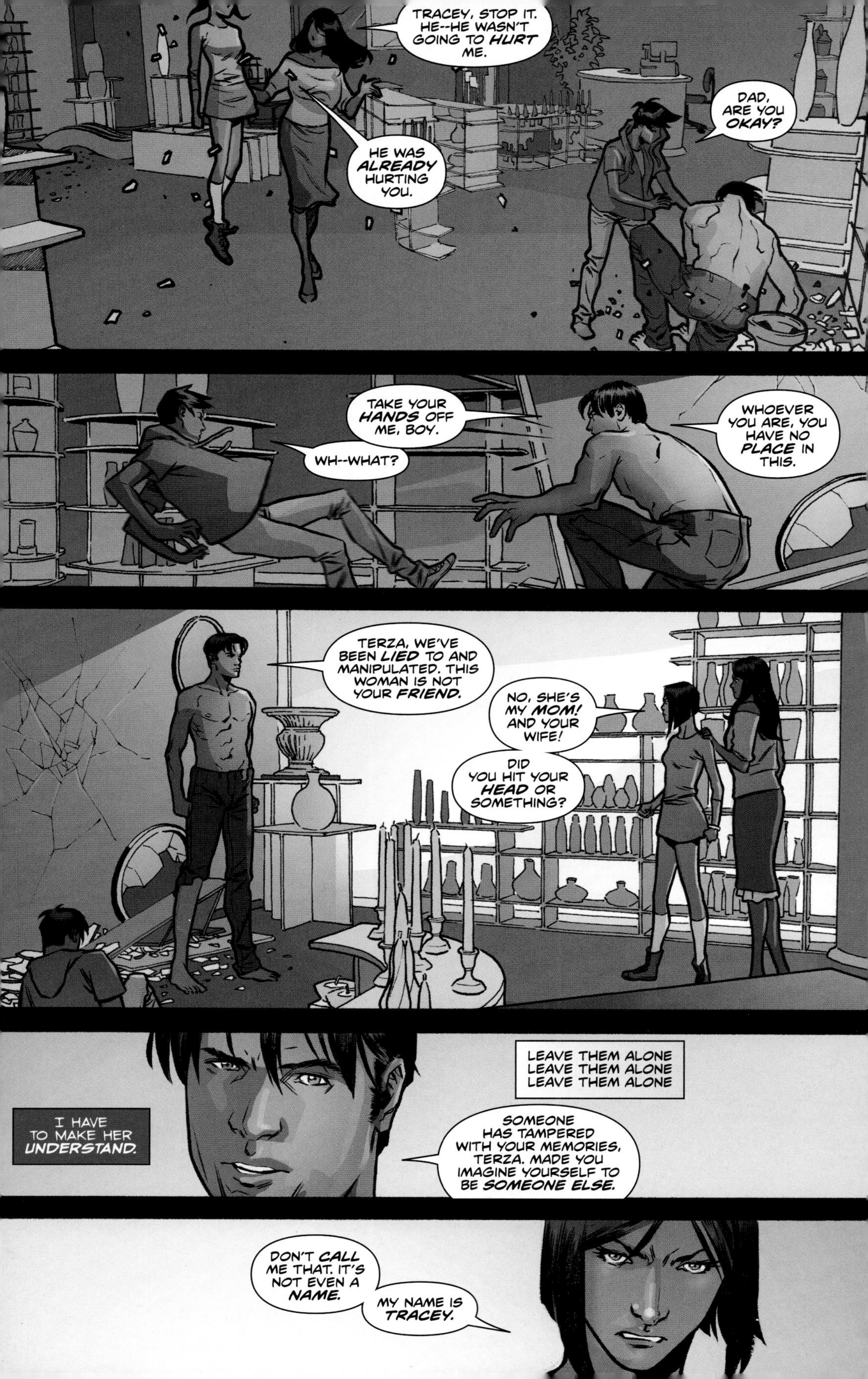
TRACEY, STOP IT. HE--HE WASN'T GOING TO HURT ME.
HE WAS ALREADY HURTING YOU.
DAD, ARE YOU OKAY?
TAKE YOUR HANDS OFF ME, BOY.
WH--WHAT?
WHOEVER YOU ARE, YOU HAVE NO PLACE IN THIS.
TERZA, WE'VE BEEN LIED TO AND MANIPULATED. THIS WOMAN IS NOT YOUR FRIEND.
NO, SHE'S MY MOM! AND YOUR WIFE!
DID YOU HIT YOUR HEAD OR SOMETHING?
I HAVE TO MAKE HER UNDERSTAND.
LEAVE THEM ALONE
LEAVE THEM ALONE
LEAVE THEM ALONE
SOMEONE HAS TAMPERED WITH YOUR MEMORIES, TERZA. MADE YOU IMAGINE YOURSELF TO BE SOMEONE ELSE.
DON'T CALL ME THAT. IT'S NOT EVEN A NAME.
MY NAME IS TRACEY.

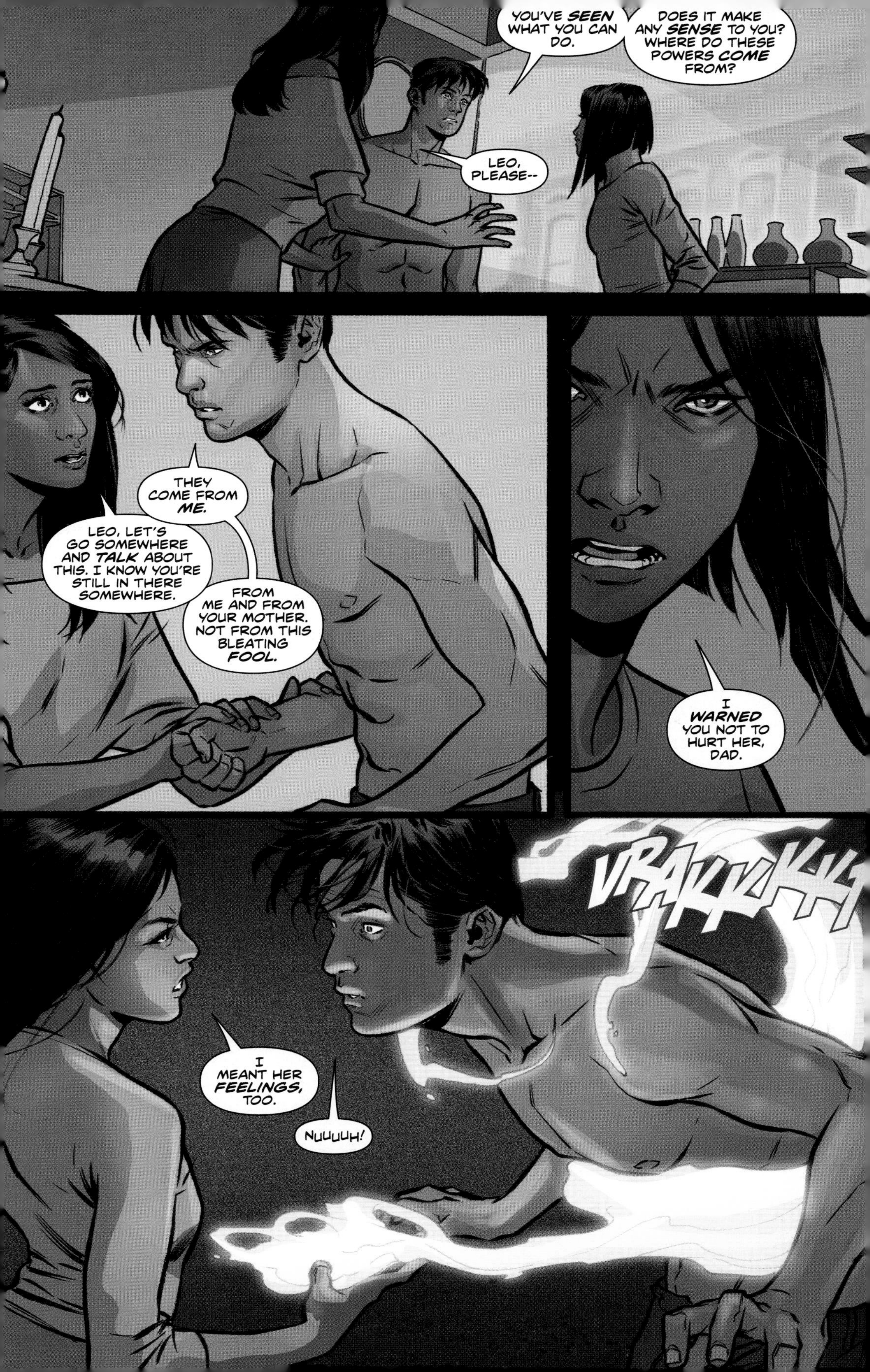
YOU'VE SEEN WHAT YOU CAN DO.
DOES IT MAKE ANY SENSE TO YOU? WHERE DO THESE POWERS COME FROM?
LEO, PLEASE--
THEY COME FROM ME.
LEO, LET'S GO SOMEWHERE AND TALK ABOUT THIS. I KNOW YOU'RE STILL IN THERE SOMEWHERE.
FROM ME AND FROM YOUR MOTHER. NOT FROM THIS BLEATING FOOL.
I WARNED YOU NOT TO HURT HER, DAD.
VRAKKKK!
I MEANT HER FEELINGS, TOO.
NUUUUH!

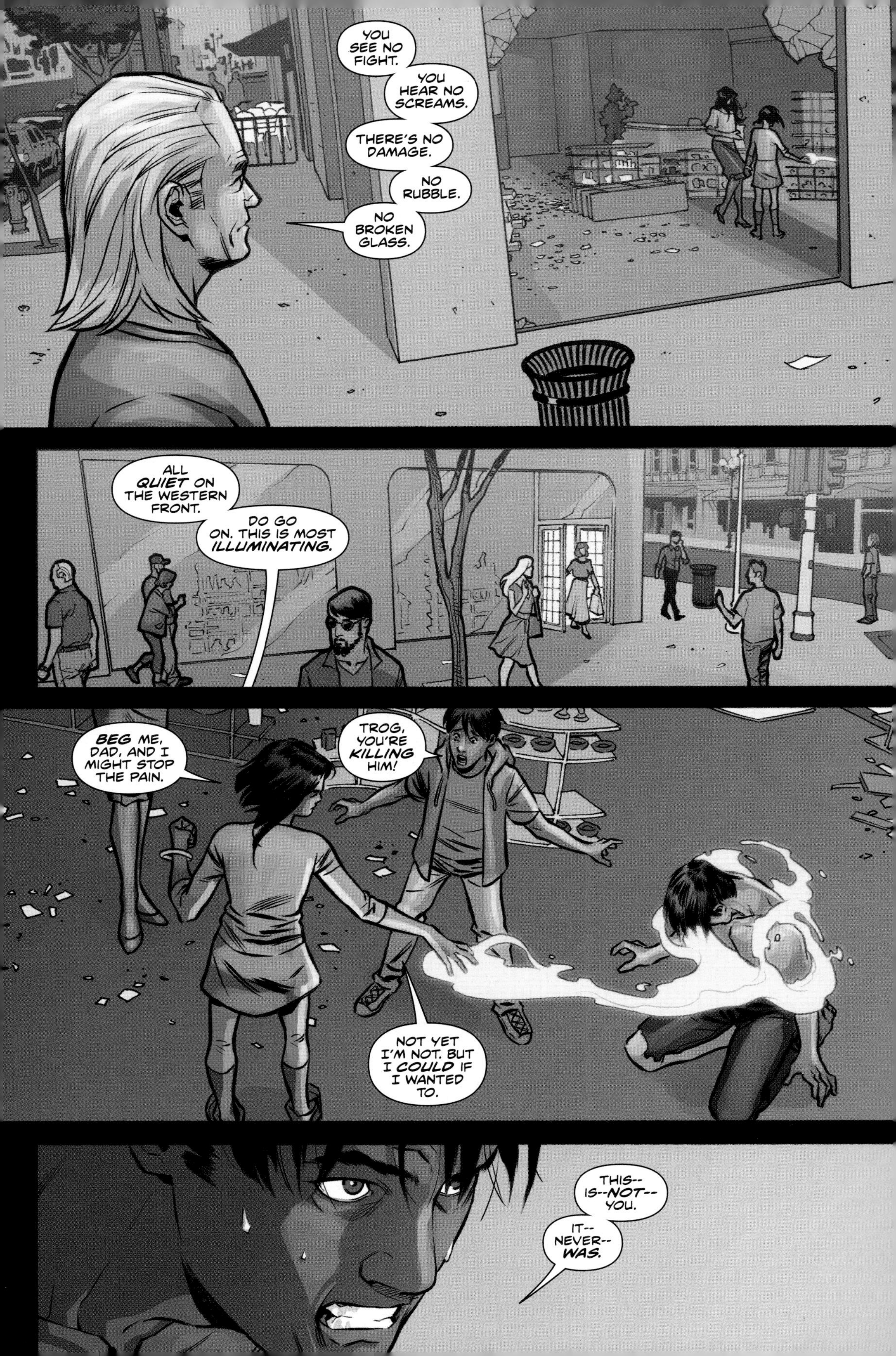
YOU SEE NO FIGHT.
YOU HEAR NO SCREAMS.
THERE'S NO DAMAGE.
NO RUBBLE.
NO BROKEN GLASS.
ALL QUIET ON THE WESTERN FRONT.
DO GO ON. THIS IS MOST ILLUMINATING.
BEG ME, DAD, AND I MIGHT STOP THE PAIN.
TROG, YOU'RE KILLING HIM!
NOT YET I'M NOT. BUT I COULD IF I WANTED TO.
THIS--IS--NOT--YOU.
IT--NEVER--WAS.

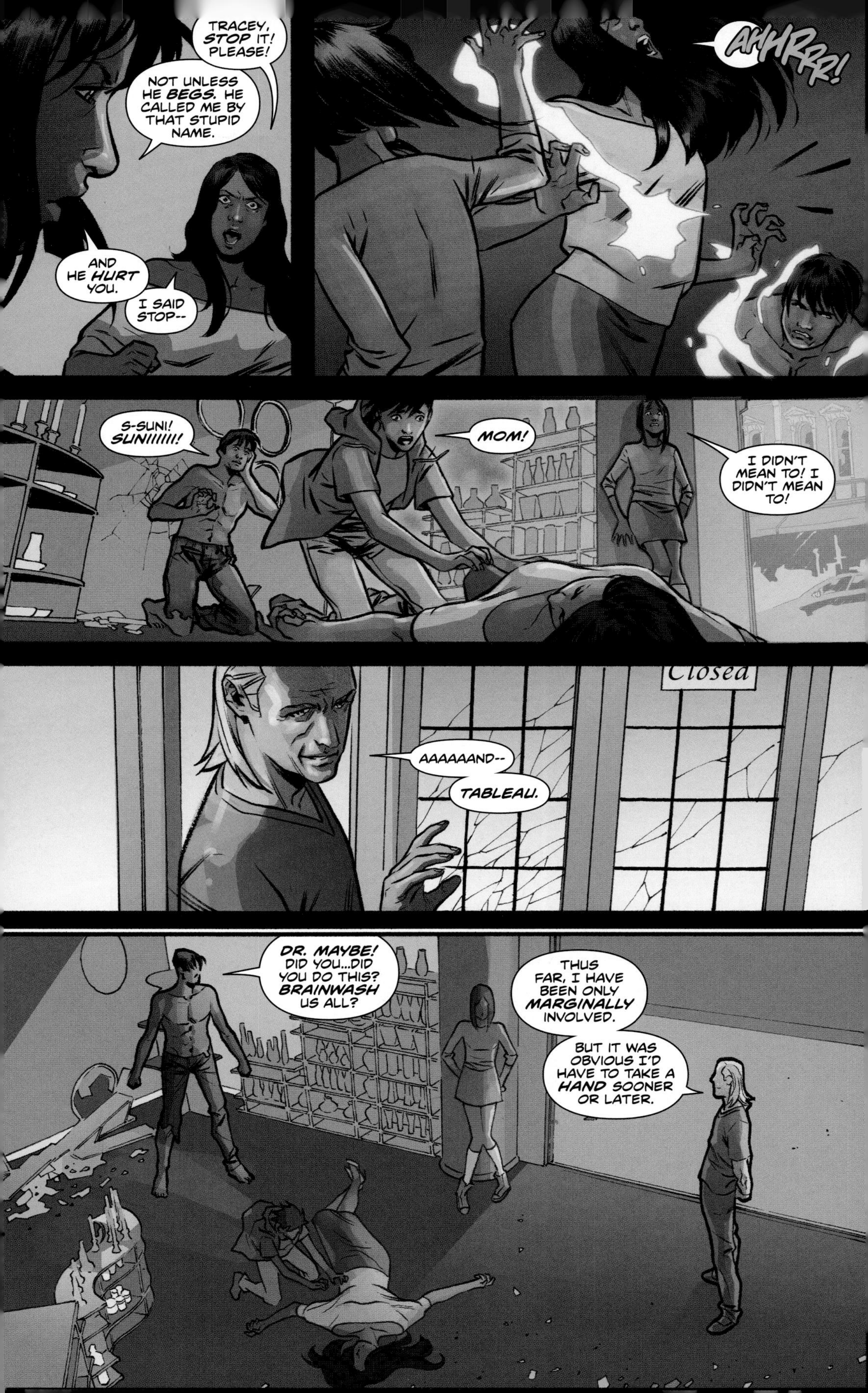

TRACEY, STOP IT! PLEASE!
NOT UNLESS HE BEGS. HE CALLED ME BY THAT STUPID NAME.
AND HE HURT YOU.
I SAID STOP--
AHHRRR!
S-SUN! SUNIIIIIII!
MOM!
I DIDN'T MEAN TO! I DIDN'T MEAN TO!
Closed
AAAAAAND--
TABLEAU.
DR. MAYBE! DID YOU...DID YOU DO THIS? BRAINWASH US ALL?
THUS FAR, I HAVE BEEN ONLY MARGINALLY INVOLVED.
BUT IT WAS OBVIOUS I'D HAVE TO TAKE A HAND SOONER OR LATER.

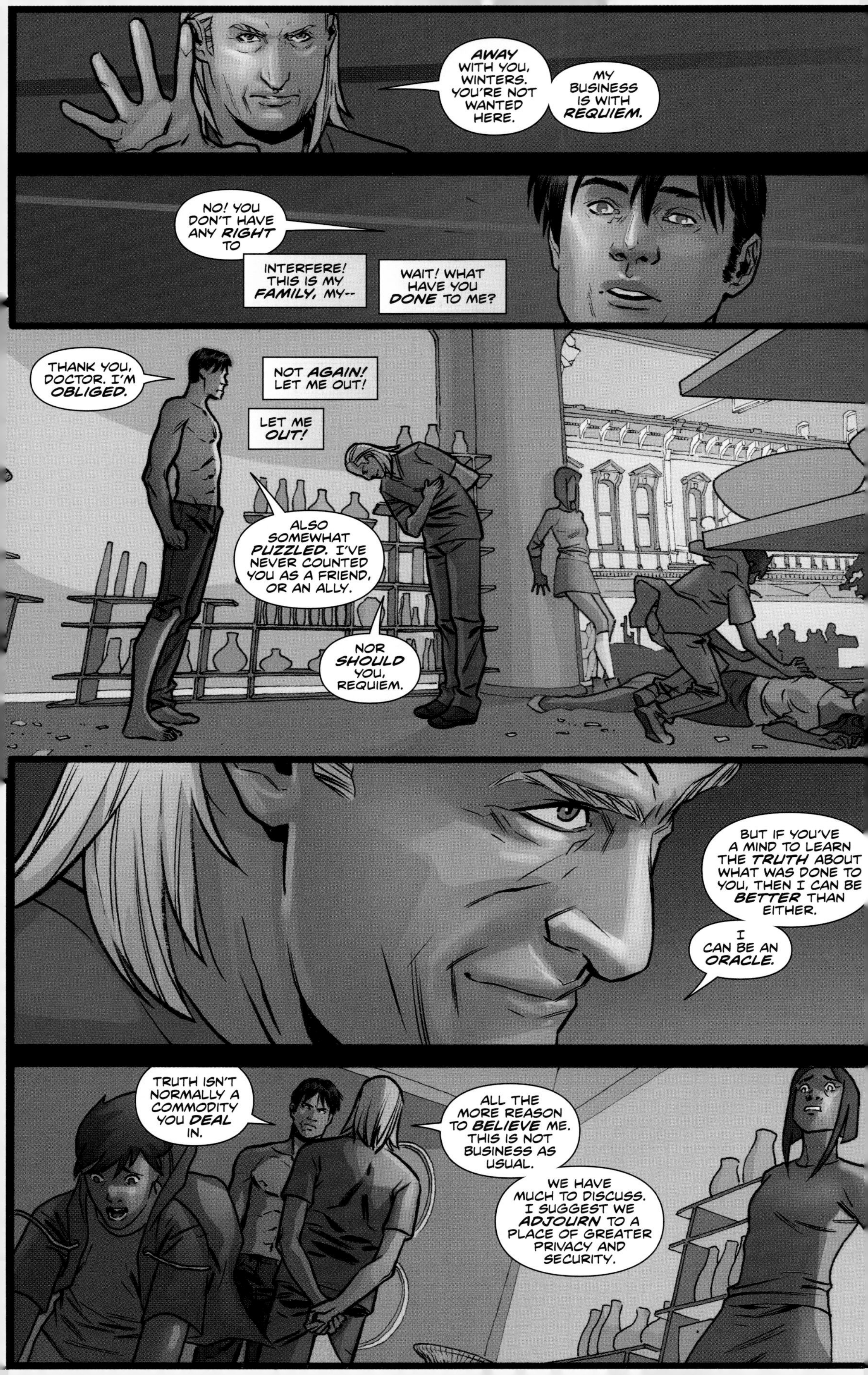
AWAY WITH YOU, WINTERS. YOU'RE NOT WANTED HERE.
MY BUSINESS IS WITH REQUIEM.
NO! YOU DON'T HAVE ANY RIGHT TO
INTERFERE! THIS IS MY FAMILY, MY--
WAIT! WHAT HAVE YOU DONE TO ME?
THANK YOU, DOCTOR. I'M OBLIGED.
NOT AGAIN! LET ME OUT!
LET ME OUT!
ALSO SOMEWHAT PUZZLED. I'VE NEVER COUNTED YOU AS A FRIEND, OR AN ALLY.
NOR SHOULD YOU, REQUIEM.
BUT IF YOU'VE A MIND TO LEARN THE TRUTH ABOUT WHAT WAS DONE TO YOU, THEN I CAN BE BETTER THAN EITHER.
I CAN BE AN ORACLE.
TRUTH ISN'T NORMALLY A COMMODITY YOU DEAL IN.
ALL THE MORE REASON TO BELIEVE ME. THIS IS NOT BUSINESS AS USUAL.
WE HAVE MUCH TO DISCUSS. I SUGGEST WE ADJOURN TO A PLACE OF GREATER PRIVACY AND SECURITY.

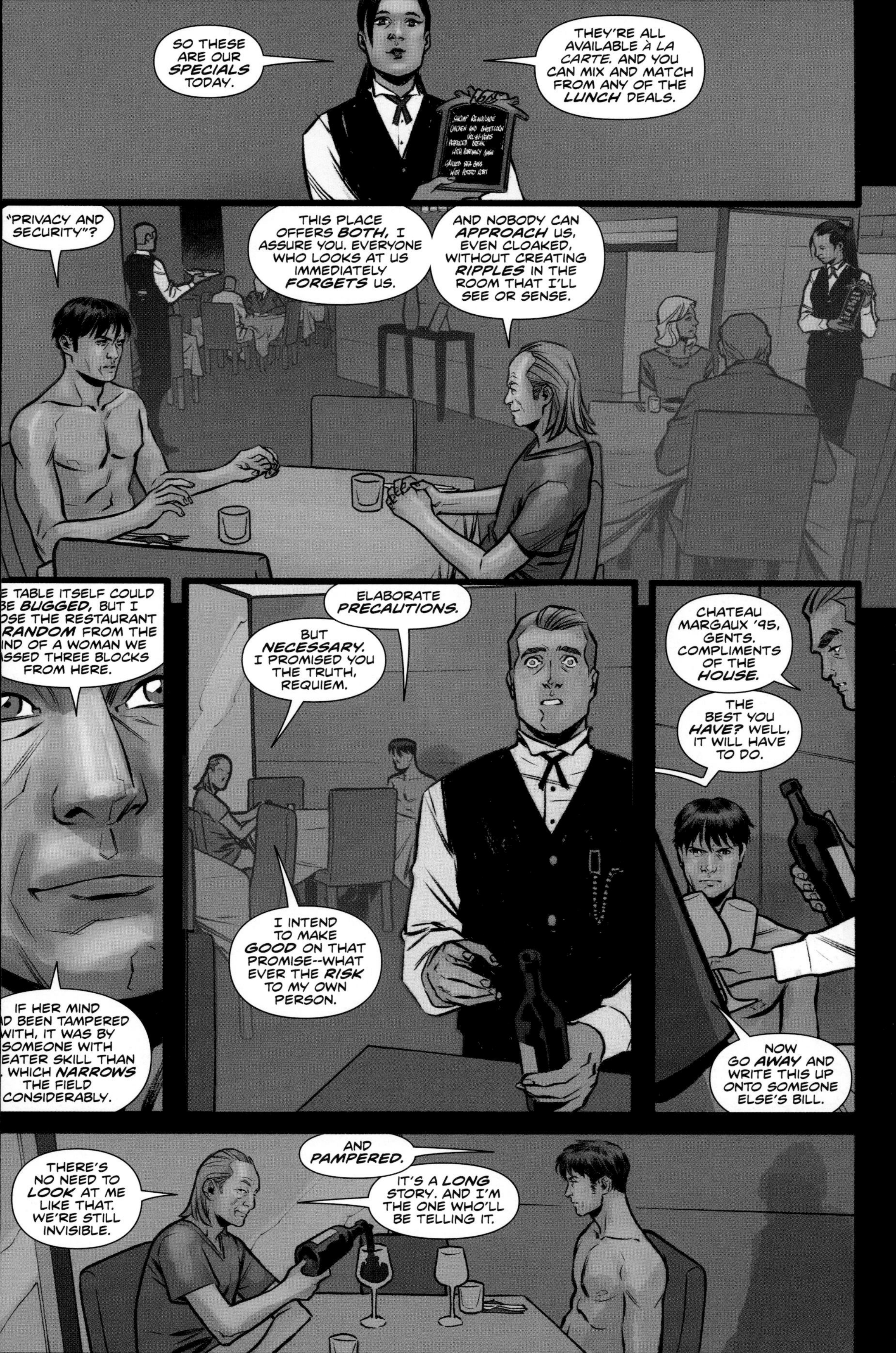
SO THESE ARE OUR SPECIALS TODAY.
THEY'RE ALL AVAILABLE À LA CARTE. AND YOU CAN MIX AND MATCH FROM ANY OF THE LUNCH DEALS.
"PRIVACY AND SECURITY"?
THIS PLACE OFFERS BOTH, I ASSURE YOU. EVERYONE WHO LOOKS AT US IMMEDIATELY FORGETS US.
AND NOBODY CAN APPROACH US, EVEN CLOAKED, WITHOUT CREATING RIPPLES IN THE ROOM THAT I'LL SEE OR SENSE.
E TABLE ITSELF COULD BE BUGGED, BUT I OSE THE RESTAURANT RANDOM FROM THE IND OF A WOMAN WE ASSED THREE BLOCKS FROM HERE.
IF HER MIND D BEEN TAMPERED WITH, IT WAS BY SOMEONE WITH EATER SKILL THAN . WHICH NARROWS THE FIELD CONSIDERABLY.
ELABORATE PRECAUTIONS.
BUT NECESSARY. I PROMISED YOU THE TRUTH, REQUIEM.
I INTEND TO MAKE GOOD ON THAT PROMISE--WHAT EVER THE RISK TO MY OWN PERSON.
CHATEAU MARGAUX '95, GENTS. COMPLIMENTS OF THE HOUSE.
THE BEST YOU HAVE? WELL, IT WILL HAVE TO DO.
NOW GO AWAY AND WRITE THIS UP ONTO SOMEONE ELSE'S BILL.
THERE'S NO NEED TO LOOK AT ME LIKE THAT. WE'RE STILL INVISIBLE.
AND PAMPERED.
IT'S A LONG STORY. AND I'M THE ONE WHO'LL BE TELLING IT.

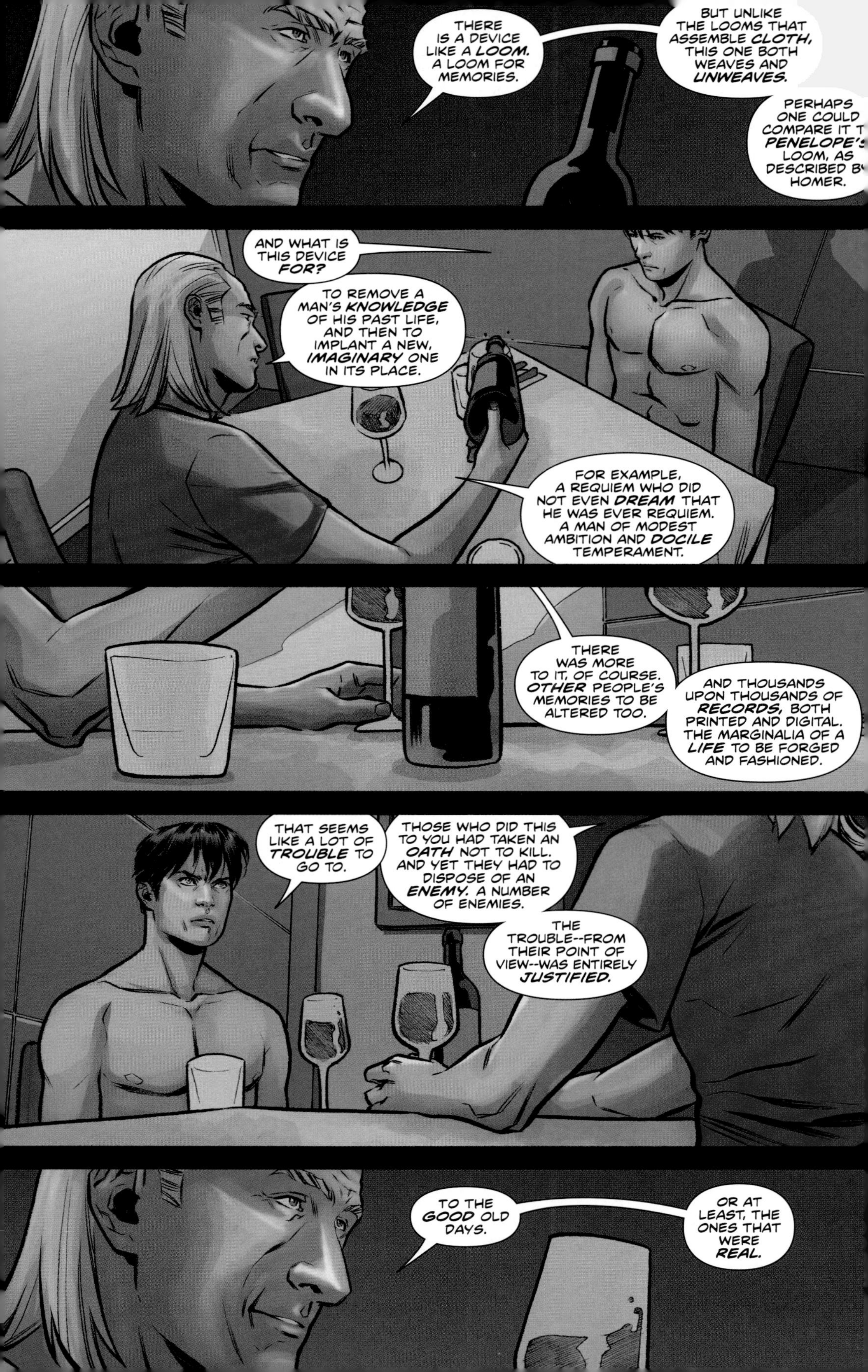
THERE IS A DEVICE LIKE A LOOM. A LOOM FOR MEMORIES.
BUT UNLIKE THE LOOMS THAT ASSEMBLE CLOTH, THIS ONE BOTH WEAVES AND UNWEAVES.
PERHAPS ONE COULD COMPARE IT T PENELOPE'S LOOM, AS DESCRIBED B HOMER.
AND WHAT IS THIS DEVICE FOR?
TO REMOVE A MAN'S KNOWLEDGE OF HIS PAST LIFE, AND THEN TO IMPLANT A NEW, IMAGINARY ONE IN ITS PLACE.
FOR EXAMPLE, A REQUIEM WHO DID NOT EVEN DREAM THAT HE WAS EVER REQUIEM. A MAN OF MODEST AMBITION AND DOCILE TEMPERAMENT.
THERE WAS MORE TO IT, OF COURSE. OTHER PEOPLE'S MEMORIES TO BE ALTERED TOO.
AND THOUSANDS UPON THOUSANDS OF RECORDS, BOTH PRINTED AND DIGITAL. THE MARGINALIA OF A LIFE TO BE FORGED AND FASHIONED.
THAT SEEMS LIKE A LOT OF TROUBLE TO GO TO.
THOSE WHO DID THIS TO YOU HAD TAKEN AN OATH NOT TO KILL. AND YET THEY HAD TO DISPOSE OF AN ENEMY. A NUMBER OF ENEMIES.
THE TROUBLE--FROM THEIR POINT OF VIEW--WAS ENTIRELY JUSTIFIED.
TO THE GOOD OLD DAYS.
OR AT LEAST, THE ONES THAT WERE REAL.

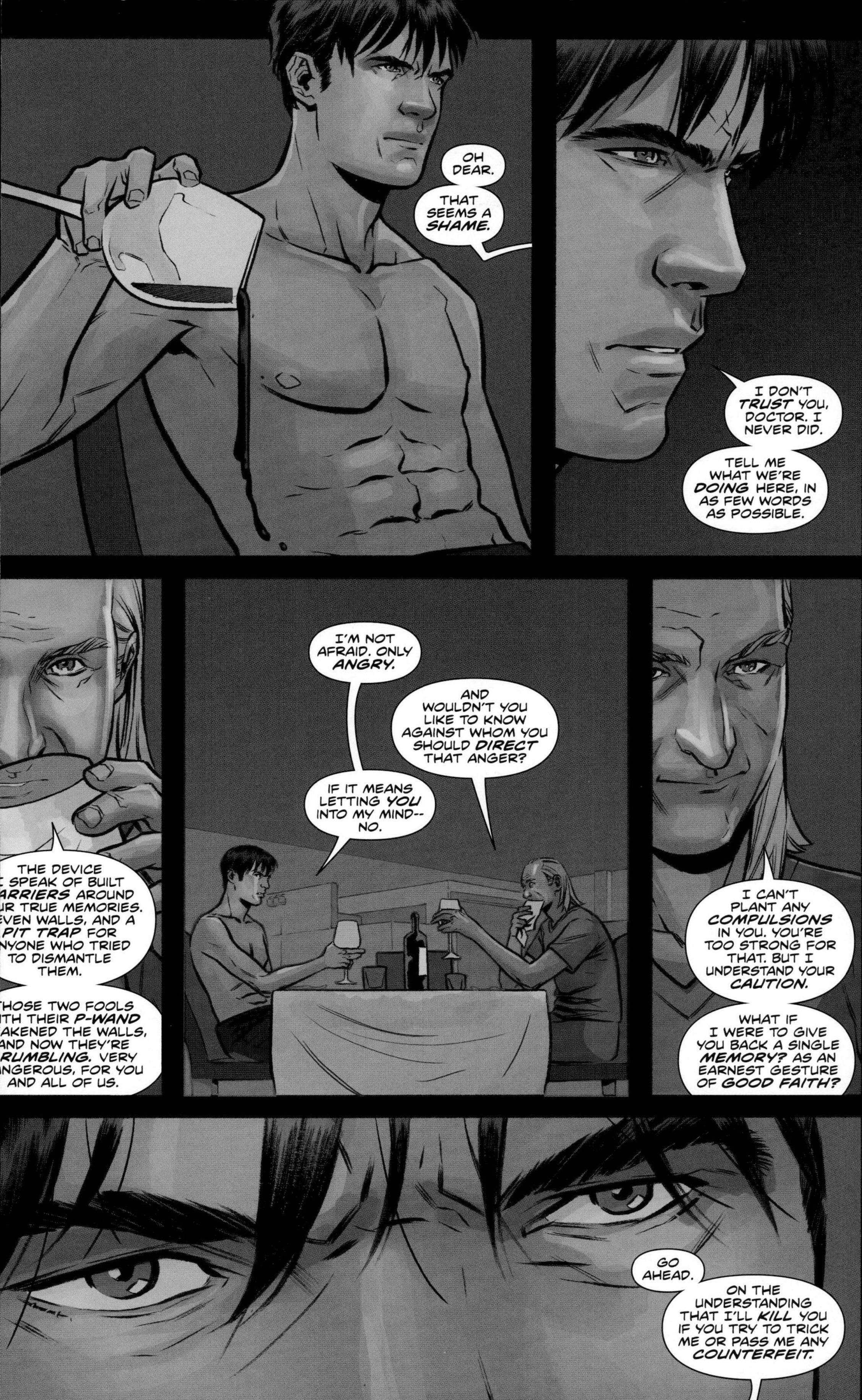

OH DEAR.
THAT SEEMS A SHAME.
I DON'T TRUST YOU, DOCTOR. I NEVER DID.
TELL ME WHAT WE'RE DOING HERE, IN AS FEW WORDS AS POSSIBLE.
THE DEVICE SPEAK OF BUILT ARRIERS AROUND UR TRUE MEMORIES. EVEN WALLS, AND A PIT TRAP FOR NYONE WHO TRIED TO DISMANTLE THEM.
THOSE TWO FOOLS ITH THEIR P-WAND AKENED THE WALLS, AND NOW THEY'RE RUMBLING. VERY NGEROUS, FOR YOU AND ALL OF US.
I'M NOT AFRAID. ONLY ANGRY.
AND WOULDN'T YOU LIKE TO KNOW AGAINST WHOM YOU SHOULD DIRECT THAT ANGER?
IF IT MEANS LETTING YOU INTO MY MIND-- NO.
I CAN'T PLANT ANY COMPULSIONS IN YOU. YOU'RE TOO STRONG FOR THAT. BUT I UNDERSTAND YOUR CAUTION.
WHAT IF I WERE TO GIVE YOU BACK A SINGLE MEMORY? AS AN EARNEST GESTURE OF GOOD FAITH?
GO AHEAD.
ON THE UNDERSTANDING THAT I'LL KILL YOU IF YOU TRY TO TRICK ME OR PASS ME ANY COUNTERFEIT.

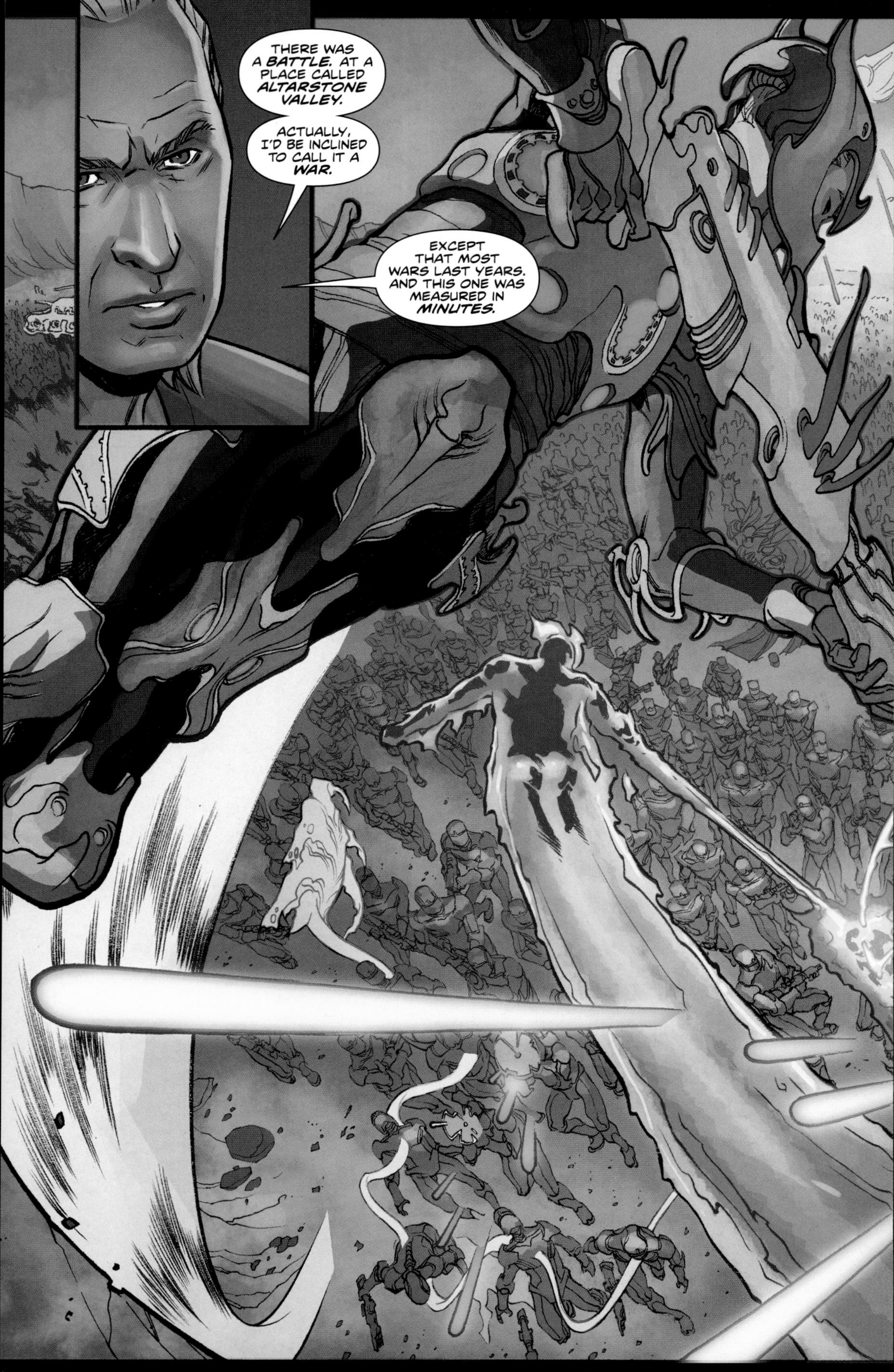
THERE WAS A BATTLE. AT A PLACE CALLED ALTARSTONE VALLEY.
ACTUALLY, I'D BE INCLINED TO CALL IT A WAR.
EXCEPT THAT MOST WARS LAST YEARS. AND THIS ONE WAS MEASURED IN MINUTES.

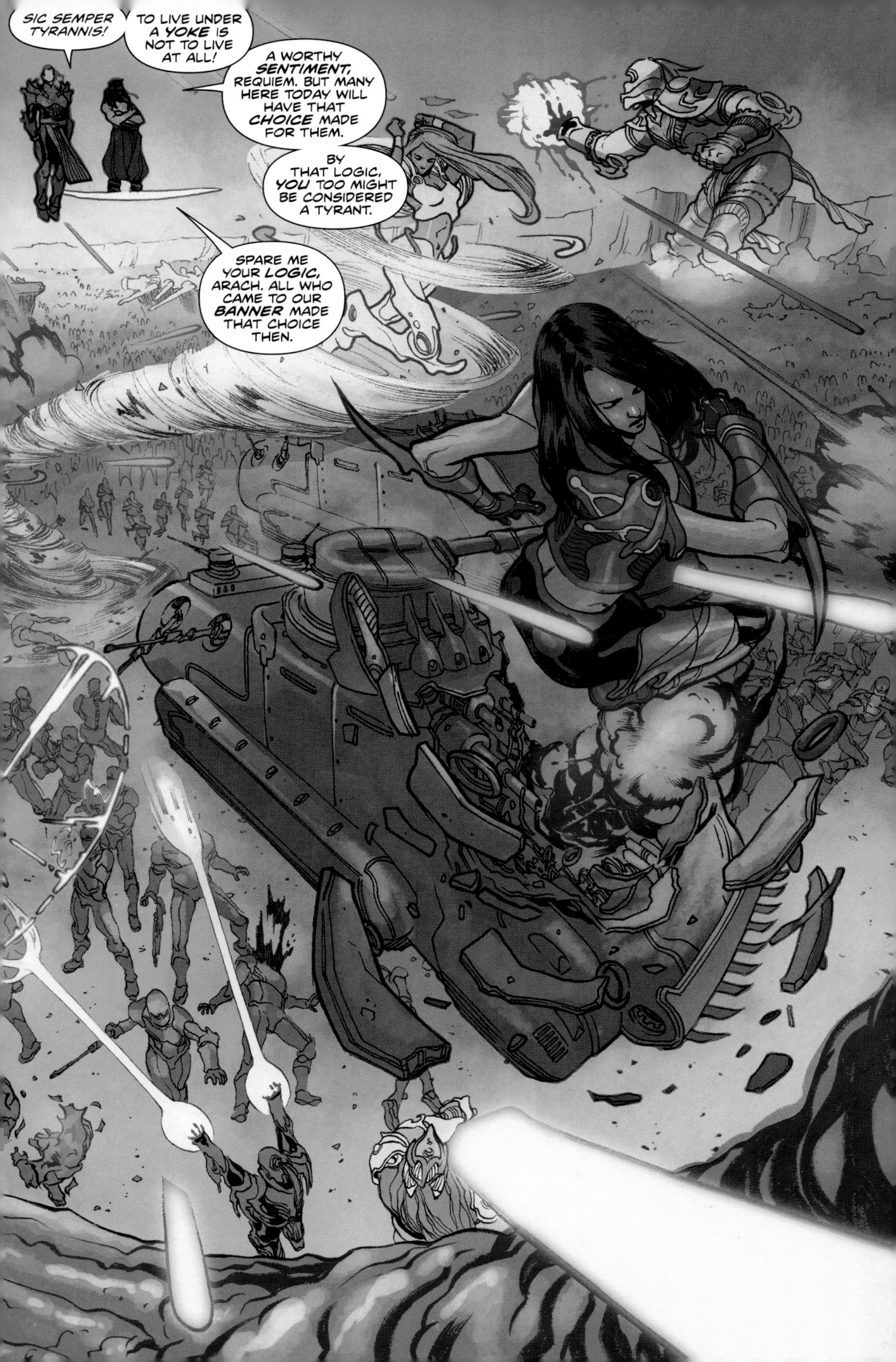
SIC SEMPER TYRANNIS!
TO LIVE UNDER A YOKE IS NOT TO LIVE AT ALL!
A WORTHY SENTIMENT, REQUIEM. BUT MANY HERE TODAY WILL HAVE THAT CHOICE MADE FOR THEM.
BY THAT LOGIC, YOU TOO MIGHT BE CONSIDERED A TYRANT.
SPARE ME YOUR LOGIC, ARACH. ALL WHO CAME TO OUR BANNER MADE THAT CHOICE THEN.

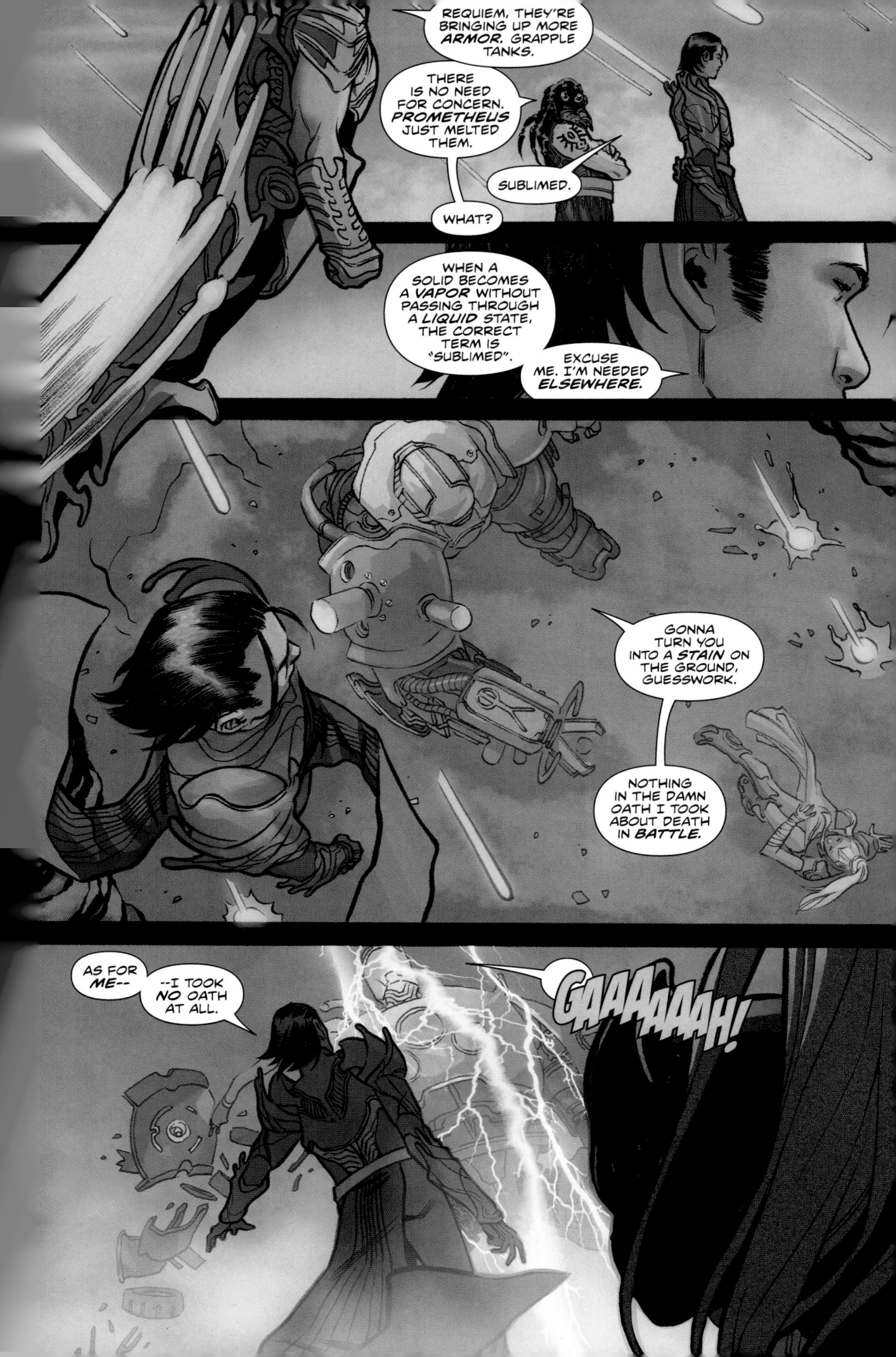
REQUIEM, THEY'RE BRINGING UP MORE ARMOR. GRAPPLE TANKS.
THERE IS NO NEED FOR CONCERN. PROMETHEUS JUST MELTED THEM.
SUBLIMED.
WHAT?
WHEN A SOLID BECOMES A VAPOR WITHOUT PASSING THROUGH A LIQUID STATE, THE CORRECT TERM IS "SUBLIMED".
EXCUSE ME. I'M NEEDED ELSEWHERE.
GONNA TURN YOU INTO A STAIN ON THE GROUND, GUESSWORK.
NOTHING IN THE DAMN OATH I TOOK ABOUT DEATH IN BATTLE.
AS FOR ME--
--I TOOK NO OATH AT ALL.
GAAAAAAH!

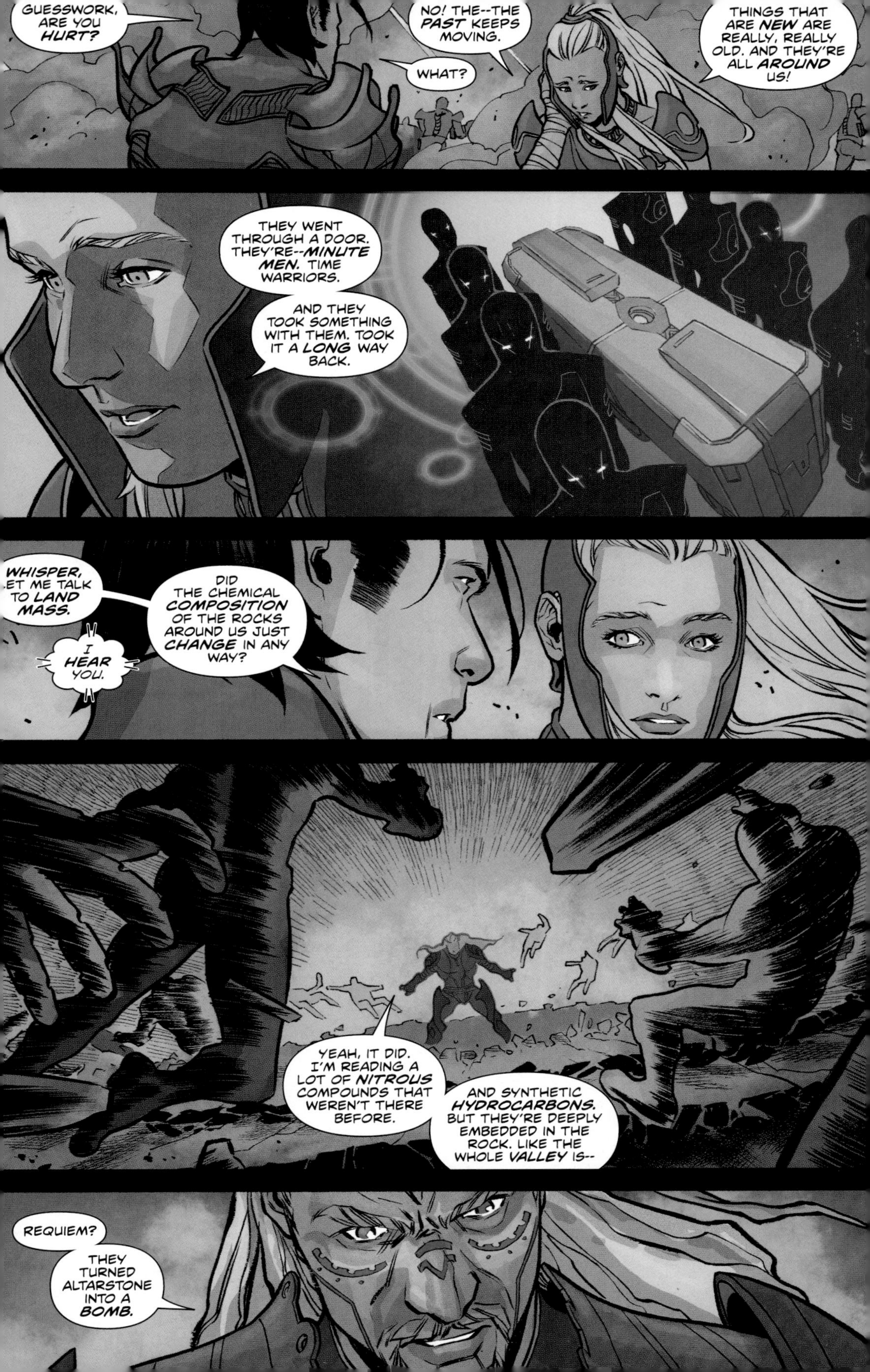
GUESSWORK, ARE YOU HURT?
NO! THE--THE PAST KEEPS MOVING.
WHAT?
THINGS THAT ARE NEW ARE REALLY, REALLY OLD. AND THEY'RE ALL AROUND US!
THEY WENT THROUGH A DOOR. THEY'RE--MINUTE MEN. TIME WARRIORS.
AND THEY TOOK SOMETHING WITH THEM. TOOK IT A LONG WAY BACK.
WHISPER, LET ME TALK TO LAND MASS.
I HEAR YOU.
DID THE CHEMICAL COMPOSITION OF THE ROCKS AROUND US JUST CHANGE IN ANY WAY?
YEAH, IT DID. I'M READING A LOT OF NITROUS COMPOUNDS THAT WEREN'T THERE BEFORE.
AND SYNTHETIC HYDROCARBONS. BUT THEY'RE DEEPLY EMBEDDED IN THE ROCK. LIKE THE WHOLE VALLEY IS--
REQUIEM?
THEY TURNED ALTARSTONE INTO A BOMB.

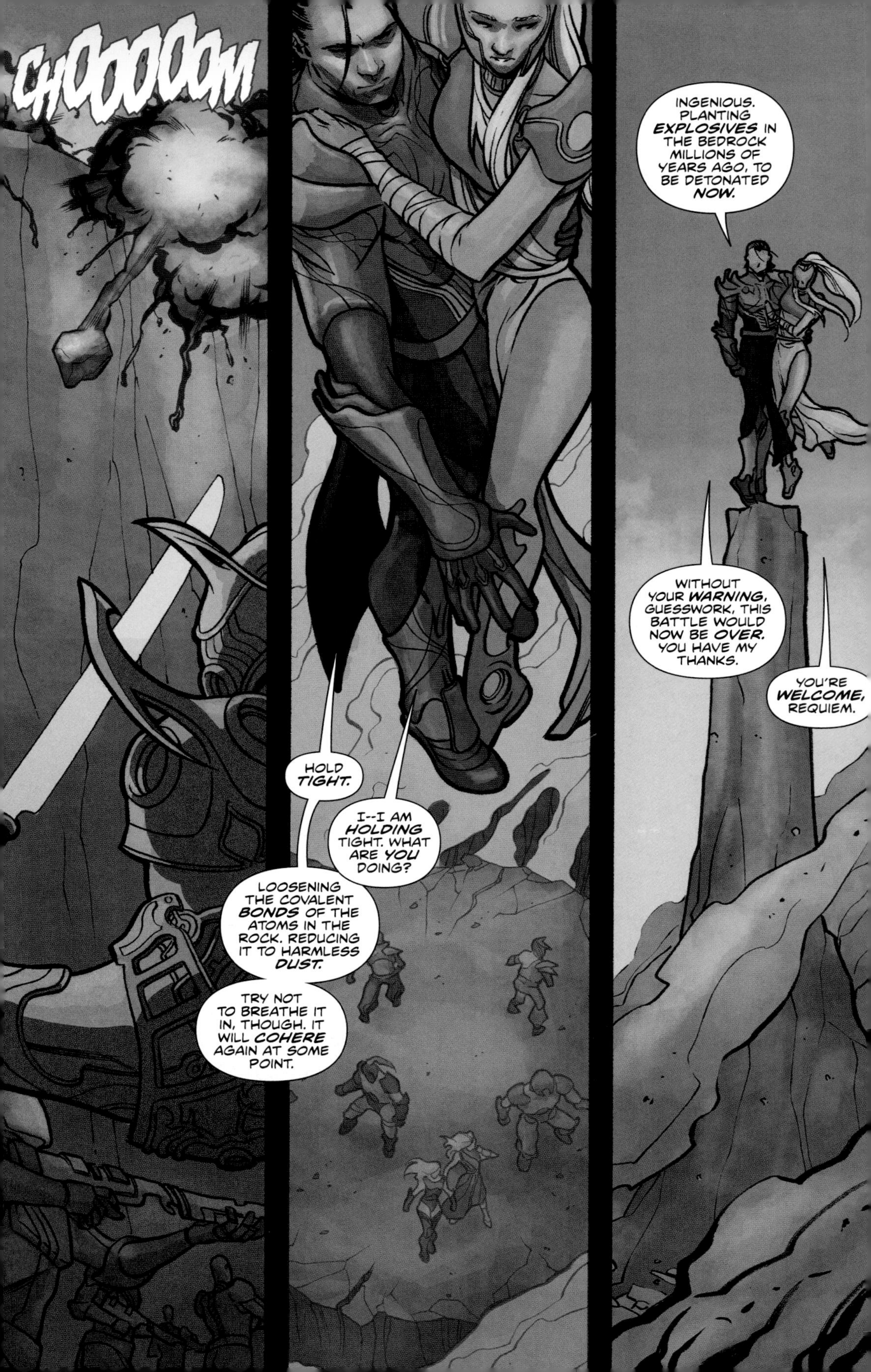
CHOOOOOM
HOLD TIGHT.
I--I AM HOLDING TIGHT. WHAT ARE YOU DOING?
LOOSENING THE COVALENT BONDS OF THE ATOMS IN THE ROCK. REDUCING IT TO HARMLESS DUST.
TRY NOT TO BREATHE IT IN, THOUGH. IT WILL COHERE AGAIN AT SOME POINT.
INGENIOUS. PLANTING EXPLOSIVES IN THE BEDROCK MILLIONS OF YEARS AGO, TO BE DETONATED NOW.
WITHOUT YOUR WARNING, GUESSWORK, THIS BATTLE WOULD NOW BE OVER. YOU HAVE MY THANKS.
YOU'RE WELCOME, REQUIEM.

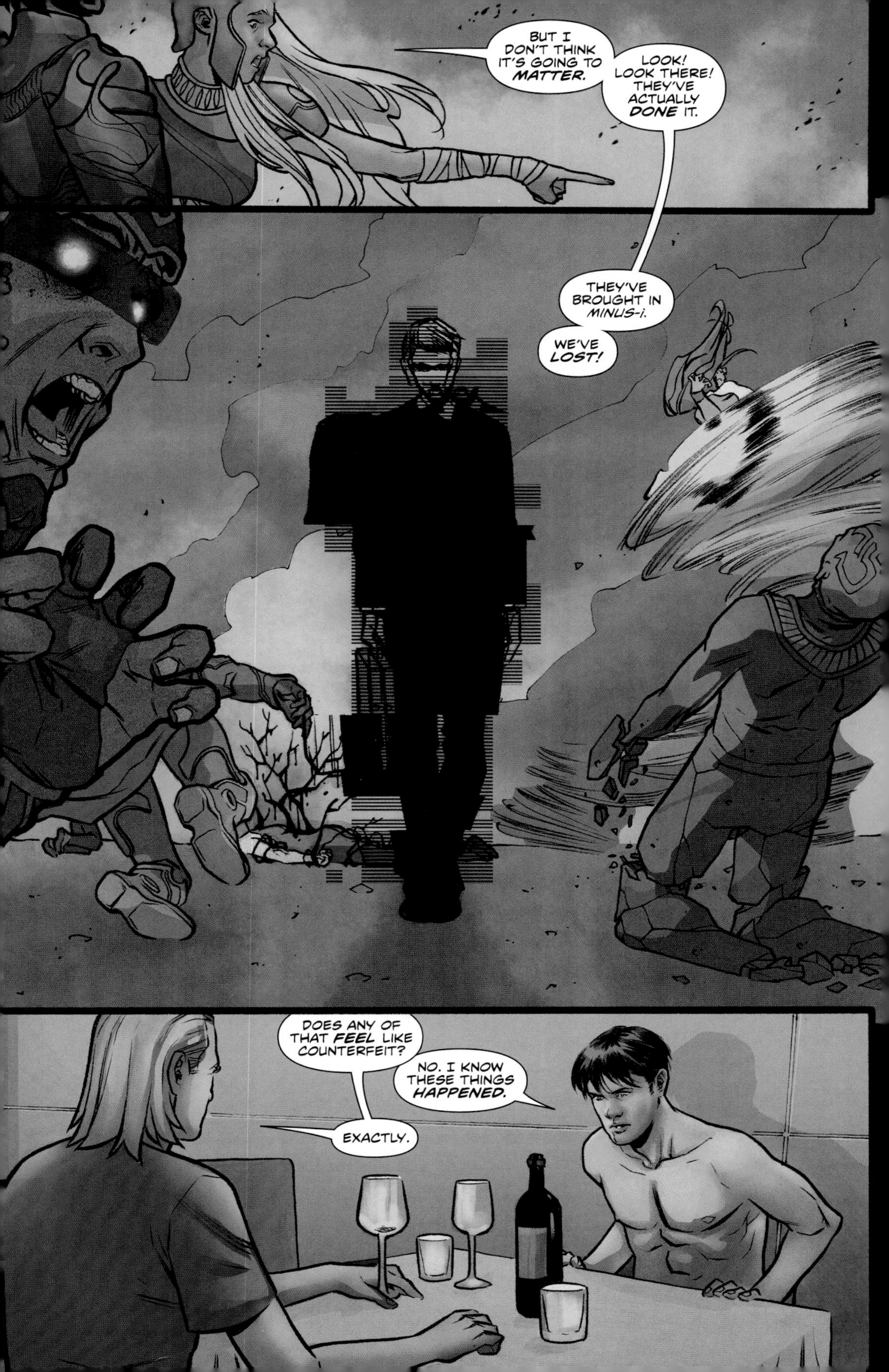
BUT I DON'T THINK IT'S GOING TO MATTER.
LOOK! LOOK THERE! THEY'VE ACTUALLY DONE IT.
THEY'VE BROUGHT IN MINUS-i.
WE'VE LOST!
DOES ANY OF THAT FEEL LIKE COUNTERFEIT?
NO. I KNOW THESE THINGS HAPPENED.
EXACTLY.

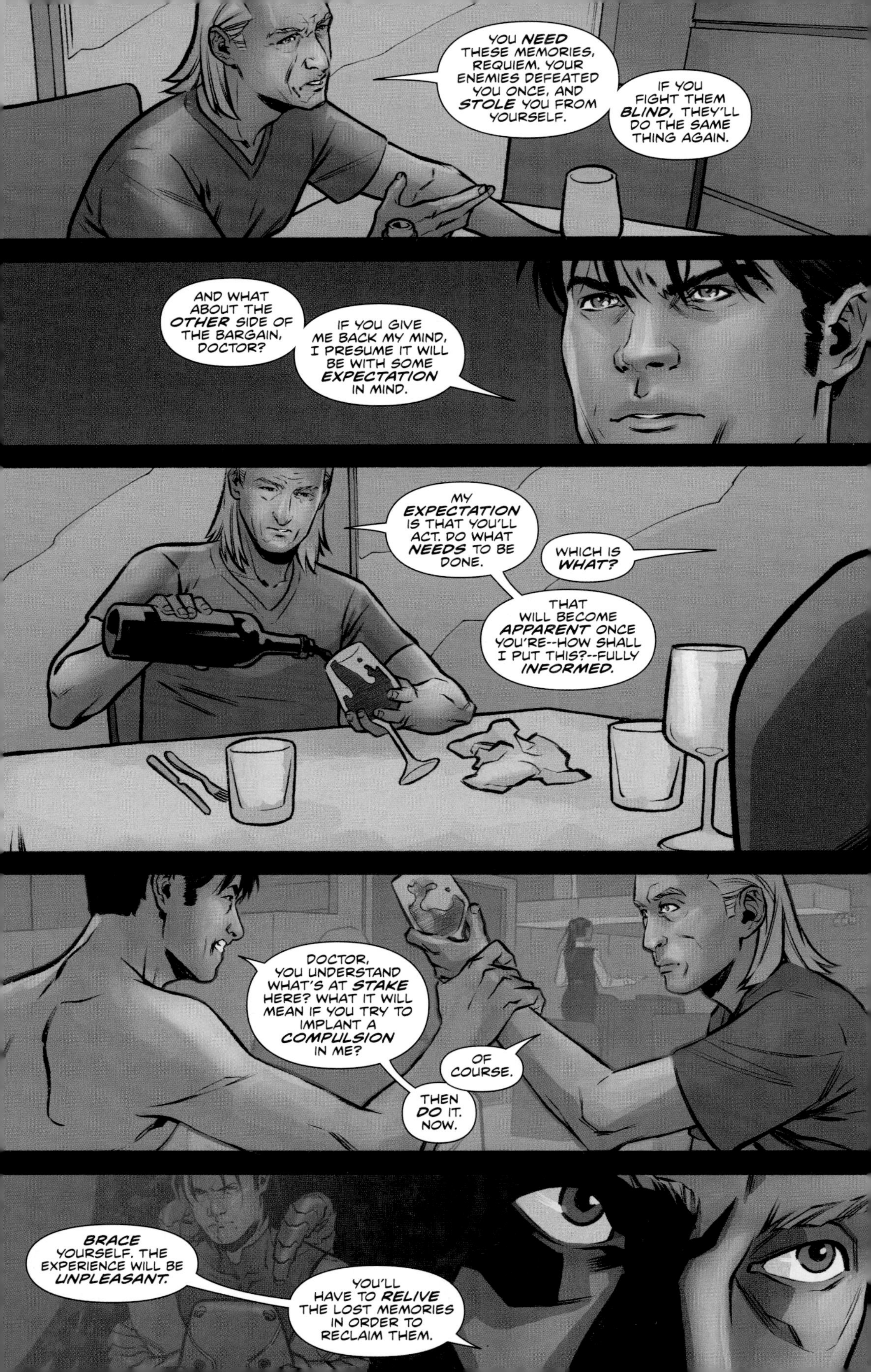
YOU NEED THESE MEMORIES, REQUIEM. YOUR ENEMIES DEFEATED YOU ONCE, AND STOLE YOU FROM YOURSELF.
IF YOU FIGHT THEM BLIND, THEY'LL DO THE SAME THING AGAIN.
AND WHAT ABOUT THE OTHER SIDE OF THE BARGAIN, DOCTOR?
IF YOU GIVE ME BACK MY MIND, I PRESUME IT WILL BE WITH SOME EXPECTATION IN MIND.
MY EXPECTATION IS THAT YOU'LL ACT. DO WHAT NEEDS TO BE DONE.
WHICH IS WHAT?
THAT WILL BECOME APPARENT ONCE YOU'RE--HOW SHALL I PUT THIS?--FULLY INFORMED.
DOCTOR, YOU UNDERSTAND WHAT'S AT STAKE HERE? WHAT IT WILL MEAN IF YOU TRY TO IMPLANT A COMPULSION IN ME?
OF COURSE.
THEN DO IT. NOW.
BRACE YOURSELF. THE EXPERIENCE WILL BE UNPLEASANT.
YOU'LL HAVE TO RELIVE THE LOST MEMORIES IN ORDER TO RECLAIM THEM.

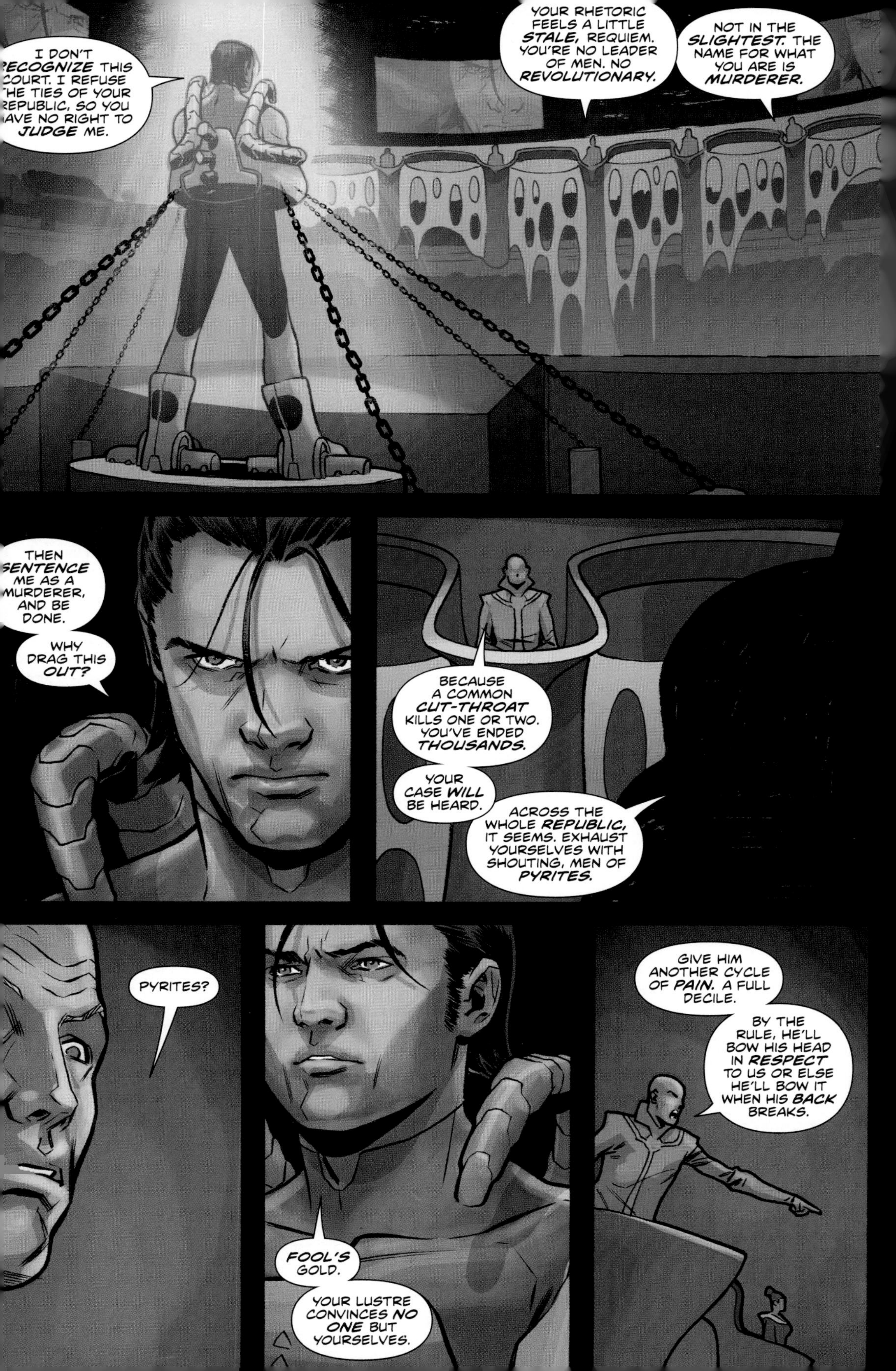
I DON'T RECOGNIZE THIS COURT. I REFUSE THE TIES OF YOUR REPUBLIC, SO YOU HAVE NO RIGHT TO JUDGE ME.
YOUR RHETORIC FEELS A LITTLE STALE, REQUIEM. YOU'RE NO LEADER OF MEN. NO REVOLUTIONARY.
NOT IN THE SLIGHTEST. THE NAME FOR WHAT YOU ARE IS MURDERER.
THEN SENTENCE ME AS A MURDERER, AND BE DONE.
WHY DRAG THIS OUT?
BECAUSE A COMMON CUT-THROAT KILLS ONE OR TWO. YOU'VE ENDED THOUSANDS.
YOUR CASE WILL BE HEARD.
ACROSS THE WHOLE REPUBLIC, IT SEEMS. EXHAUST YOURSELVES WITH SHOUTING, MEN OF PYRITES.
PYRITES?
FOOL'S GOLD.
YOUR LUSTRE CONVINCES NO ONE BUT YOURSELVES.
GIVE HIM ANOTHER CYCLE OF PAIN. A FULL DECILE.
BY THE RULE, HE'LL BOW HIS HEAD IN RESPECT TO US OR ELSE HE'LL BOW IT WHEN HIS BACK BREAKS.

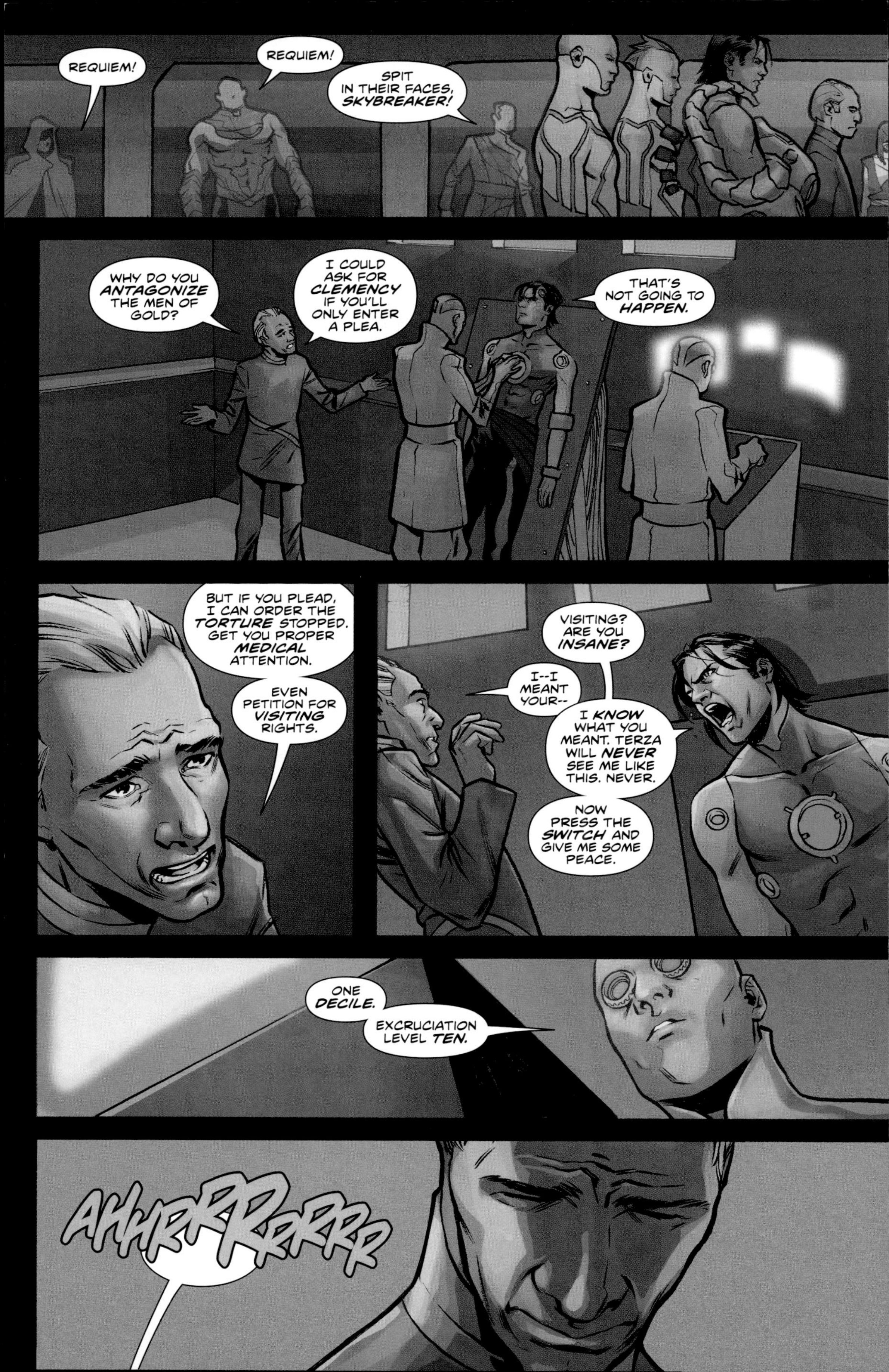
REQUIEM!
REQUIEM!
SPIT IN THEIR FACES, SKYBREAKER!
WHY DO YOU ANTAGONIZE THE MEN OF GOLD?
I COULD ASK FOR CLEMENCY IF YOU'LL ONLY ENTER A PLEA.
THAT'S NOT GOING TO HAPPEN.
BUT IF YOU PLEAD, I CAN ORDER THE TORTURE STOPPED. GET YOU PROPER MEDICAL ATTENTION.
EVEN PETITION FOR VISITING RIGHTS.
VISITING? ARE YOU INSANE?
I--I MEANT YOUR--
I KNOW WHAT YOU MEANT. TERZA WILL NEVER SEE ME LIKE THIS. NEVER.
NOW PRESS THE SWITCH AND GIVE ME SOME PEACE.
ONE DECILE.
EXCRUCIATION LEVEL TEN.
AHHRRRrrrrr

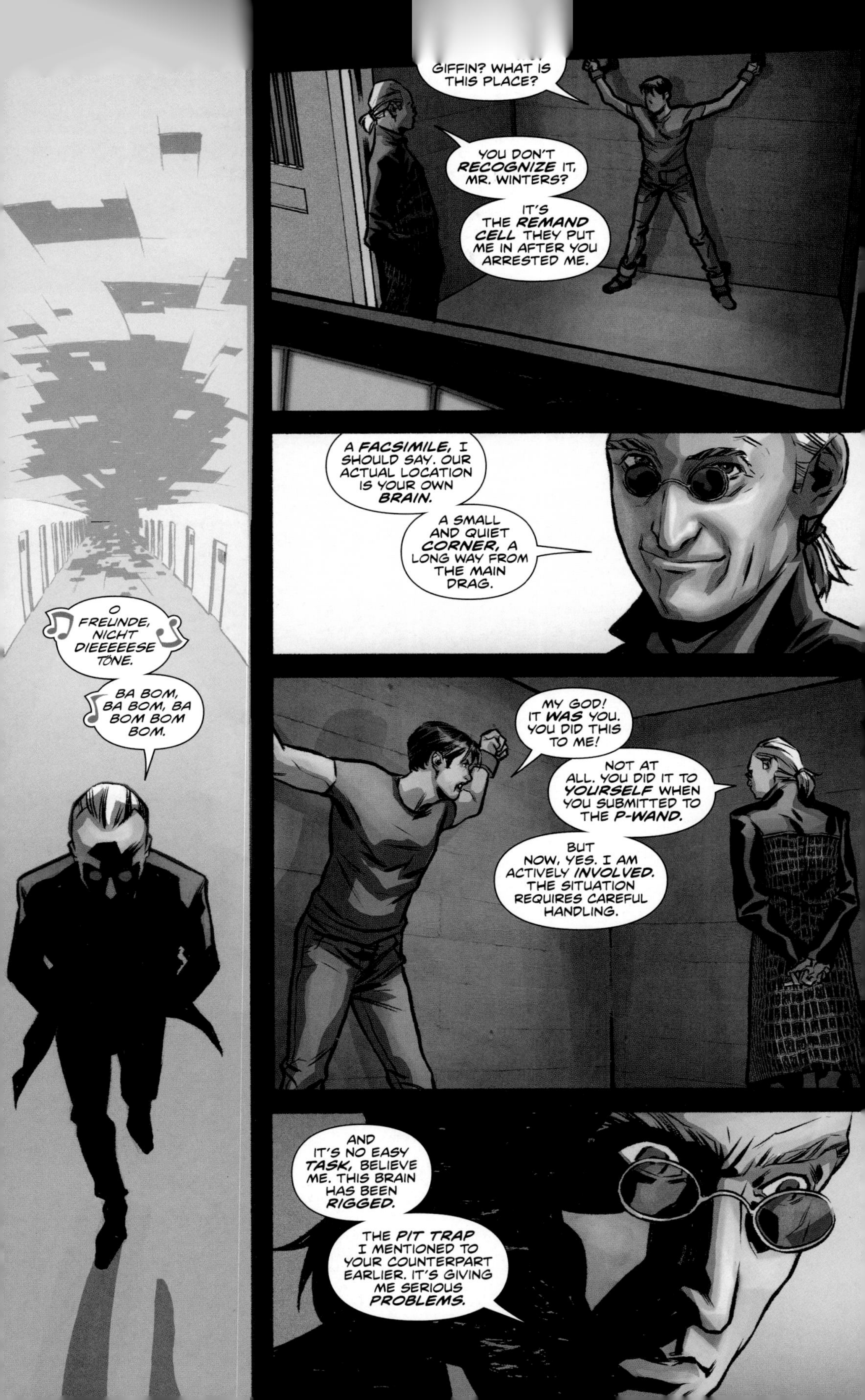

GIFFIN? WHAT IS THIS PLACE?
YOU DON'T RECOGNIZE IT, MR. WINTERS?
IT'S THE REMAND CELL THEY PUT ME IN AFTER YOU ARRESTED ME.
A FACSIMILE, I SHOULD SAY. OUR ACTUAL LOCATION IS YOUR OWN BRAIN.
A SMALL AND QUIET CORNER, A LONG WAY FROM THE MAIN DRAG.
MY GOD! IT WAS YOU. YOU DID THIS TO ME!
NOT AT ALL. YOU DID IT TO YOURSELF WHEN YOU SUBMITTED TO THE P-WAND.
BUT NOW, YES. I AM ACTIVELY INVOLVED. THE SITUATION REQUIRES CAREFUL HANDLING.
AND IT'S NO EASY TASK, BELIEVE ME. THIS BRAIN HAS BEEN RIGGED.
THE PIT TRAP I MENTIONED TO YOUR COUNTERPART EARLIER. IT'S GIVING ME SERIOUS PROBLEMS.
O FREUNDE, NICHT DIEEEEESE TÖNE.
BA BOM, BA BOM, BA BOM BOM BOM.

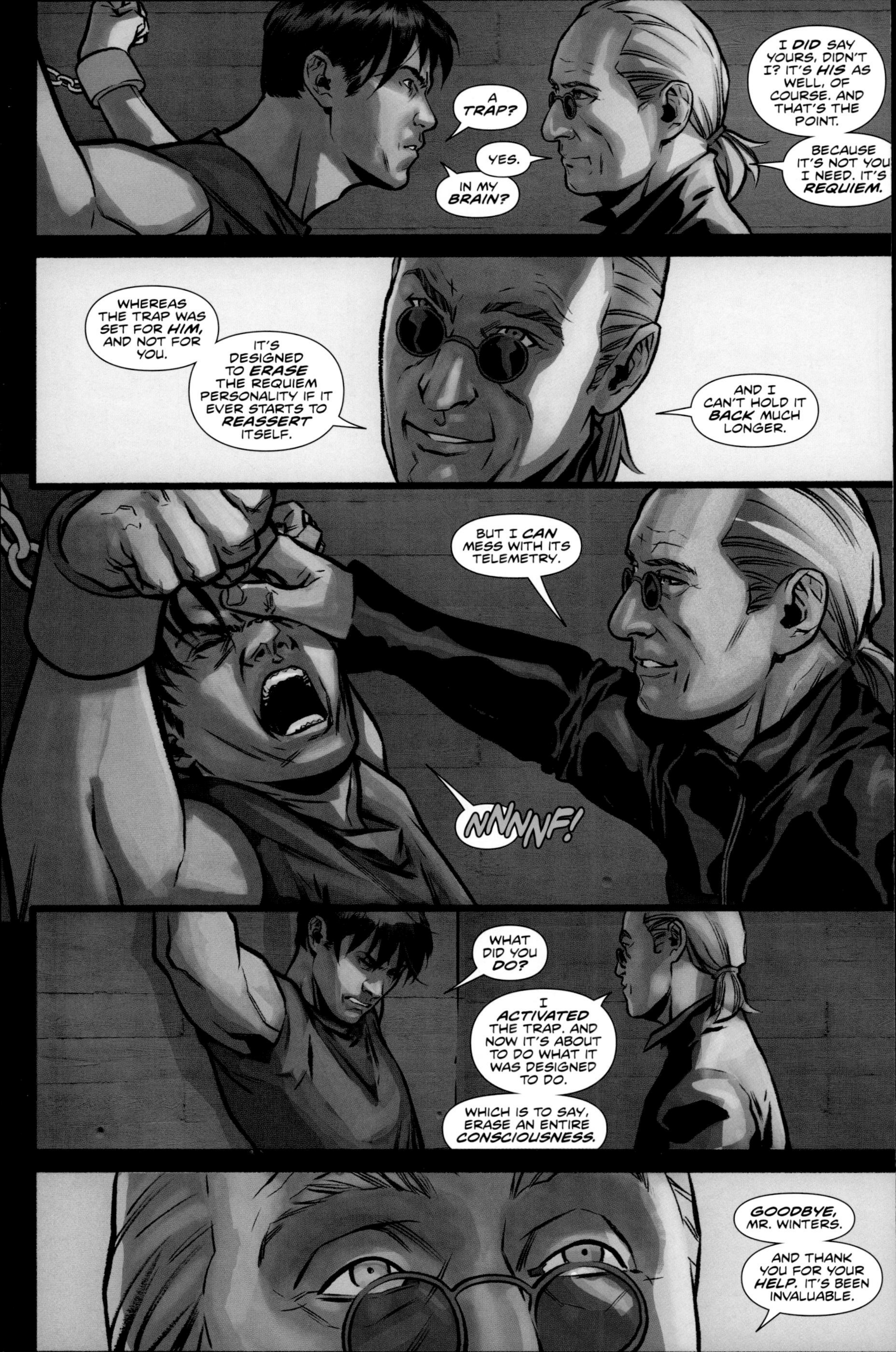
A TRAP?
YES.
IN MY BRAIN?
I DID SAY YOURS, DIDN'T I? IT'S HIS AS WELL, OF COURSE. AND THAT'S THE POINT.
BECAUSE IT'S NOT YOU I NEED. IT'S REQUIEM.
WHEREAS THE TRAP WAS SET FOR HIM, AND NOT FOR YOU.
IT'S DESIGNED TO ERASE THE REQUIEM PERSONALITY IF IT EVER STARTS TO REASSERT ITSELF.
AND I CAN'T HOLD IT BACK MUCH LONGER.
BUT I CAN MESS WITH ITS TELEMETRY.
NNNNF!
WHAT DID YOU DO?
I ACTIVATED THE TRAP. AND NOW IT'S ABOUT TO DO WHAT IT WAS DESIGNED TO DO.
WHICH IS TO SAY, ERASE AN ENTIRE CONSCIOUSNESS.
GOODBYE, MR. WINTERS.
AND THANK YOU FOR YOUR HELP. IT'S BEEN INVALUABLE.

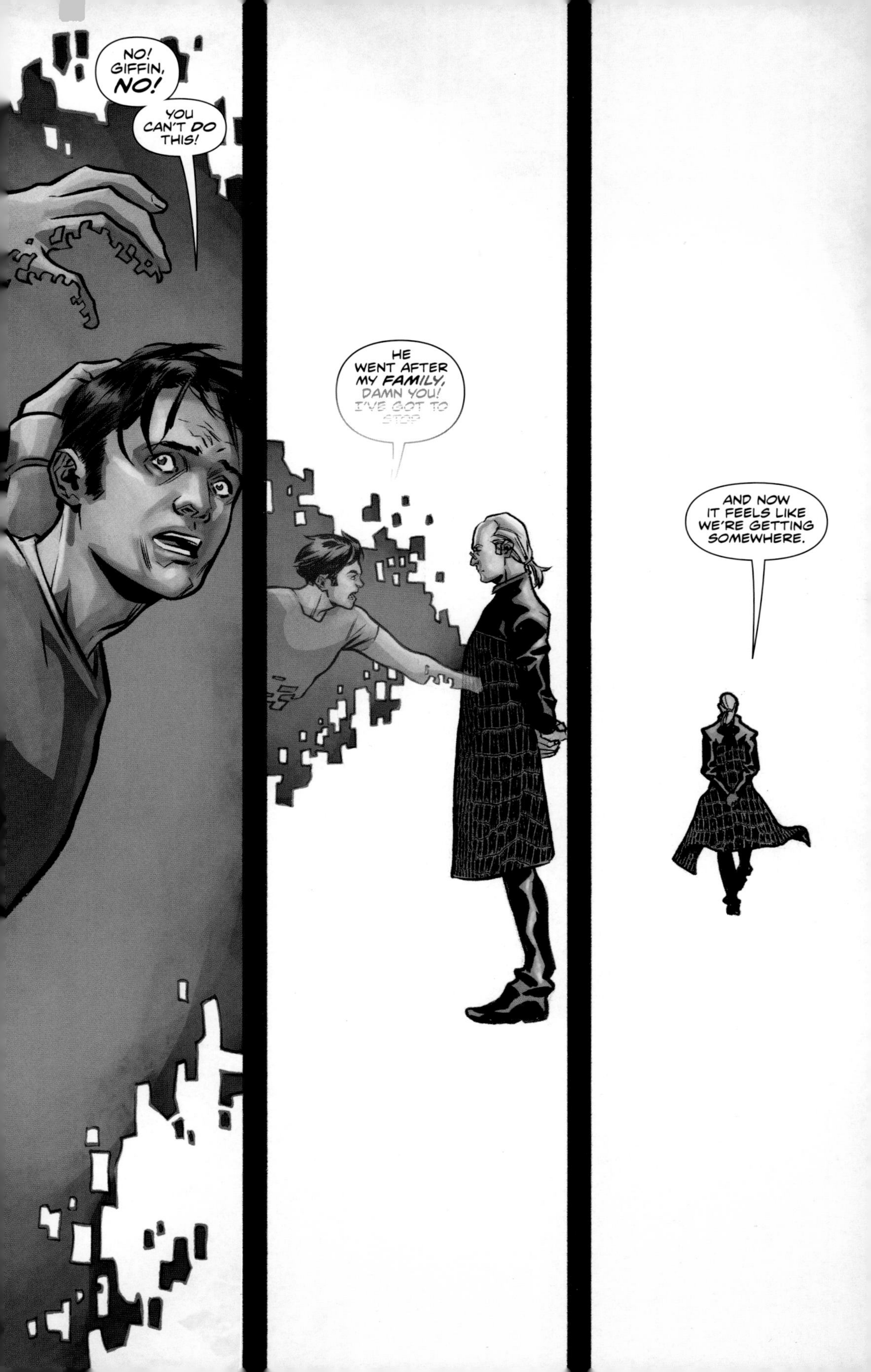
NO! GIFFIN, NO!
YOU CAN'T DO THIS!
HE WENT AFTER MY FAMILY, DAMN YOU! I'VE GOT TO STOP
AND NOW IT FEELS LIKE WE'RE GETTING SOMEWHERE.

"WE'RE IN A **RACE**. THE TRUTH, AGAINST THE BIGGEST **LIE** EVER TOLD."
Chapter 13

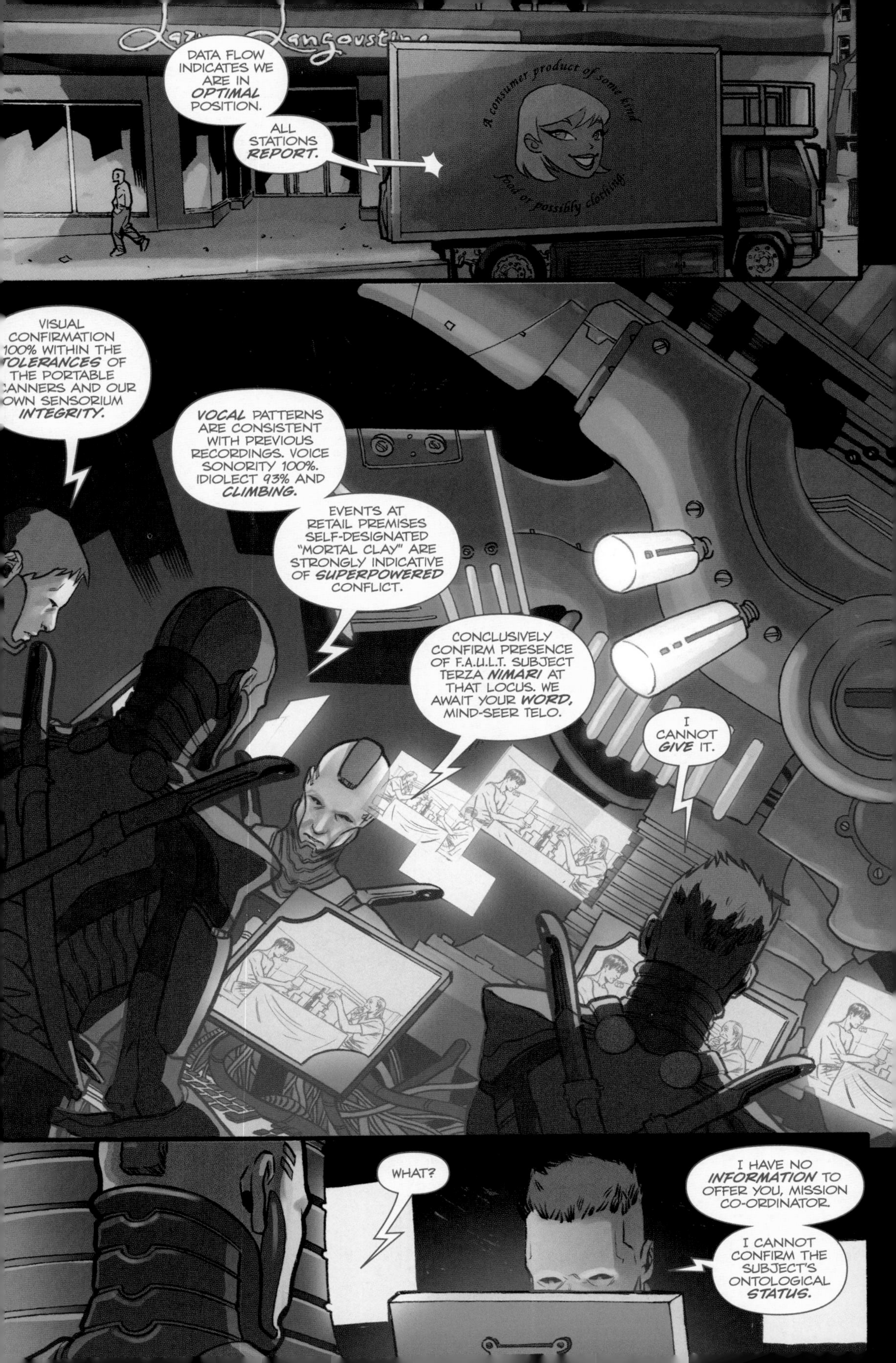
DATA FLOW INDICATES WE ARE IN OPTIMAL POSITION.
ALL STATIONS REPORT.
A consumer product of some kind
food or possibly clothing
VISUAL CONFIRMATION 100% WITHIN THE TOLERANCES OF THE PORTABLE CANNERS AND OUR OWN SENSORIUM INTEGRITY.
VOCAL PATTERNS ARE CONSISTENT WITH PREVIOUS RECORDINGS. VOICE SONORITY 100%. IDIOLECT 93% AND CLIMBING.
EVENTS AT RETAIL PREMISES SELF-DESIGNATED "MORTAL CLAY" ARE STRONGLY INDICATIVE OF SUPERPOWERED CONFLICT.
CONCLUSIVELY CONFIRM PRESENCE OF F.A.U.L.T. SUBJECT TERZA NIMARI AT THAT LOCUS. WE AWAIT YOUR WORD, MIND-SEER TELO.
I CANNOT GIVE IT.
WHAT?
I HAVE NO INFORMATION TO OFFER YOU, MISSION CO-ORDINATOR.
I CANNOT CONFIRM THE SUBJECT'S ONTOLOGICAL STATUS.

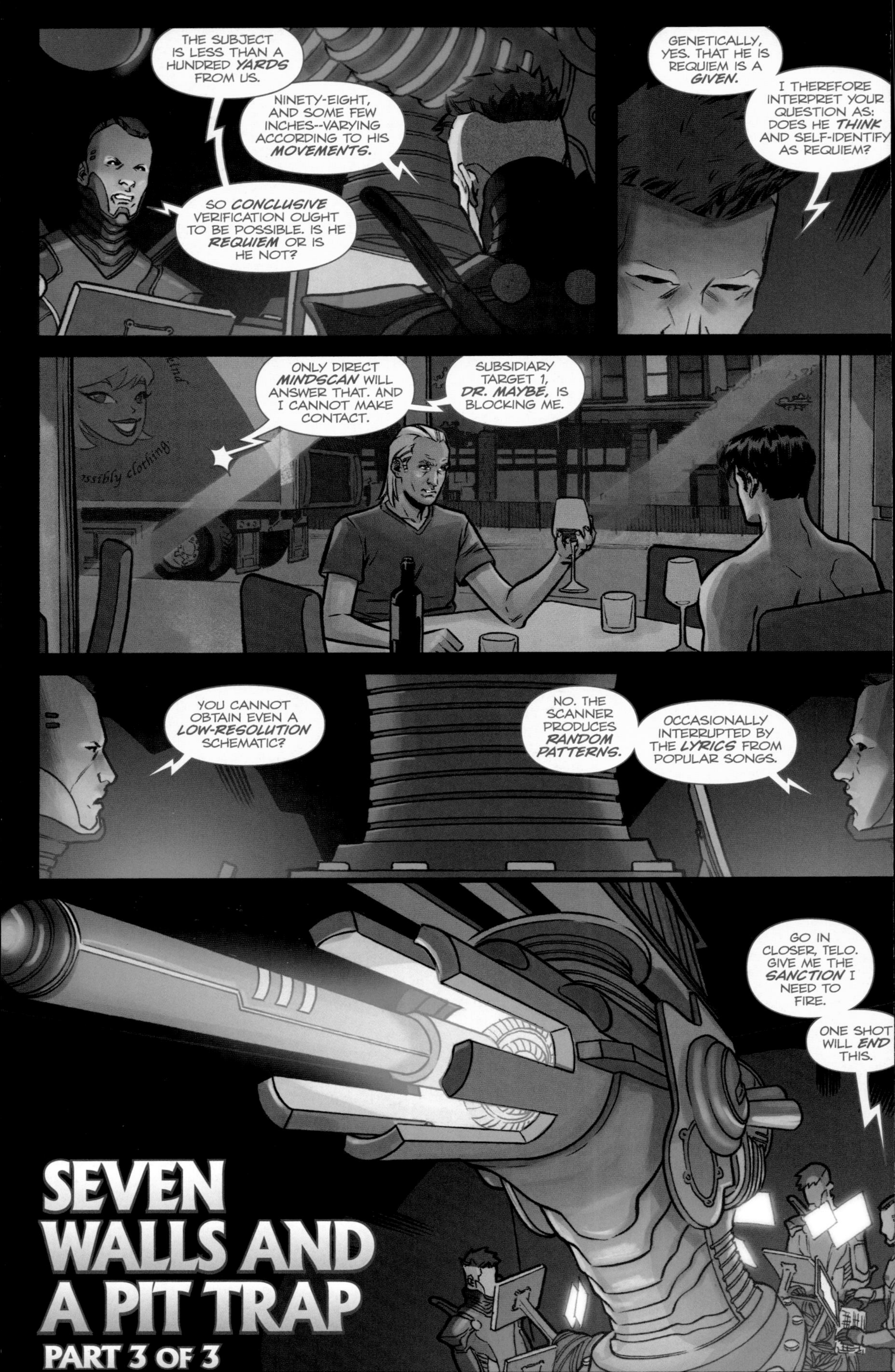

THE SUBJECT IS LESS THAN A HUNDRED YARDS FROM US.
NINETY-EIGHT, AND SOME FEW INCHES--VARYING ACCORDING TO HIS MOVEMENTS.
SO CONCLUSIVE VERIFICATION OUGHT TO BE POSSIBLE. IS HE REQUIEM OR IS HE NOT?
GENETICALLY, YES. THAT HE IS REQUIEM IS A GIVEN.
I THEREFORE INTERPRET YOUR QUESTION AS: DOES HE THINK AND SELF-IDENTIFY AS REQUIEM?
ONLY DIRECT MINDSCAN WILL ANSWER THAT. AND I CANNOT MAKE CONTACT.
SUBSIDIARY TARGET 1, DR. MAYBE, IS BLOCKING ME.
YOU CANNOT OBTAIN EVEN A LOW-RESOLUTION SCHEMATIC?
NO. THE SCANNER PRODUCES RANDOM PATTERNS.
OCCASIONALLY INTERRUPTED BY THE LYRICS FROM POPULAR SONGS.
GO IN CLOSER, TELO. GIVE ME THE SANCTION I NEED TO FIRE.
ONE SHOT WILL END THIS.
SEVEN WALLS AND A PIT TRAP
PART 3 OF 3

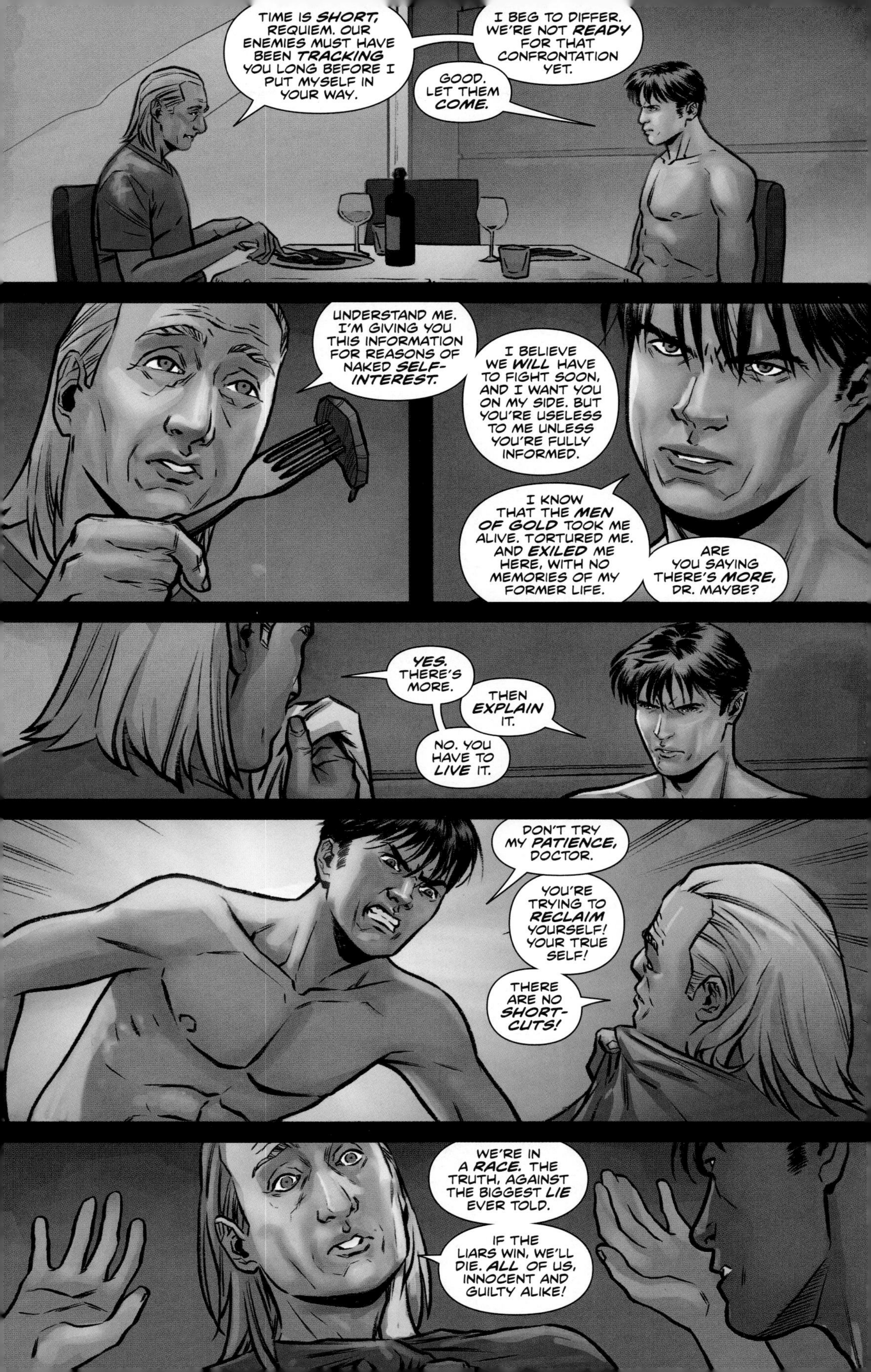
TIME IS SHORT, REQUIEM. OUR ENEMIES MUST HAVE BEEN TRACKING YOU LONG BEFORE I PUT MYSELF IN YOUR WAY.
I BEG TO DIFFER. WE'RE NOT READY FOR THAT CONFRONTATION YET.
GOOD. LET THEM COME.
UNDERSTAND ME. I'M GIVING YOU THIS INFORMATION FOR REASONS OF NAKED SELF-INTEREST.
I BELIEVE WE WILL HAVE TO FIGHT SOON, AND I WANT YOU ON MY SIDE. BUT YOU'RE USELESS TO ME UNLESS YOU'RE FULLY INFORMED.
I KNOW THAT THE MEN OF GOLD TOOK ME ALIVE. TORTURED ME. AND EXILED ME HERE, WITH NO MEMORIES OF MY FORMER LIFE.
ARE YOU SAYING THERE'S MORE, DR. MAYBE?
YES. THERE'S MORE.
THEN EXPLAIN IT.
NO. YOU HAVE TO LIVE IT.
DON'T TRY MY PATIENCE, DOCTOR.
YOU'RE TRYING TO RECLAIM YOURSELF! YOUR TRUE SELF!
THERE ARE NO SHORT-CUTS!
WE'RE IN A RACE. THE TRUTH, AGAINST THE BIGGEST LIE EVER TOLD.
IF THE LIARS WIN, WE'LL DIE. ALL OF US, INNOCENT AND GUILTY ALIKE!

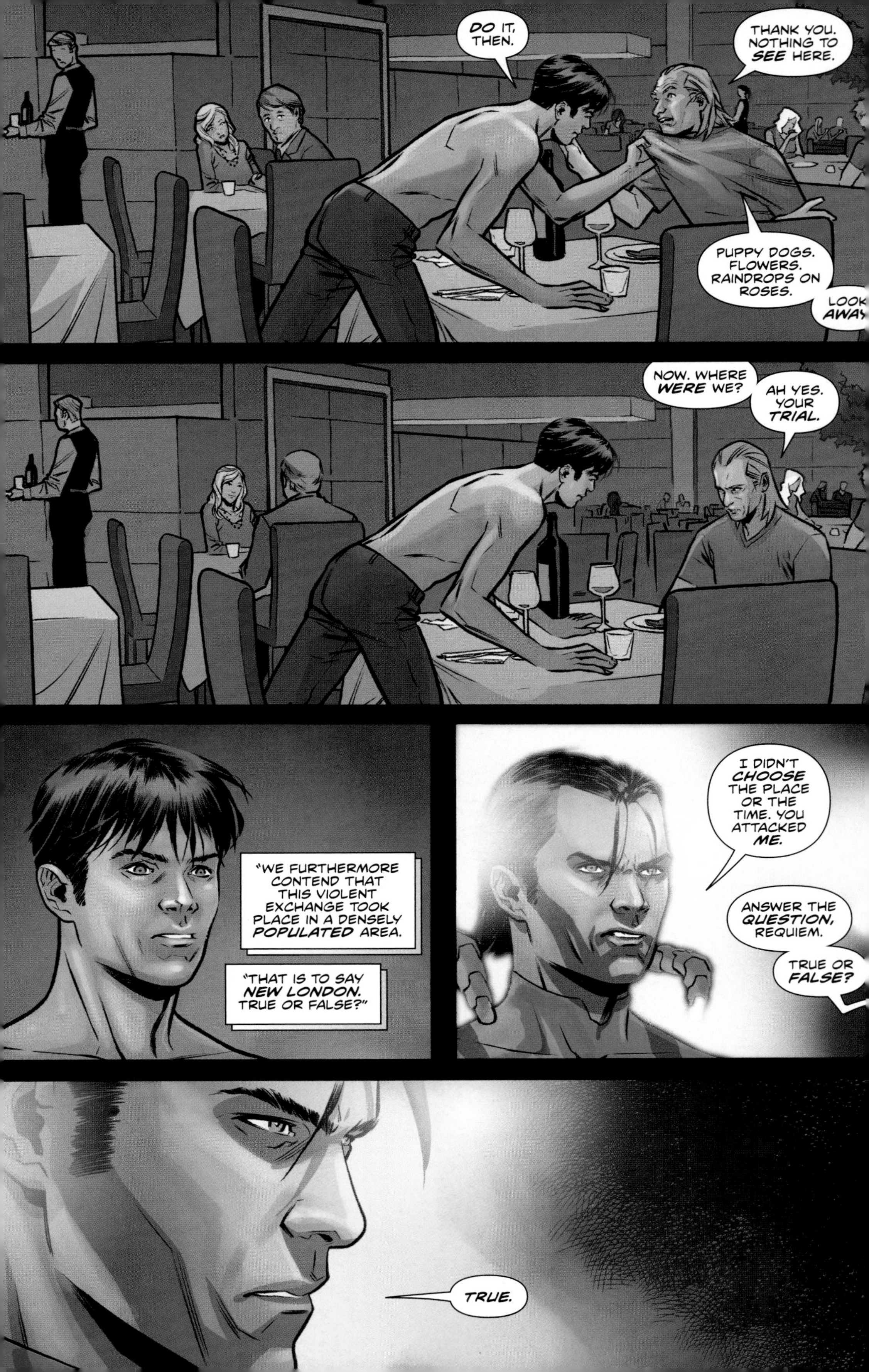
DO IT, THEN.
THANK YOU. NOTHING TO SEE HERE.
PUPPY DOGS. FLOWERS. RAINDROPS ON ROSES.
LOOK AWAY
NOW. WHERE WERE WE?
AH YES. YOUR TRIAL.
"WE FURTHERMORE CONTEND THAT THIS VIOLENT EXCHANGE TOOK PLACE IN A DENSELY POPULATED AREA.
"THAT IS TO SAY NEW LONDON. TRUE OR FALSE?"
I DIDN'T CHOOSE THE PLACE OR THE TIME. YOU ATTACKED ME.
ANSWER THE QUESTION, REQUIEM.
TRUE OR FALSE?
TRUE.

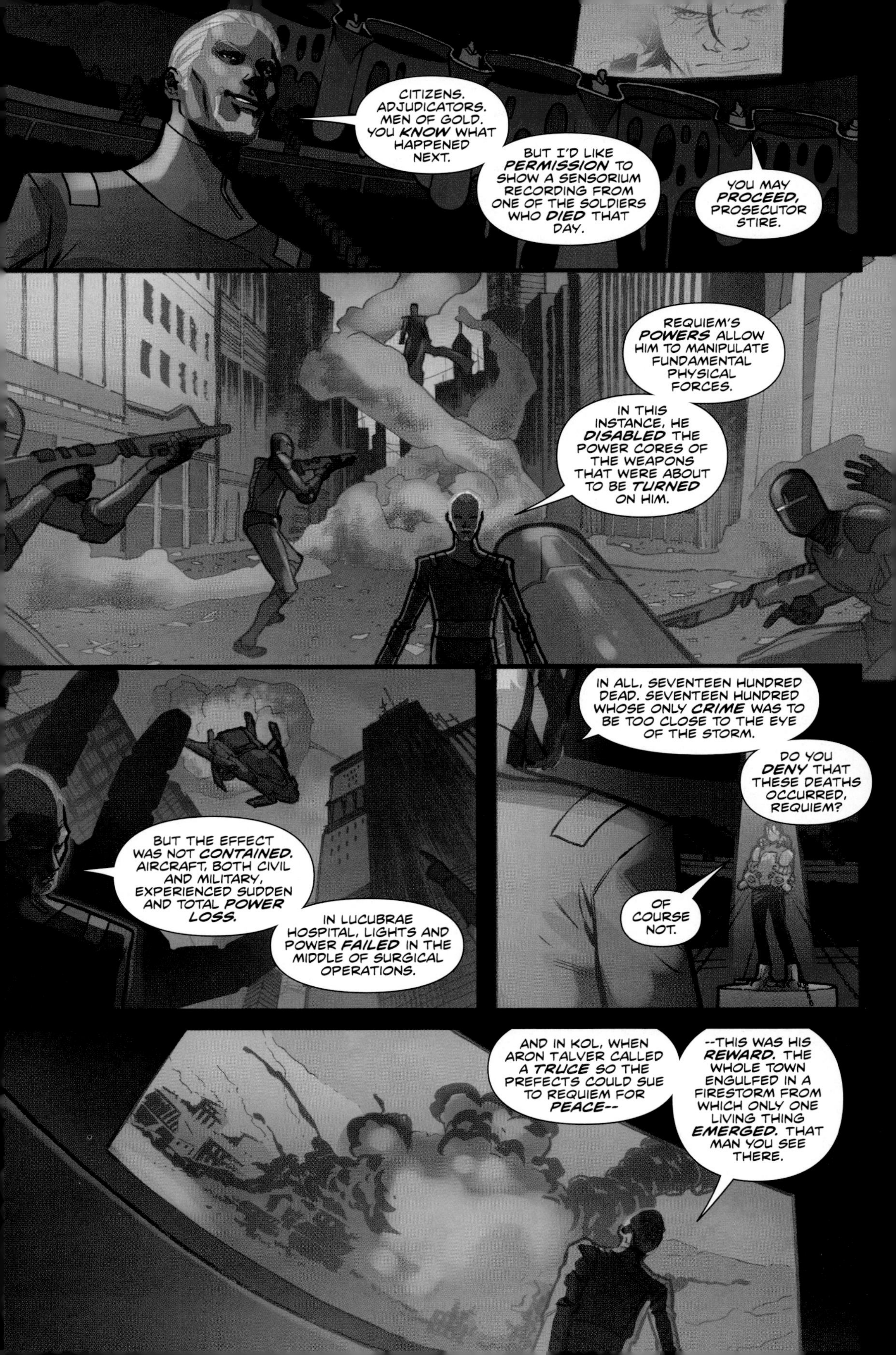
CITIZENS. ADJUDICATORS. MEN OF GOLD. YOU KNOW WHAT HAPPENED NEXT.
BUT I'D LIKE PERMISSION TO SHOW A SENSORIUM RECORDING FROM ONE OF THE SOLDIERS WHO DIED THAT DAY.
YOU MAY PROCEED, PROSECUTOR STIRE.
REQUIEM'S POWERS ALLOW HIM TO MANIPULATE FUNDAMENTAL PHYSICAL FORCES.
IN THIS INSTANCE, HE DISABLED THE POWER CORES OF THE WEAPONS THAT WERE ABOUT TO BE TURNED ON HIM.
BUT THE EFFECT WAS NOT CONTAINED. AIRCRAFT, BOTH CIVIL AND MILITARY, EXPERIENCED SUDDEN AND TOTAL POWER LOSS.
IN LUCUBRAE HOSPITAL, LIGHTS AND POWER FAILED IN THE MIDDLE OF SURGICAL OPERATIONS.
IN ALL, SEVENTEEN HUNDRED DEAD. SEVENTEEN HUNDRED WHOSE ONLY CRIME WAS TO BE TOO CLOSE TO THE EYE OF THE STORM.
DO YOU DENY THAT THESE DEATHS OCCURRED, REQUIEM?
OF COURSE NOT.
AND IN KOL, WHEN ARON TALVER CALLED A TRUCE SO THE PREFECTS COULD SUE TO REQUIEM FOR PEACE--
--THIS WAS HIS REWARD. THE WHOLE TOWN ENGULFED IN A FIRESTORM FROM WHICH ONLY ONE LIVING THING EMERGED. THAT MAN YOU SEE THERE.

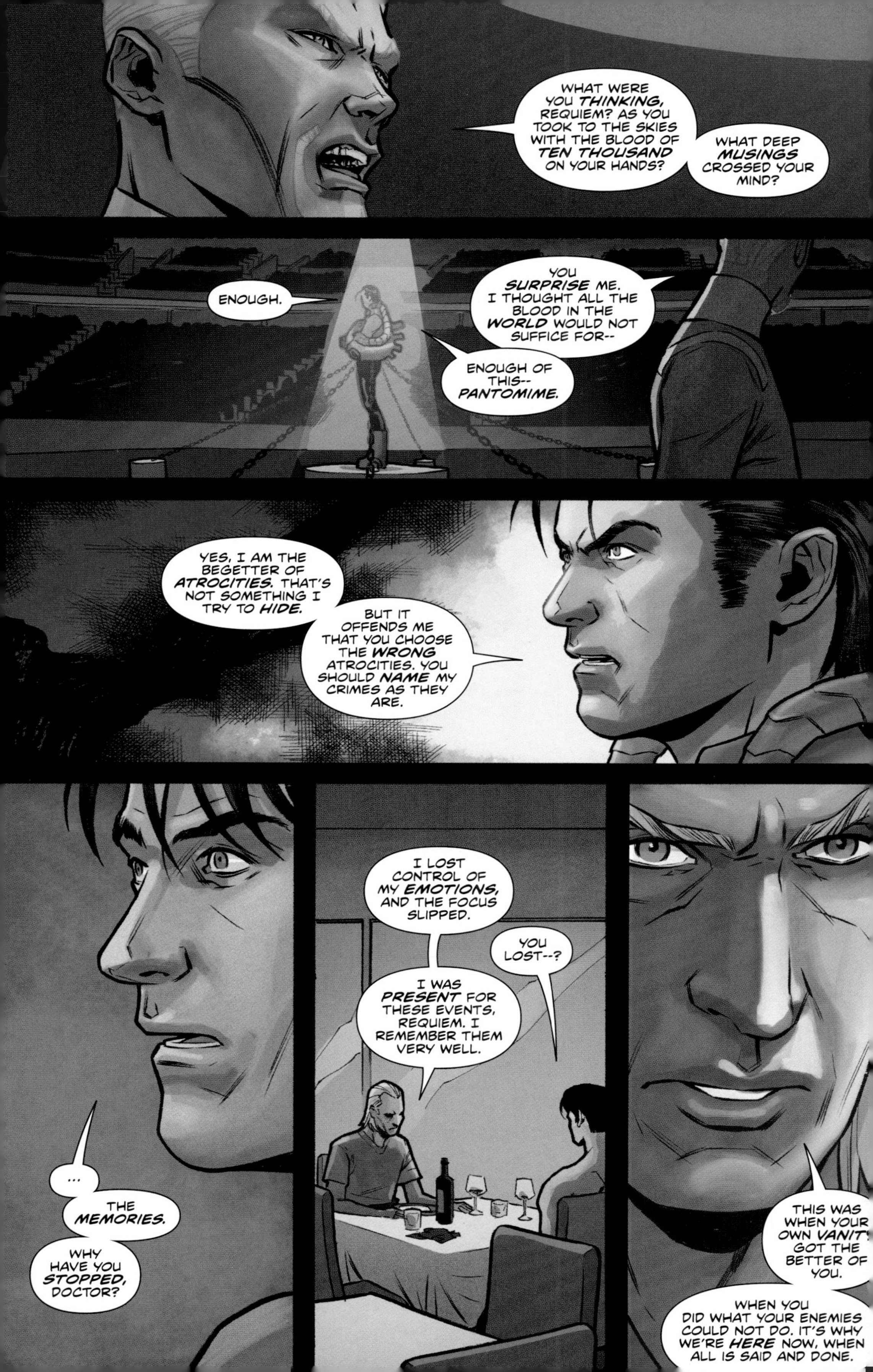
WHAT WERE YOU THINKING, REQUIEM? AS YOU TOOK TO THE SKIES WITH THE BLOOD OF TEN THOUSAND ON YOUR HANDS?
WHAT DEEP MUSINGS CROSSED YOUR MIND?
ENOUGH.
YOU SURPRISE ME. I THOUGHT ALL THE BLOOD IN THE WORLD WOULD NOT SUFFICE FOR--
ENOUGH OF THIS-- PANTOMIME.
YES, I AM THE BEGETTER OF ATROCITIES. THAT'S NOT SOMETHING I TRY TO HIDE.
BUT IT OFFENDS ME THAT YOU CHOOSE THE WRONG ATROCITIES. YOU SHOULD NAME MY CRIMES AS THEY ARE.
...
THE MEMORIES.
WHY HAVE YOU STOPPED, DOCTOR?
I LOST CONTROL OF MY EMOTIONS, AND THE FOCUS SLIPPED.
YOU LOST--?
I WAS PRESENT FOR THESE EVENTS, REQUIEM. I REMEMBER THEM VERY WELL.
THIS WAS WHEN YOUR OWN VANITY GOT THE BETTER OF YOU.
WHEN YOU DID WHAT YOUR ENEMIES COULD NOT DO. IT'S WHY WE'RE HERE NOW, WHEN ALL IS SAID AND DONE.

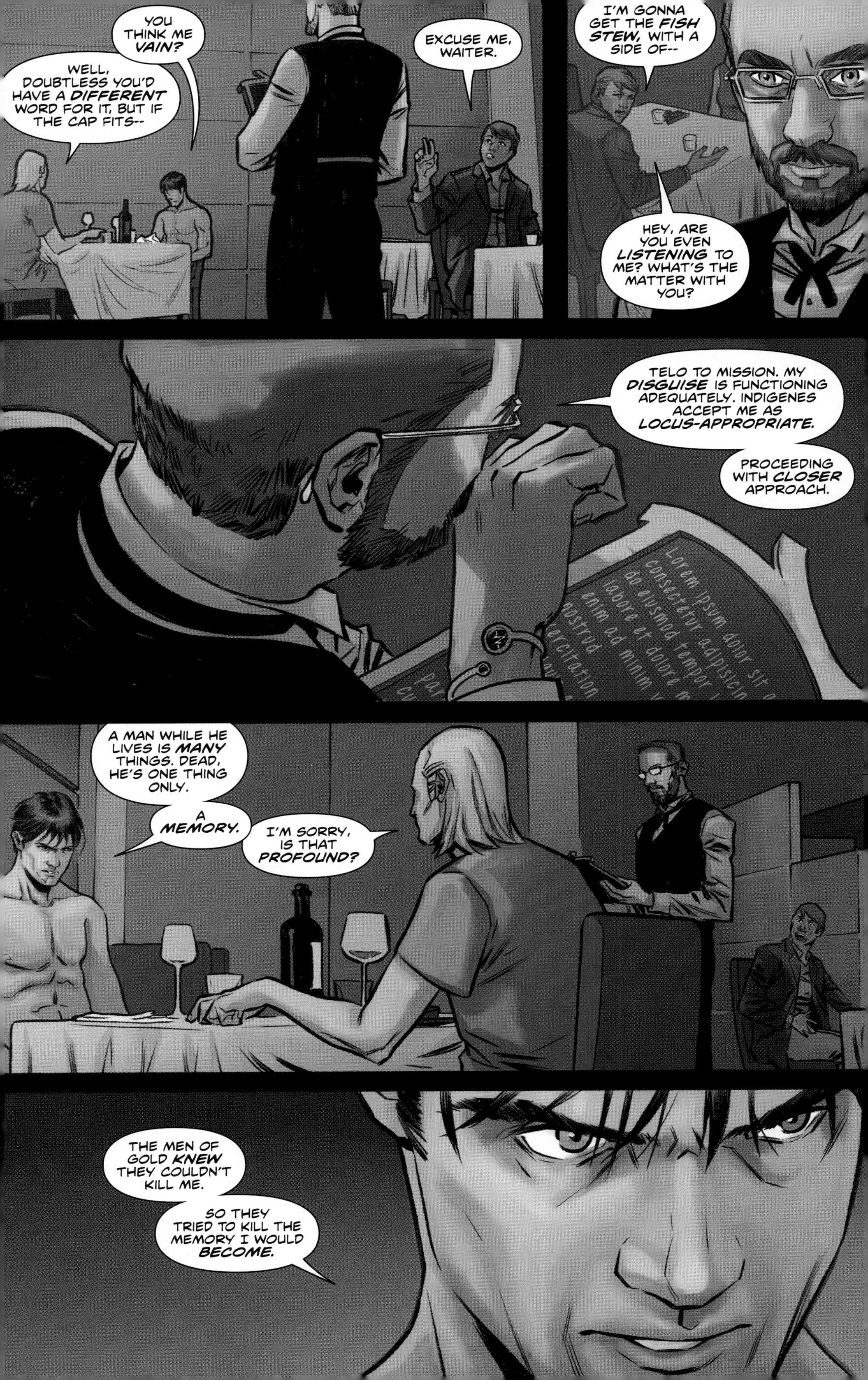
YOU THINK ME VAIN?
WELL, DOUBTLESS YOU'D HAVE A DIFFERENT WORD FOR IT, BUT IF THE CAP FITS--
EXCUSE ME, WAITER.
I'M GONNA GET THE FISH STEW, WITH A SIDE OF--
HEY, ARE YOU EVEN LISTENING TO ME? WHAT'S THE MATTER WITH YOU?
TELO TO MISSION. MY DISGUISE IS FUNCTIONING ADEQUATELY. INDIGENES ACCEPT ME AS LOCUS-APPROPRIATE.
PROCEEDING WITH CLOSER APPROACH.
A MAN WHILE HE LIVES IS MANY THINGS. DEAD, HE'S ONE THING ONLY.
A MEMORY.
I'M SORRY, IS THAT PROFOUND?
THE MEN OF GOLD KNEW THEY COULDN'T KILL ME.
SO THEY TRIED TO KILL THE MEMORY I WOULD BECOME.

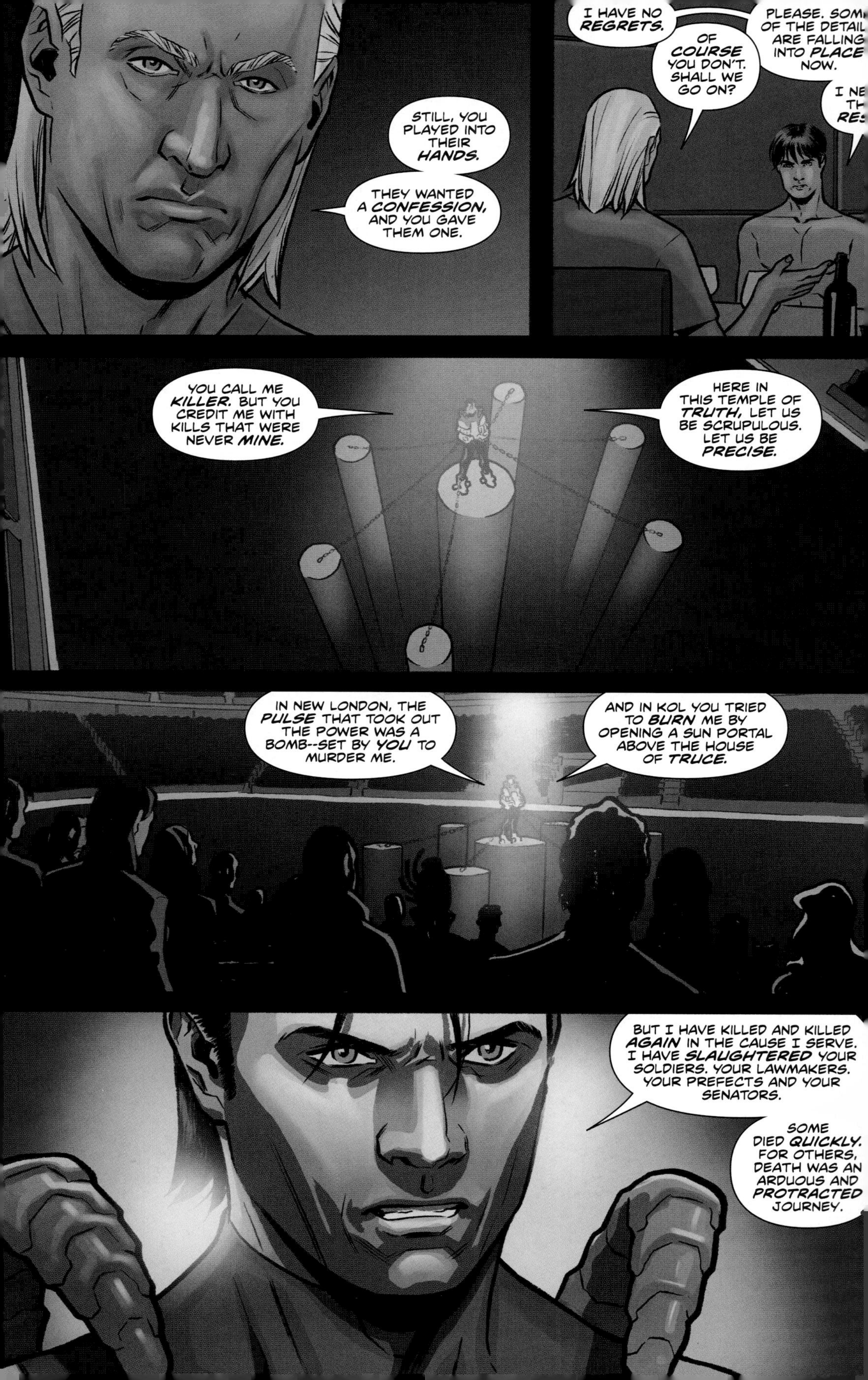

STILL, YOU PLAYED INTO THEIR ***HANDS.***
THEY WANTED A ***CONFESSION,*** AND YOU GAVE THEM ONE.
I HAVE NO ***REGRETS.***
OF ***COURSE*** YOU DON'T. SHALL WE GO ON?
PLEASE. SOM OF THE DETAIL ARE FALLING INTO ***PLACE*** NOW.
I NE TH ***RES***
YOU CALL ME ***KILLER.*** BUT YOU CREDIT ME WITH KILLS THAT WERE NEVER ***MINE.***
HERE IN THIS TEMPLE OF ***TRUTH,*** LET US BE SCRUPULOUS. LET US BE ***PRECISE.***
IN NEW LONDON, THE ***PULSE*** THAT TOOK OUT THE POWER WAS A BOMB--SET BY ***YOU*** TO MURDER ME.
AND IN KOL YOU TRIED TO ***BURN*** ME BY OPENING A SUN PORTAL ABOVE THE HOUSE OF ***TRUCE.***
BUT I HAVE KILLED AND KILLED ***AGAIN*** IN THE CAUSE I SERVE. I HAVE ***SLAUGHTERED*** YOUR SOLDIERS. YOUR LAWMAKERS. YOUR PREFECTS AND YOUR SENATORS.
SOME DIED ***QUICKLY.*** FOR OTHERS, DEATH WAS AN ARDUOUS AND ***PROTRACTED*** JOURNEY.

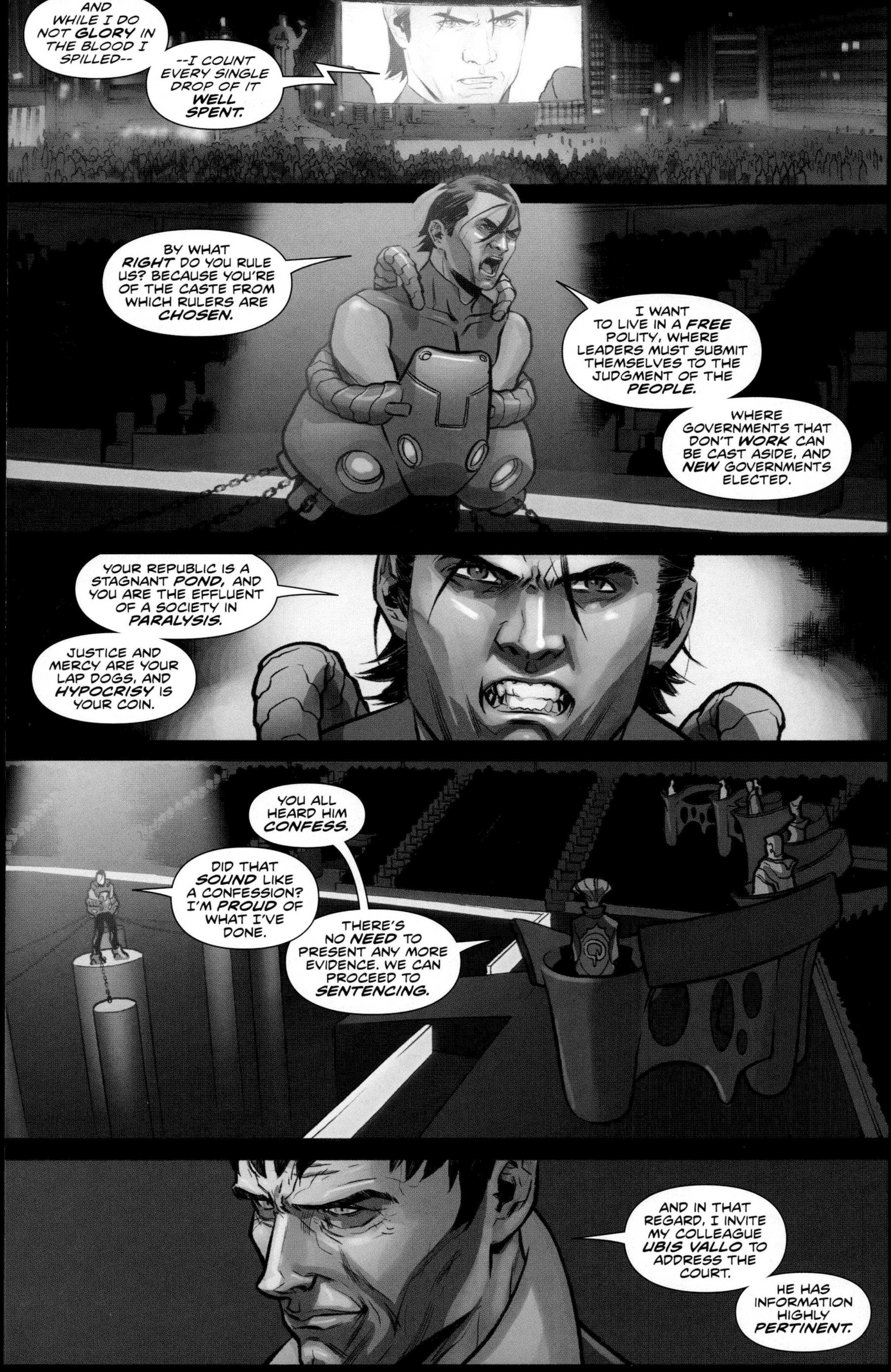
AND WHILE I DO NOT GLORY IN THE BLOOD I SPILLED--
--I COUNT EVERY SINGLE DROP OF IT WELL SPENT.
BY WHAT RIGHT DO YOU RULE US? BECAUSE YOU'RE OF THE CASTE FROM WHICH RULERS ARE CHOSEN.
I WANT TO LIVE IN A FREE POLITY, WHERE LEADERS MUST SUBMIT THEMSELVES TO THE JUDGMENT OF THE PEOPLE.
WHERE GOVERNMENTS THAT DON'T WORK CAN BE CAST ASIDE, AND NEW GOVERNMENTS ELECTED.
YOUR REPUBLIC IS A STAGNANT POND, AND YOU ARE THE EFFLUENT OF A SOCIETY IN PARALYSIS.
JUSTICE AND MERCY ARE YOUR LAP DOGS, AND HYPOCRISY IS YOUR COIN.
YOU ALL HEARD HIM CONFESS.
DID THAT SOUND LIKE A CONFESSION? I'M PROUD OF WHAT I'VE DONE.
THERE'S NO NEED TO PRESENT ANY MORE EVIDENCE. WE CAN PROCEED TO SENTENCING.
AND IN THAT REGARD, I INVITE MY COLLEAGUE UBIS VALLO TO ADDRESS THE COURT.
HE HAS INFORMATION HIGHLY PERTINENT.

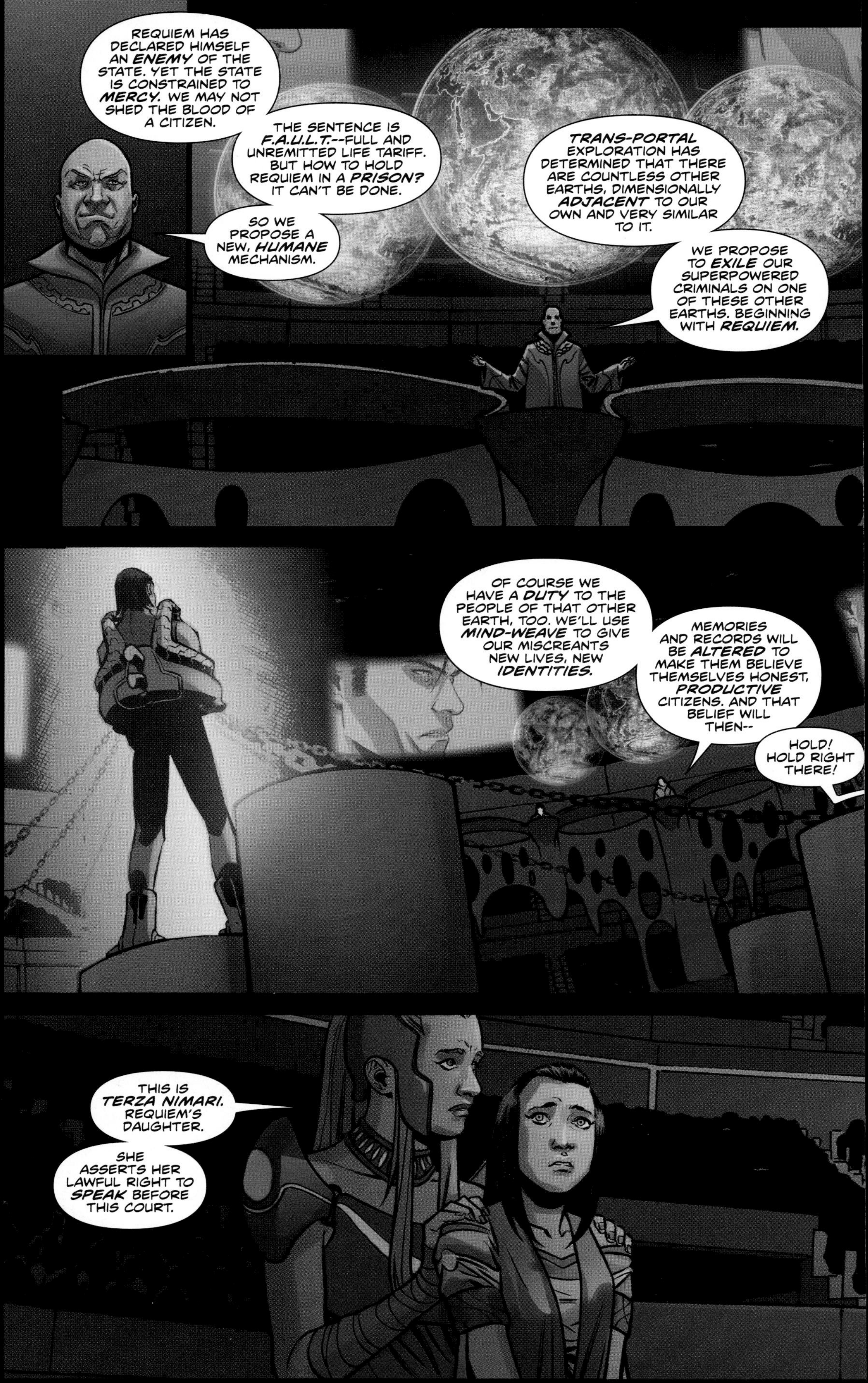
REQUIEM HAS DECLARED HIMSELF AN ENEMY OF THE STATE. YET THE STATE IS CONSTRAINED TO MERCY. WE MAY NOT SHED THE BLOOD OF A CITIZEN.
THE SENTENCE IS F.A.U.L.T.--FULL AND UNREMITTED LIFE TARIFF. BUT HOW TO HOLD REQUIEM IN A PRISON? IT CAN'T BE DONE.
SO WE PROPOSE A NEW, HUMANE MECHANISM.
TRANS-PORTAL EXPLORATION HAS DETERMINED THAT THERE ARE COUNTLESS OTHER EARTHS, DIMENSIONALLY ADJACENT TO OUR OWN AND VERY SIMILAR TO IT.
WE PROPOSE TO EXILE OUR SUPERPOWERED CRIMINALS ON ONE OF THESE OTHER EARTHS. BEGINNING WITH REQUIEM.
OF COURSE WE HAVE A DUTY TO THE PEOPLE OF THAT OTHER EARTH, TOO. WE'LL USE MIND-WEAVE TO GIVE OUR MISCREANTS NEW LIVES, NEW IDENTITIES.
MEMORIES AND RECORDS WILL BE ALTERED TO MAKE THEM BELIEVE THEMSELVES HONEST, PRODUCTIVE CITIZENS. AND THAT BELIEF WILL THEN--
HOLD! HOLD RIGHT THERE!
THIS IS TERZA NIMARI. REQUIEM'S DAUGHTER.
SHE ASSERTS HER LAWFUL RIGHT TO SPEAK BEFORE THIS COURT.

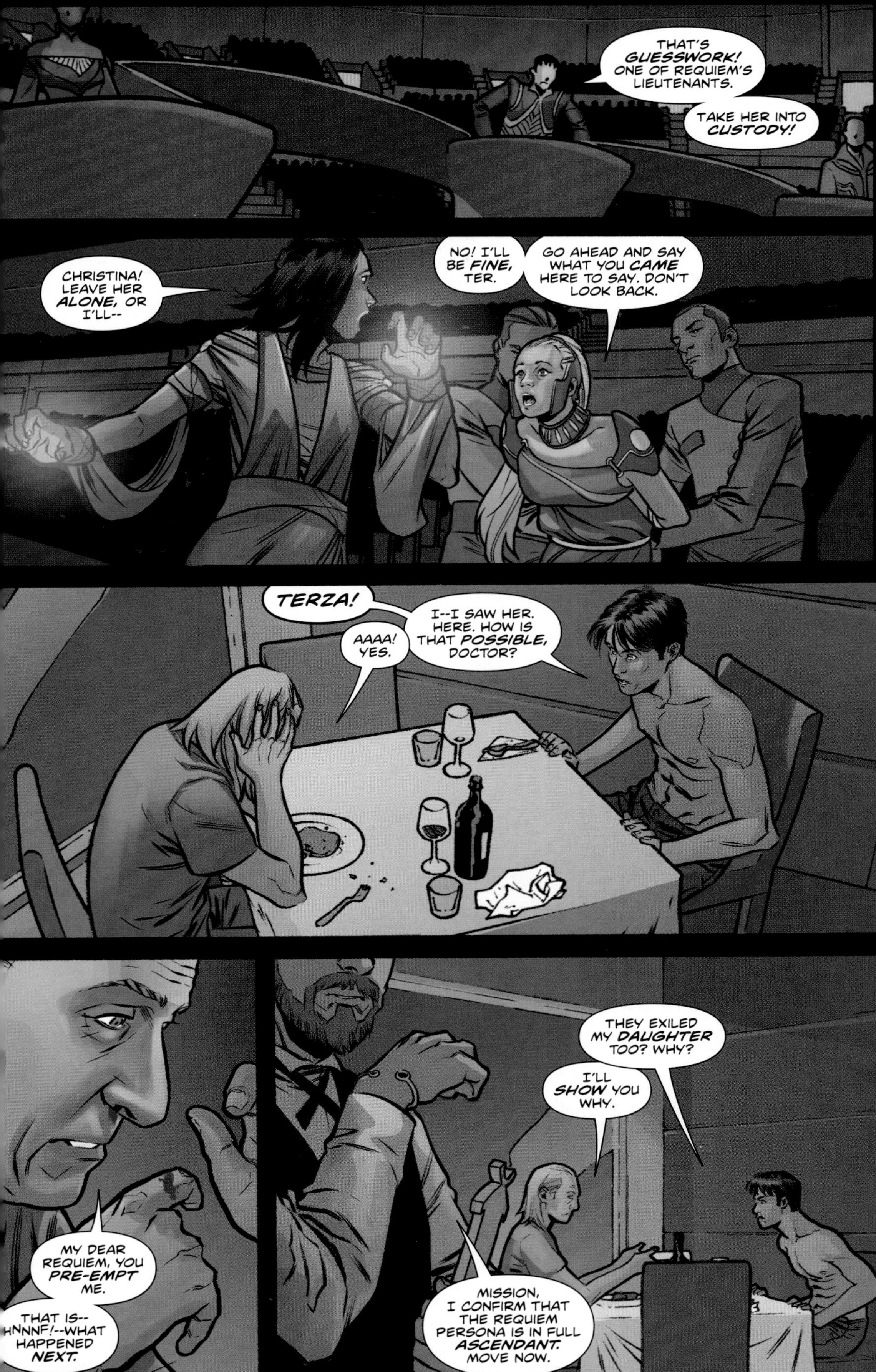
THAT'S GUESSWORK! ONE OF REQUIEM'S LIEUTENANTS.
TAKE HER INTO CUSTODY!
CHRISTINA! LEAVE HER ALONE, OR I'LL--
NO! I'LL BE FINE, TER.
GO AHEAD AND SAY WHAT YOU CAME HERE TO SAY. DON'T LOOK BACK.
TERZA!
I--I SAW HER. HERE. HOW IS THAT POSSIBLE, DOCTOR?
AAAA! YES.
MY DEAR REQUIEM, YOU PRE-EMPT ME.
THAT IS-- HNNNF!--WHAT HAPPENED NEXT.
THEY EXILED MY DAUGHTER TOO? WHY?
I'LL SHOW YOU WHY.
MISSION, I CONFIRM THAT THE REQUIEM PERSONA IS IN FULL ASCENDANT. MOVE NOW.

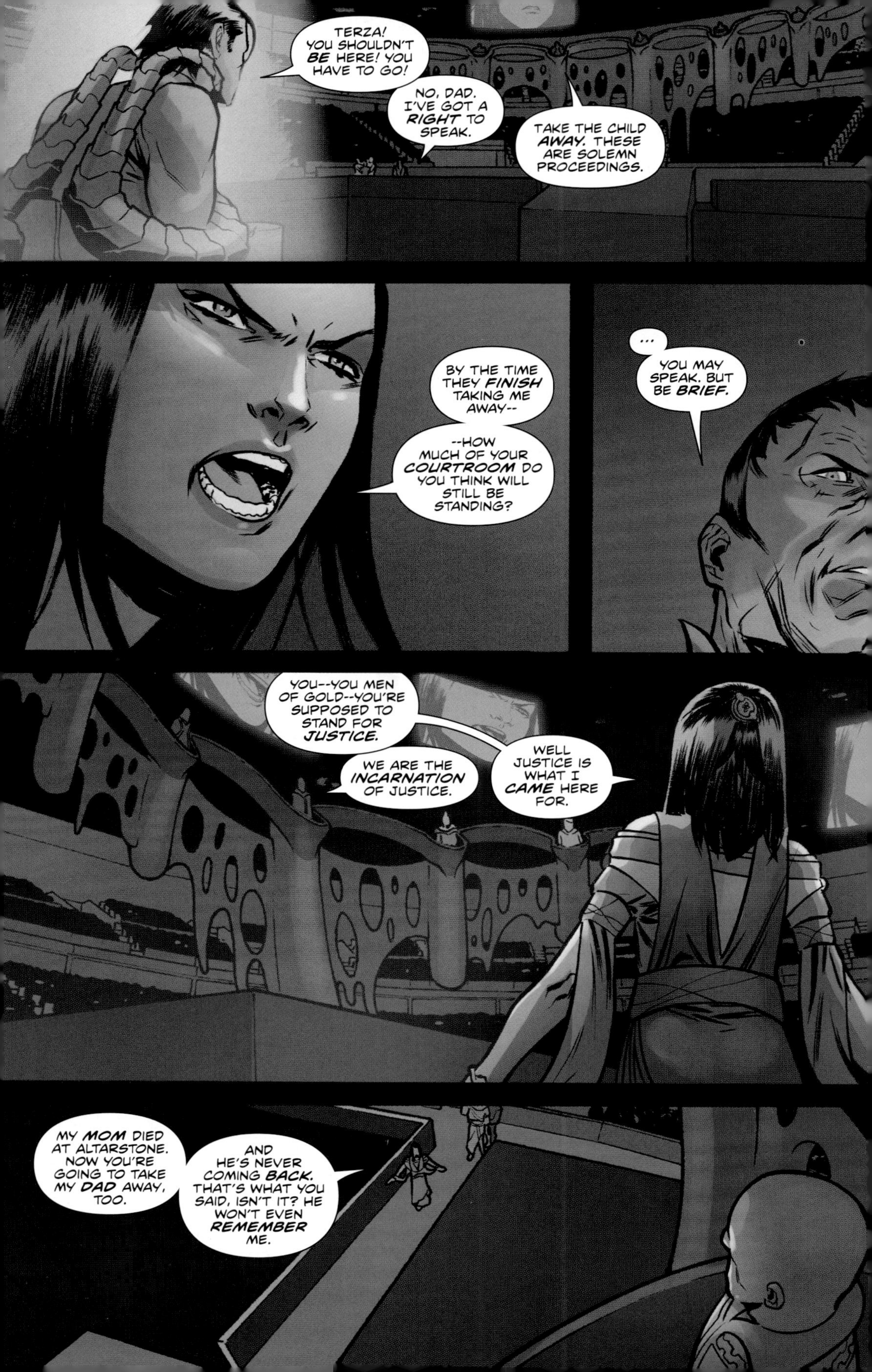
TERZA! YOU SHOULDN'T BE HERE! YOU HAVE TO GO!
NO, DAD. I'VE GOT A RIGHT TO SPEAK.
TAKE THE CHILD AWAY. THESE ARE SOLEMN PROCEEDINGS.
BY THE TIME THEY FINISH TAKING ME AWAY--
--HOW MUCH OF YOUR COURTROOM DO YOU THINK WILL STILL BE STANDING?
...
YOU MAY SPEAK. BUT BE BRIEF.
YOU--YOU MEN OF GOLD--YOU'RE SUPPOSED TO STAND FOR JUSTICE.
WE ARE THE INCARNATION OF JUSTICE.
WELL JUSTICE IS WHAT I CAME HERE FOR.
MY MOM DIED AT ALTARSTONE. NOW YOU'RE GOING TO TAKE MY DAD AWAY, TOO.
AND HE'S NEVER COMING BACK. THAT'S WHAT YOU SAID, ISN'T IT? HE WON'T EVEN REMEMBER ME.

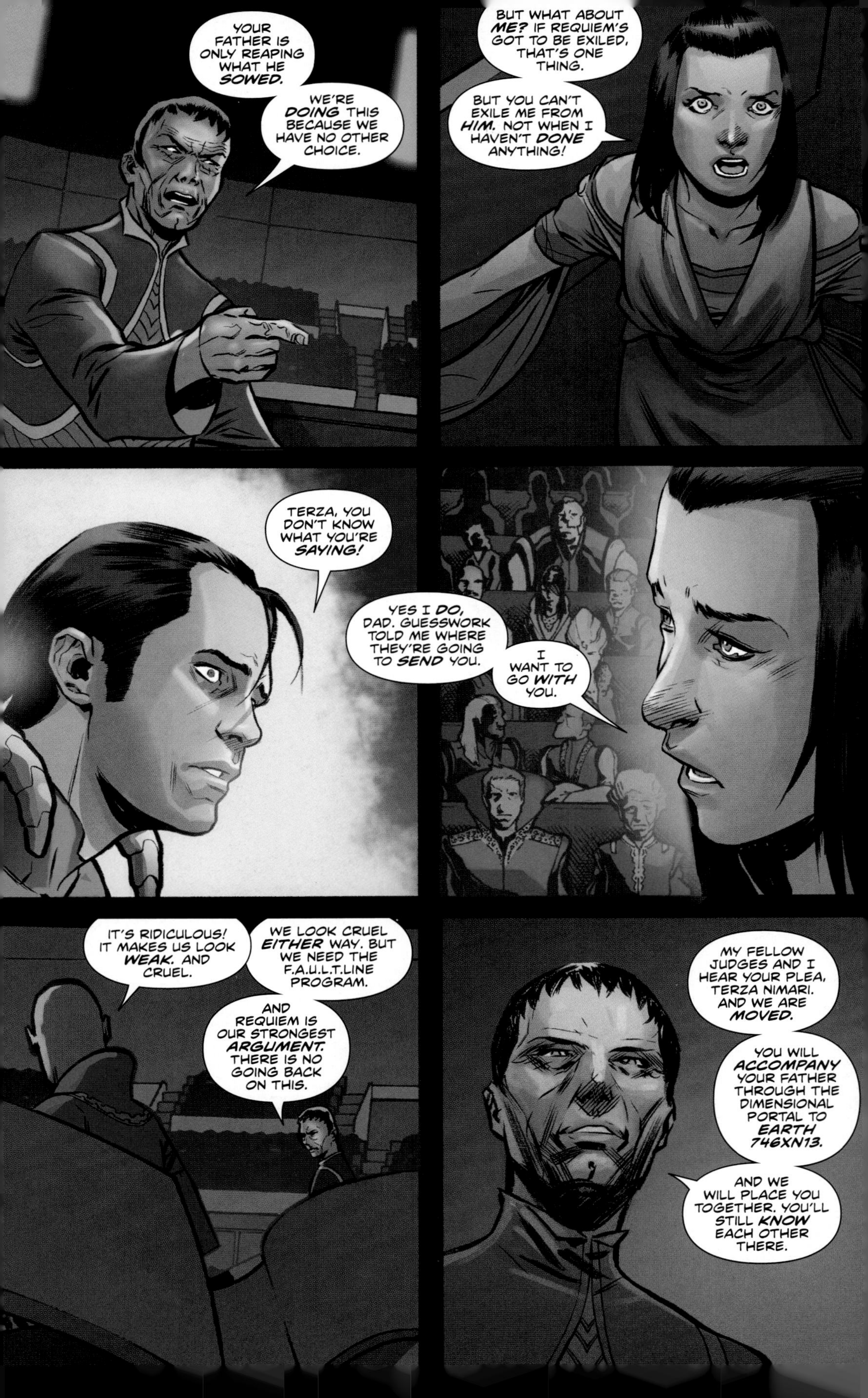
YOUR FATHER IS ONLY REAPING WHAT HE SOWED.
WE'RE DOING THIS BECAUSE WE HAVE NO OTHER CHOICE.
BUT WHAT ABOUT ME? IF REQUIEM'S GOT TO BE EXILED, THAT'S ONE THING.
BUT YOU CAN'T EXILE ME FROM HIM. NOT WHEN I HAVEN'T DONE ANYTHING!
TERZA, YOU DON'T KNOW WHAT YOU'RE SAYING!
YES I DO, DAD. GUESSWORK TOLD ME WHERE THEY'RE GOING TO SEND YOU.
I WANT TO GO WITH YOU.
IT'S RIDICULOUS! IT MAKES US LOOK WEAK. AND CRUEL.
WE LOOK CRUEL EITHER WAY. BUT WE NEED THE F.A.U.L.T.LINE PROGRAM.
AND REQUIEM IS OUR STRONGEST ARGUMENT. THERE IS NO GOING BACK ON THIS.
MY FELLOW JUDGES AND I HEAR YOUR PLEA, TERZA NIMARI. AND WE ARE MOVED.
YOU WILL ACCOMPANY YOUR FATHER THROUGH THE DIMENSIONAL PORTAL TO EARTH 746XN13.
AND WE WILL PLACE YOU TOGETHER. YOU'LL STILL KNOW EACH OTHER THERE.

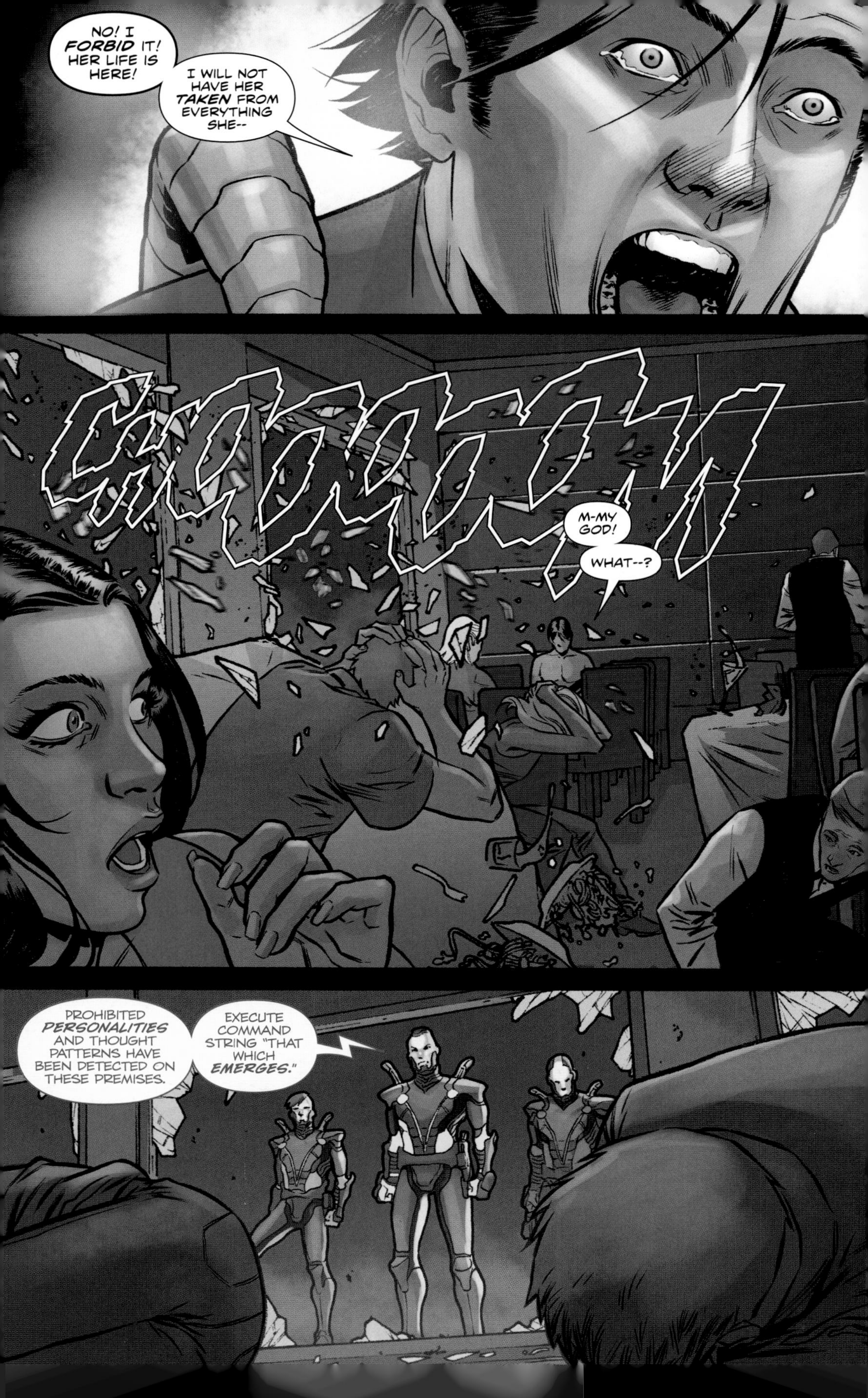
NO! I FORBID IT! HER LIFE IS HERE!
I WILL NOT HAVE HER TAKEN FROM EVERYTHING SHE--
M-MY GOD!
WHAT--?
PROHIBITED PERSONALITIES AND THOUGHT PATTERNS HAVE BEEN DETECTED ON THESE PREMISES.
EXECUTE COMMAND STRING "THAT WHICH EMERGES."

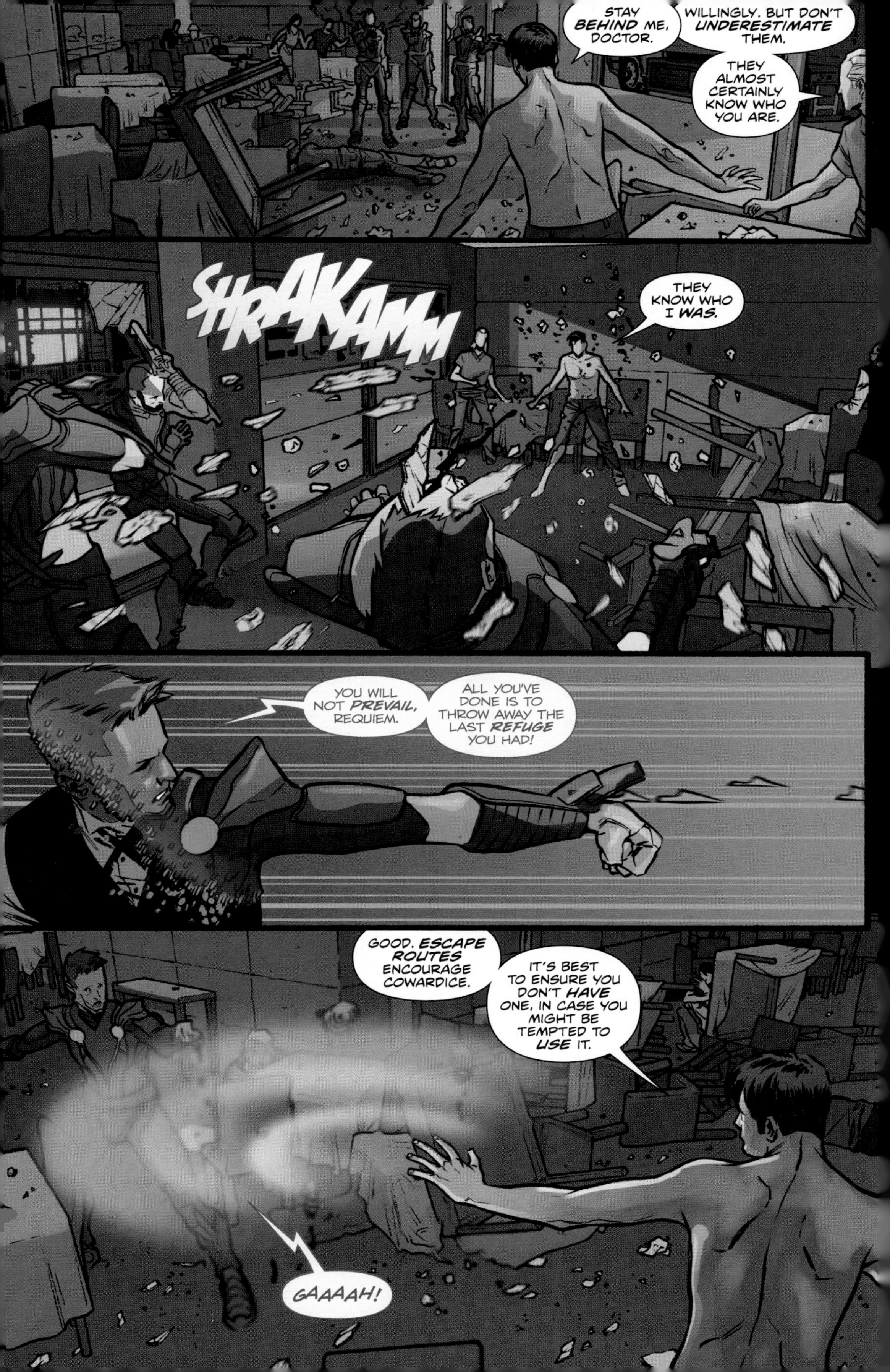
STAY BEHIND ME, DOCTOR.
WILLINGLY. BUT DON'T UNDERESTIMATE THEM.
THEY ALMOST CERTAINLY KNOW WHO YOU ARE.
SHRAKAMM
THEY KNOW WHO I WAS.
YOU WILL NOT PREVAIL, REQUIEM.
ALL YOU'VE DONE IS TO THROW AWAY THE LAST REFUGE YOU HAD!
GOOD. ESCAPE ROUTES ENCOURAGE COWARDICE.
IT'S BEST TO ENSURE YOU DON'T HAVE ONE, IN CASE YOU MIGHT BE TEMPTED TO USE IT.
GAAAAH!

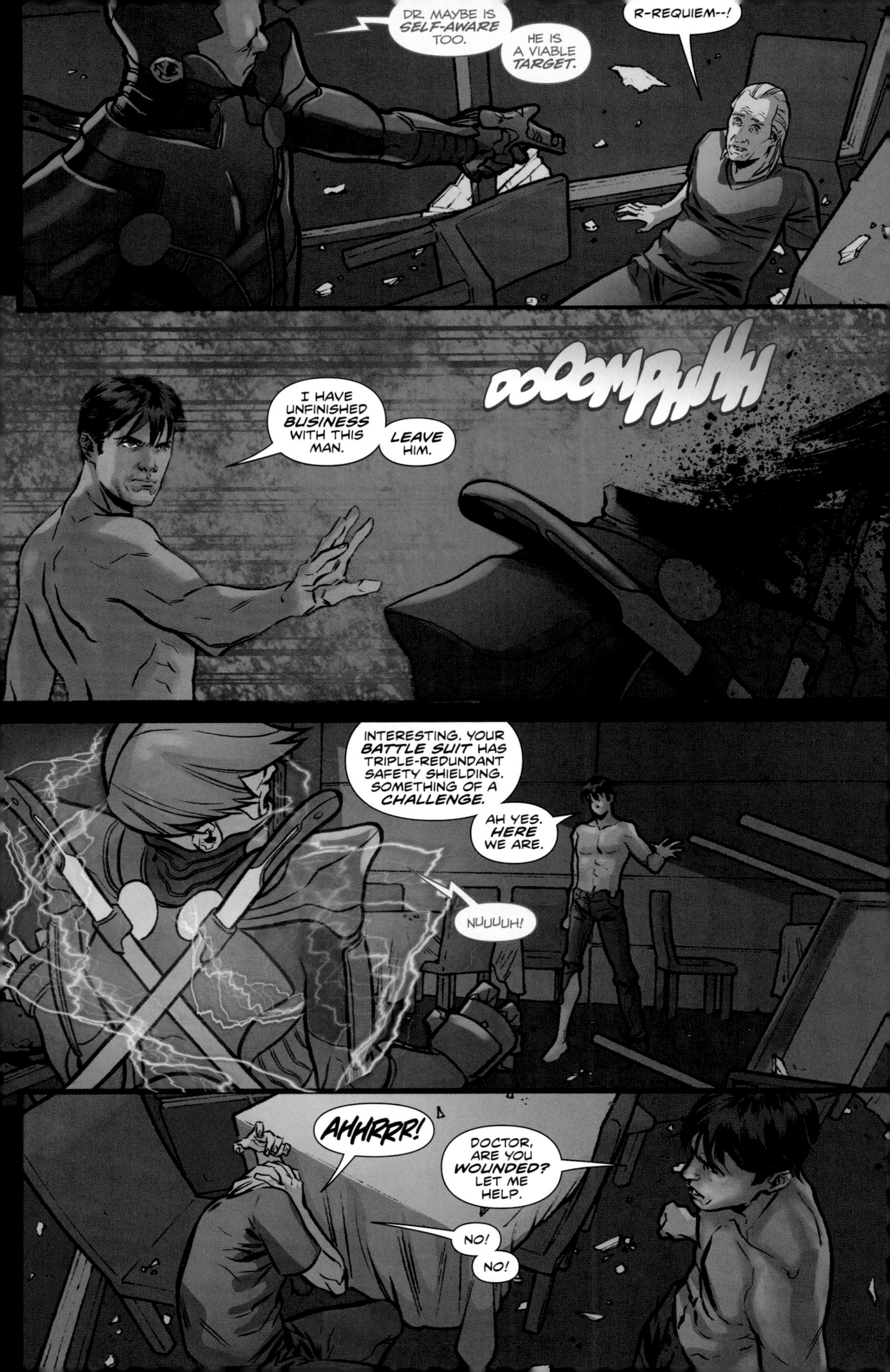

DR. MAYBE IS SELF-AWARE TOO.
HE IS A VIABLE TARGET.
R-REQUIEM--!
I HAVE UNFINISHED BUSINESS WITH THIS MAN.
LEAVE HIM.
DOOOOMPHHH
INTERESTING. YOUR BATTLE SUIT HAS TRIPLE-REDUNDANT SAFETY SHIELDING. SOMETHING OF A CHALLENGE.
AH YES. HERE WE ARE.
NUUUUH!
AHHRRR!
DOCTOR, ARE YOU WOUNDED? LET ME HELP.
NO!
NO!

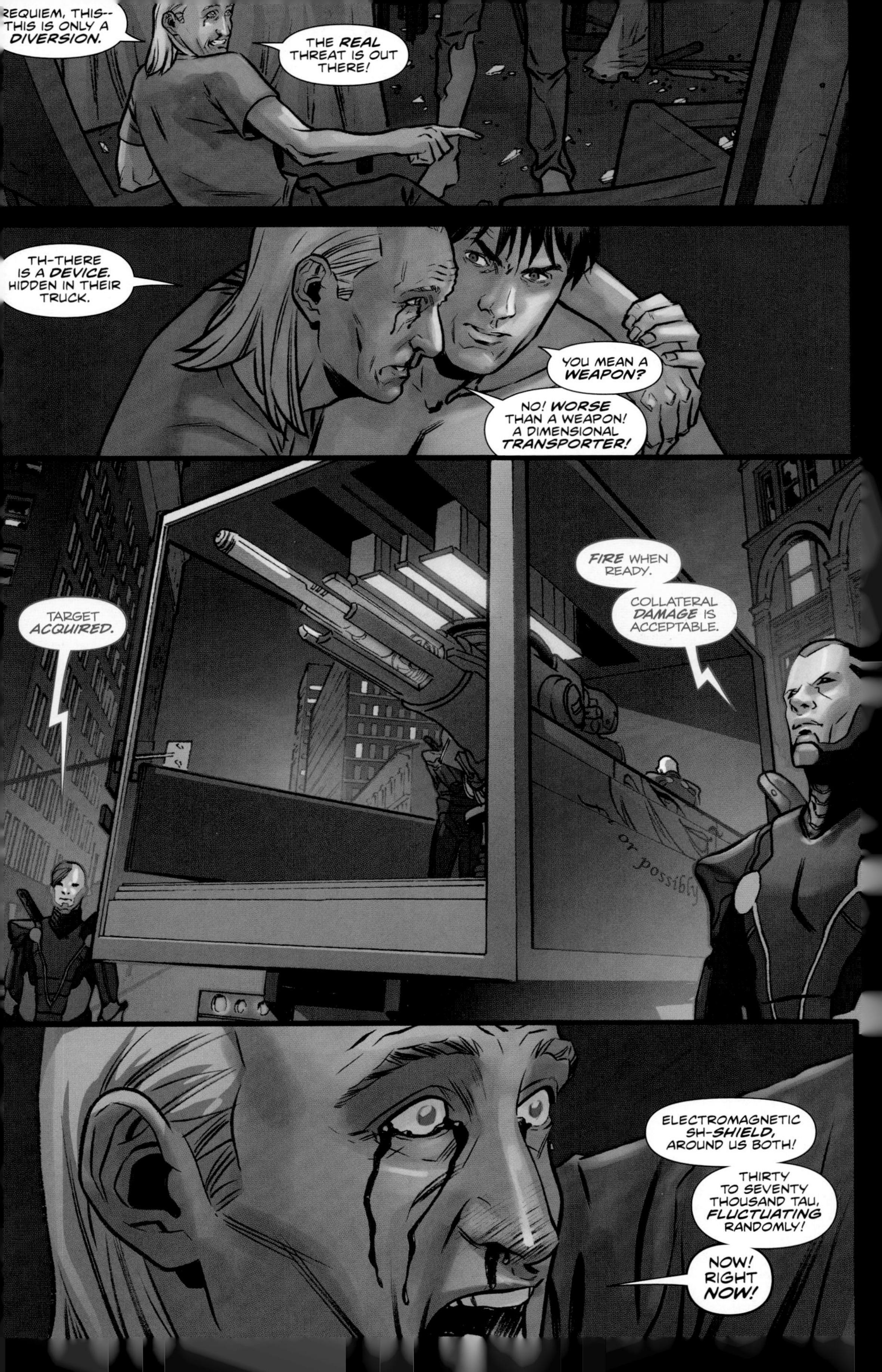
REQUIEM, THIS-- THIS IS ONLY A DIVERSION.
THE REAL THREAT IS OUT THERE!
TH-THERE IS A DEVICE. HIDDEN IN THEIR TRUCK.
YOU MEAN A WEAPON?
NO! WORSE THAN A WEAPON! A DIMENSIONAL TRANSPORTER!
TARGET ACQUIRED.
FIRE WHEN READY.
COLLATERAL DAMAGE IS ACCEPTABLE.
or possibly
ELECTROMAGNETIC SH-SHIELD, AROUND US BOTH!
THIRTY TO SEVENTY THOUSAND TAU, FLUCTUATING RANDOMLY!
NOW! RIGHT NOW!

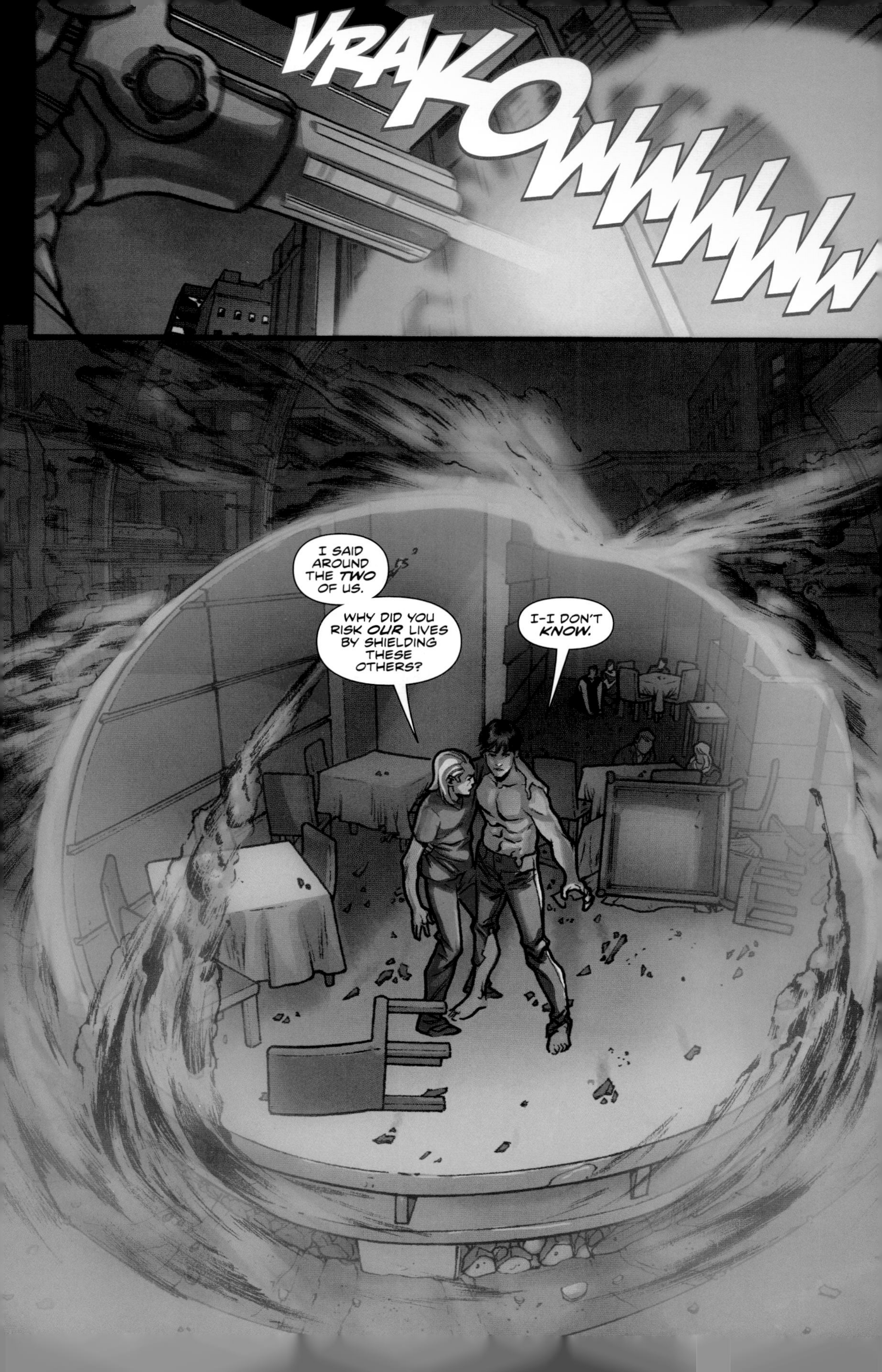
VRAKOWWWWW
I SAID AROUND THE *TWO* OF US.
WHY DID YOU RISK *OUR* LIVES BY SHIELDING THESE OTHERS?
I-I DON'T *KNOW.*

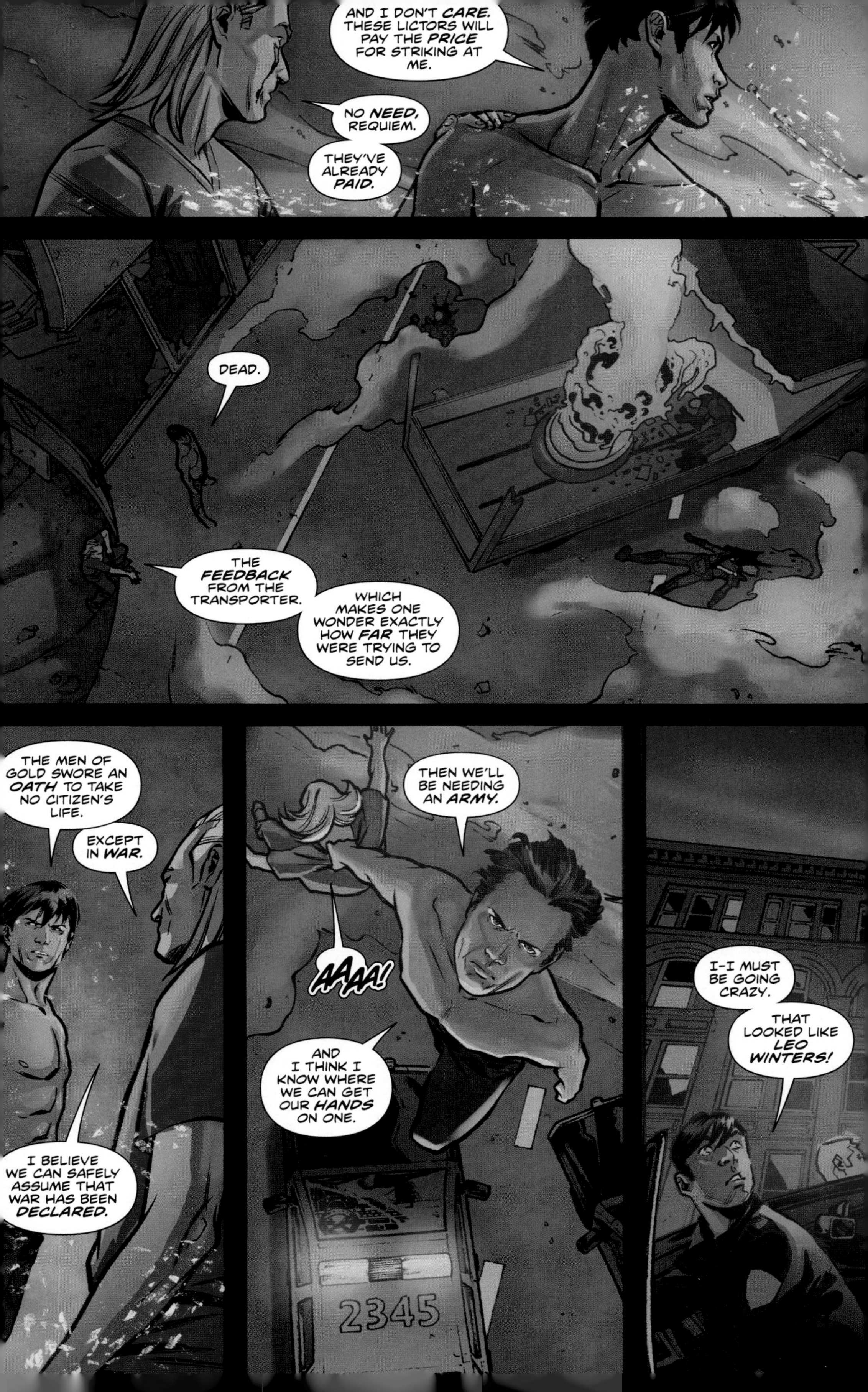
AND I DON'T CARE. THESE LICTORS WILL PAY THE PRICE FOR STRIKING AT ME.
NO NEED, REQUIEM.
THEY'VE ALREADY PAID.
DEAD.
THE FEEDBACK FROM THE TRANSPORTER.
WHICH MAKES ONE WONDER EXACTLY HOW FAR THEY WERE TRYING TO SEND US.
THE MEN OF GOLD SWORE AN OATH TO TAKE NO CITIZEN'S LIFE.
EXCEPT IN WAR.
I BELIEVE WE CAN SAFELY ASSUME THAT WAR HAS BEEN DECLARED.
THEN WE'LL BE NEEDING AN ARMY.
AAAA!
AND I THINK I KNOW WHERE WE CAN GET OUR HANDS ON ONE.
2345
I-I MUST BE GOING CRAZY.
THAT LOOKED LIKE LEO WINTERS!

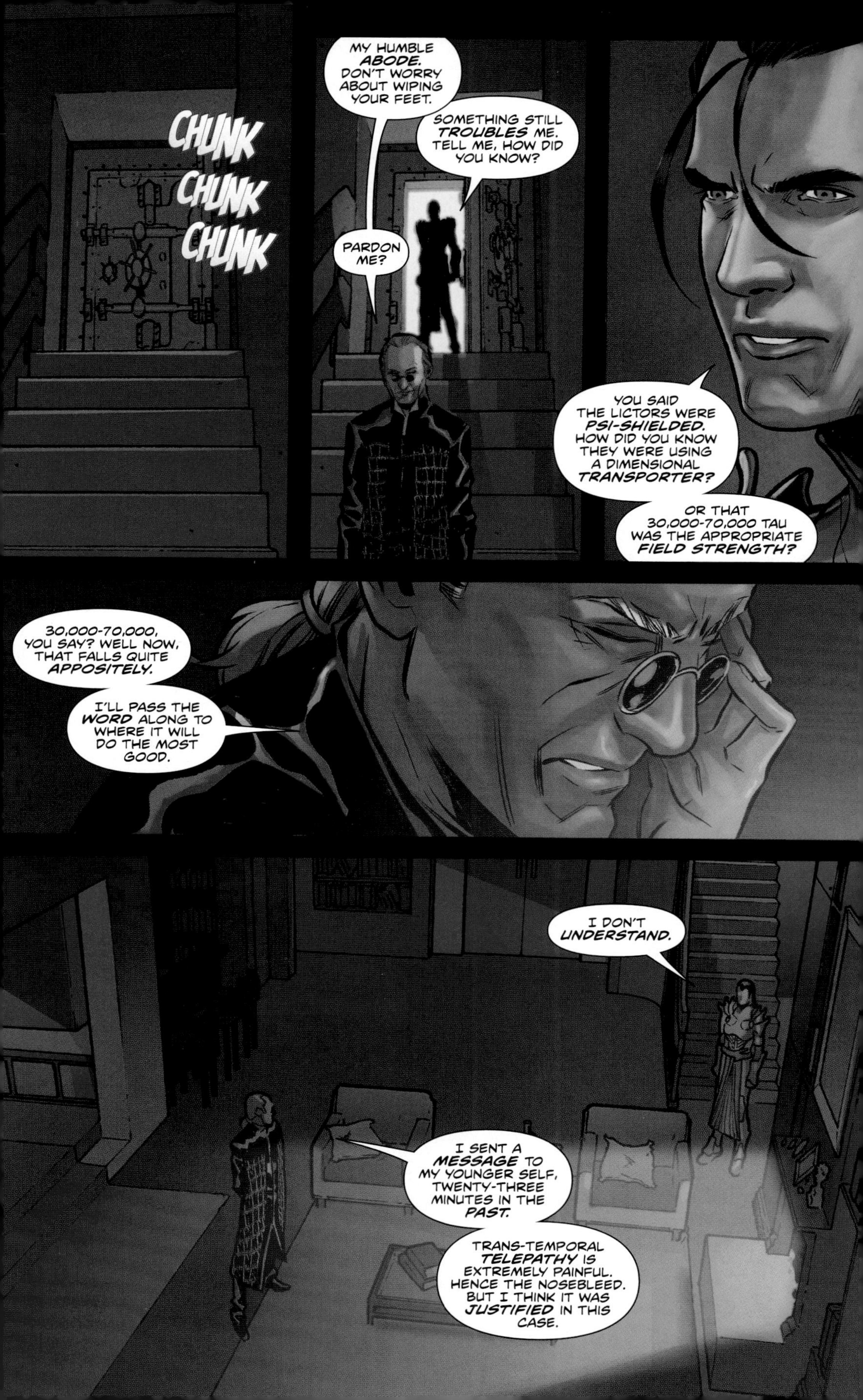
CHUNK
CHUNK
CHUNK
MY HUMBLE ABODE. DON'T WORRY ABOUT WIPING YOUR FEET.
SOMETHING STILL TROUBLES ME. TELL ME, HOW DID YOU KNOW?
PARDON ME?
YOU SAID THE LICTORS WERE PSI-SHIELDED. HOW DID YOU KNOW THEY WERE USING A DIMENSIONAL TRANSPORTER?
OR THAT 30,000-70,000 TAU WAS THE APPROPRIATE FIELD STRENGTH?
30,000-70,000, YOU SAY? WELL NOW, THAT FALLS QUITE APPOSITELY.
I'LL PASS THE WORD ALONG TO WHERE IT WILL DO THE MOST GOOD.
I DON'T UNDERSTAND.
I SENT A MESSAGE TO MY YOUNGER SELF, TWENTY-THREE MINUTES IN THE PAST.
TRANS-TEMPORAL TELEPATHY IS EXTREMELY PAINFUL. HENCE THE NOSEBLEED. BUT I THINK IT WAS JUSTIFIED IN THIS CASE.

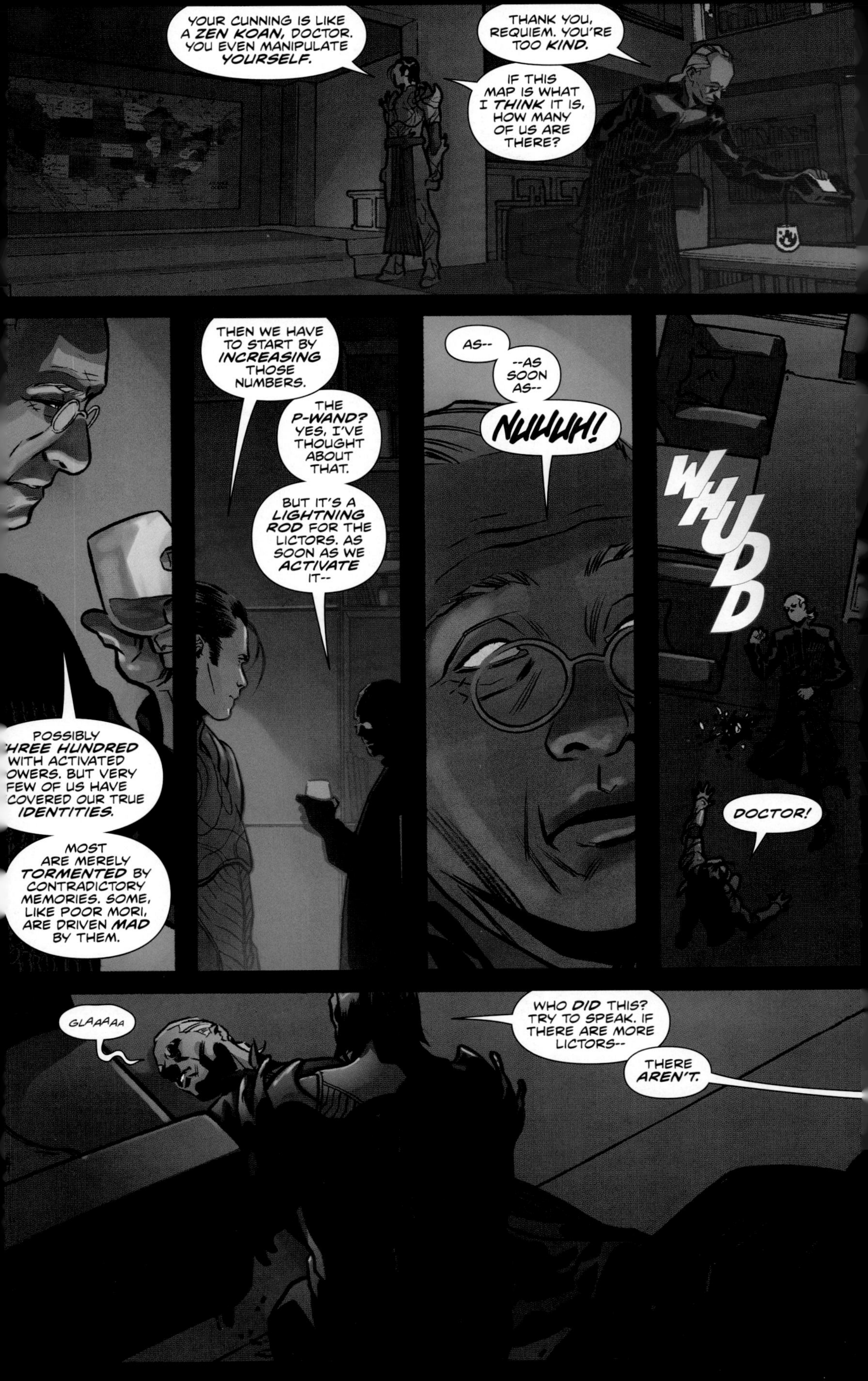
YOUR CUNNING IS LIKE A ZEN KOAN, DOCTOR. YOU EVEN MANIPULATE YOURSELF.
THANK YOU, REQUIEM. YOU'RE TOO KIND.
IF THIS MAP IS WHAT I THINK IT IS, HOW MANY OF US ARE THERE?
POSSIBLY THREE HUNDRED WITH ACTIVATED POWERS. BUT VERY FEW OF US HAVE RECOVERED OUR TRUE IDENTITIES.
MOST ARE MERELY TORMENTED BY CONTRADICTORY MEMORIES. SOME, LIKE POOR MORI, ARE DRIVEN MAD BY THEM.
THEN WE HAVE TO START BY INCREASING THOSE NUMBERS.
THE P-WAND? YES, I'VE THOUGHT ABOUT THAT.
BUT IT'S A LIGHTNING ROD FOR THE LICTORS. AS SOON AS WE ACTIVATE IT--
AS--
--AS SOON AS--
NUUUH!
WHUDD
DOCTOR!
GLAAAAA
WHO DID THIS? TRY TO SPEAK. IF THERE ARE MORE LICTORS--
THERE AREN'T.

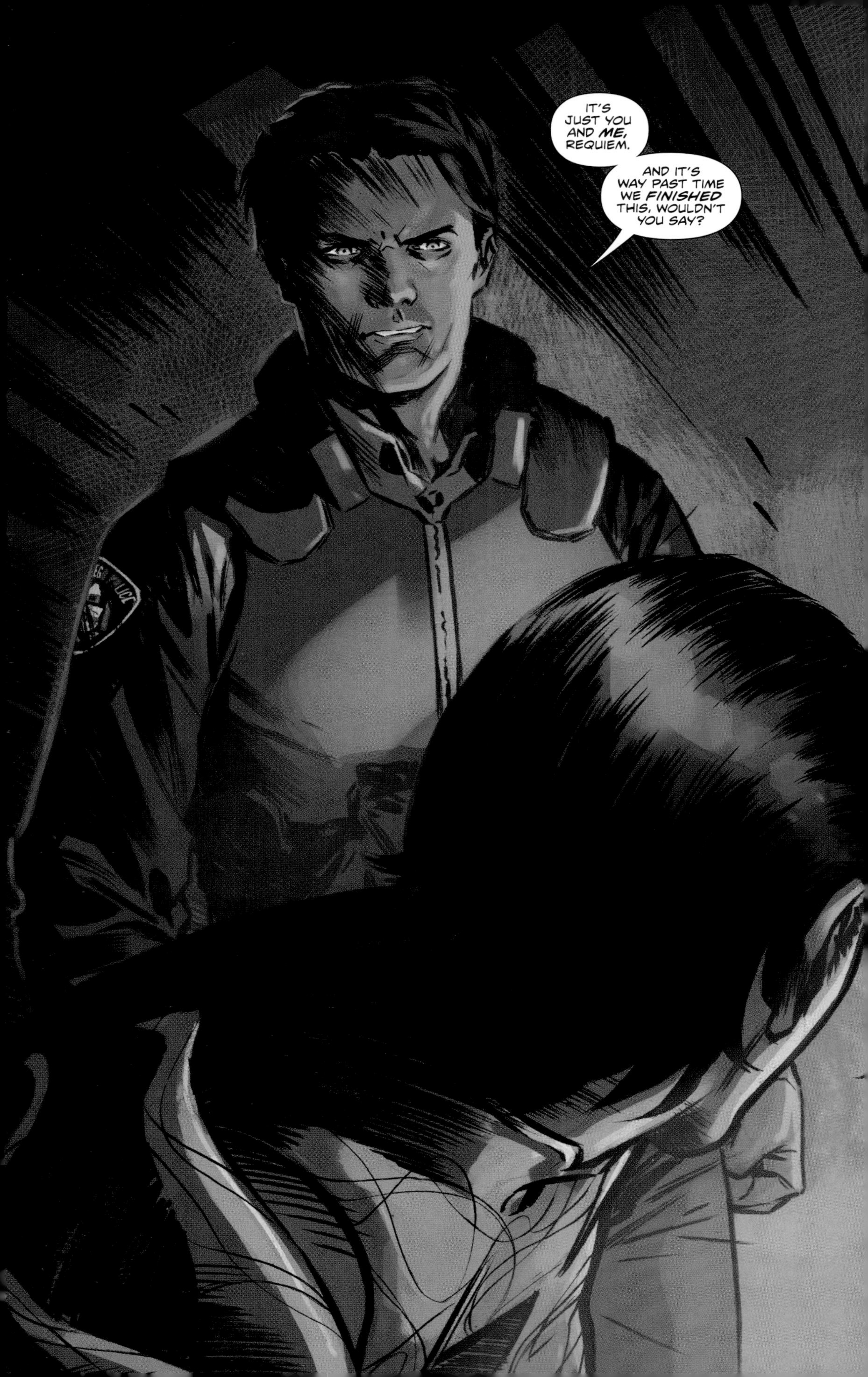
IT'S JUST YOU AND ME, REQUIEM.
AND IT'S WAY PAST TIME WE FINISHED THIS, WOULDN'T YOU SAY?

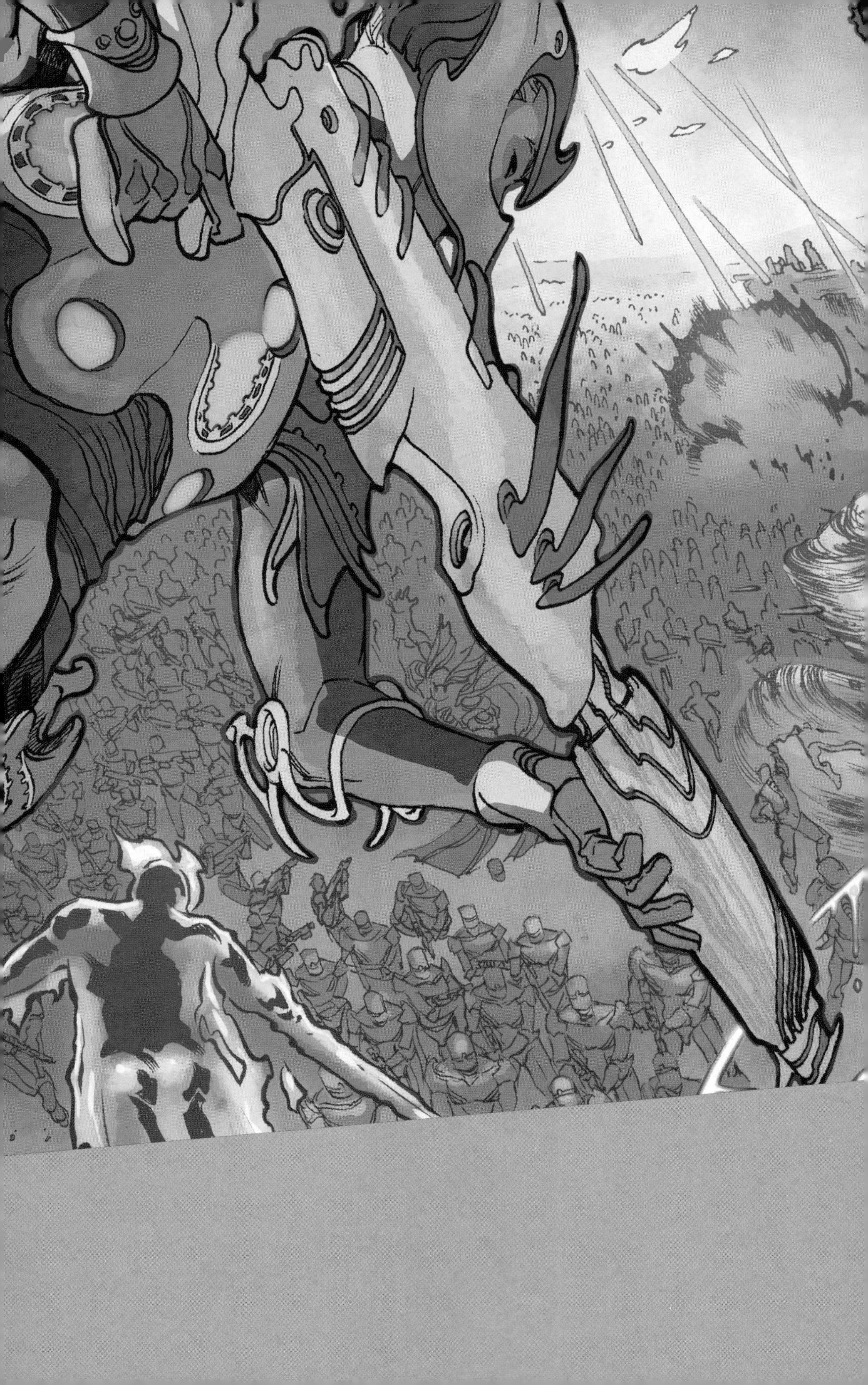

COVER GALLERY

ISSUE TEN
STEPHANIE HANS

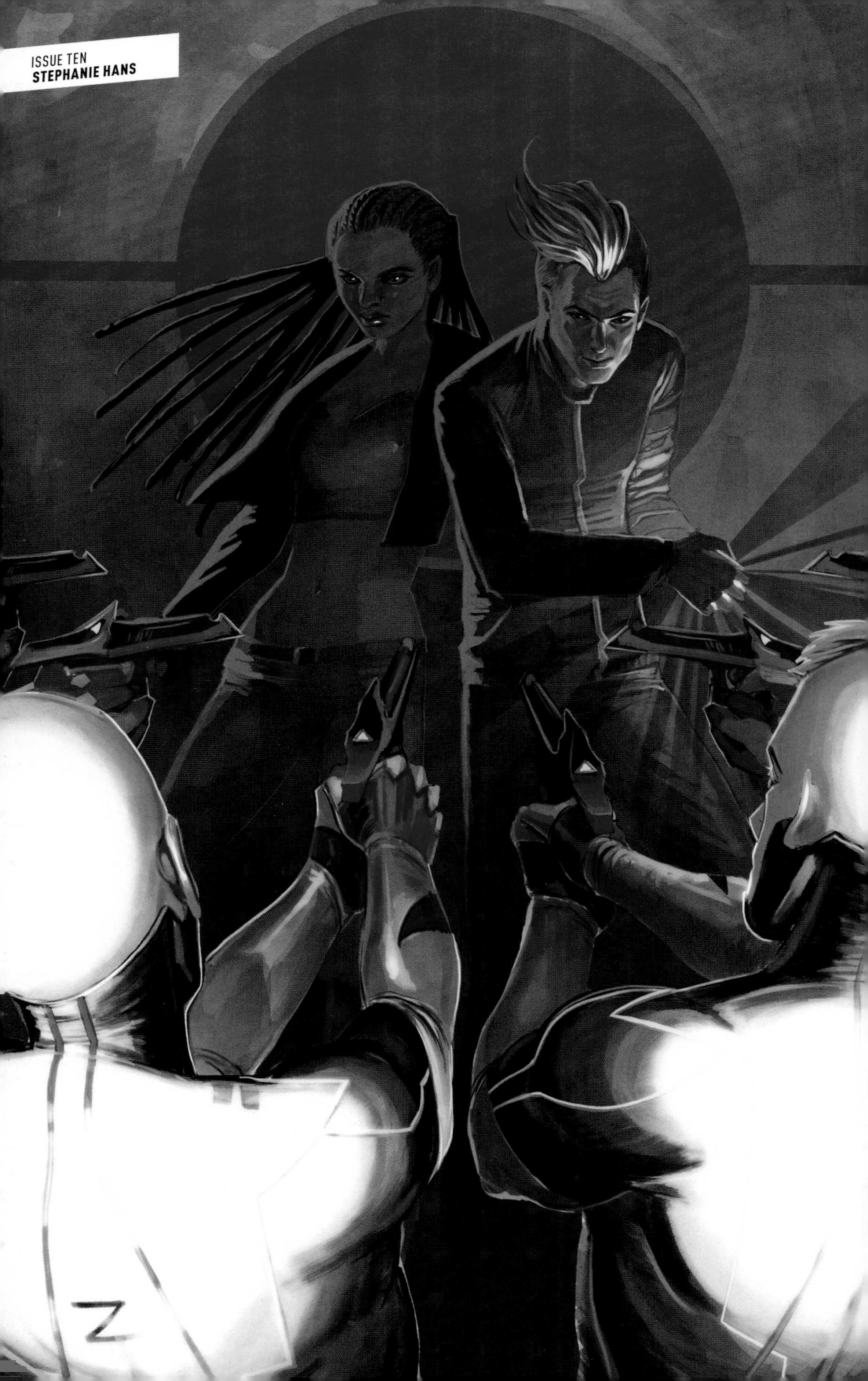

ISSUE ELEVEN
TOMMY LEE EDWARDS

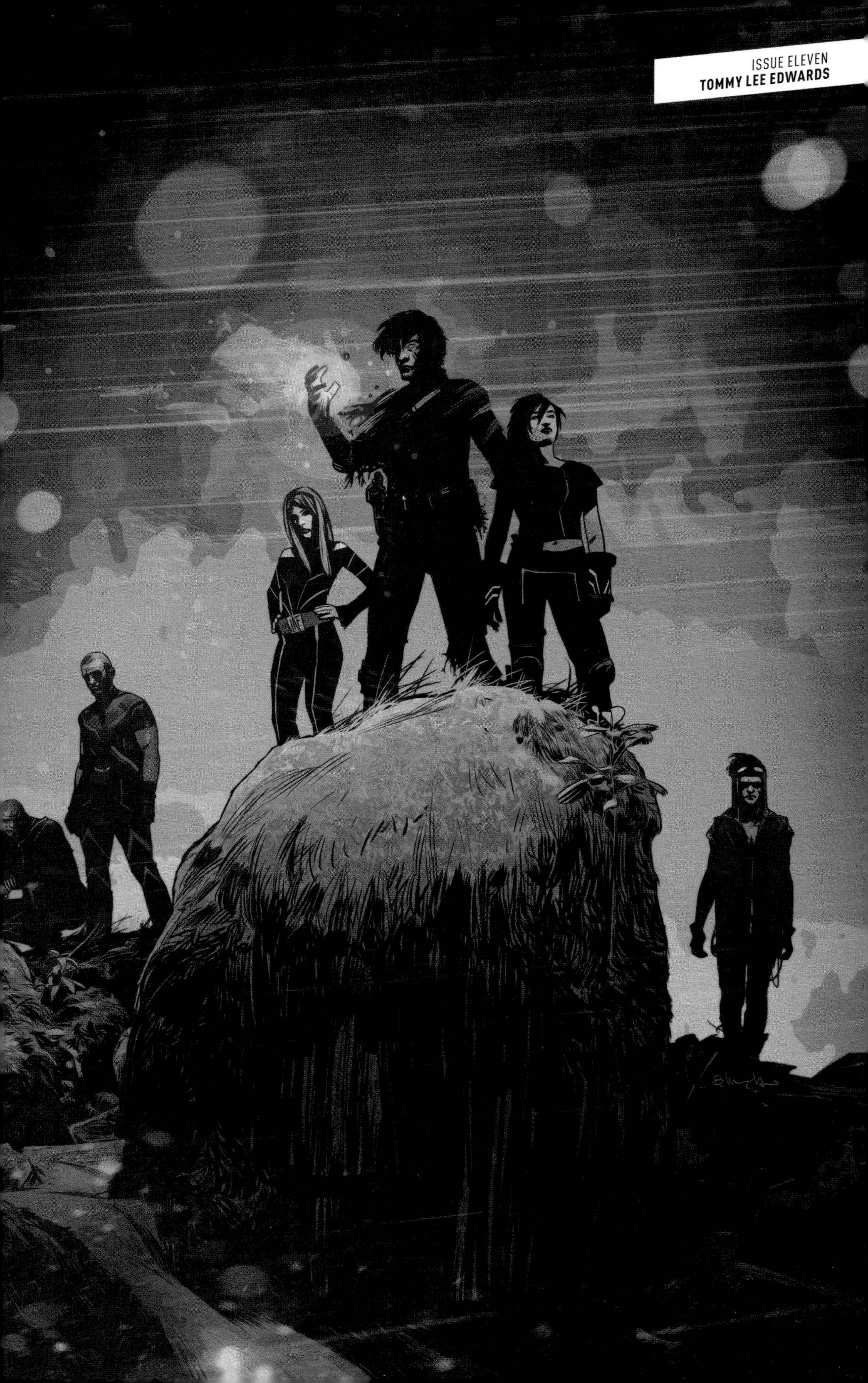

ISSUE TWELVE
STEPHANIE HANS

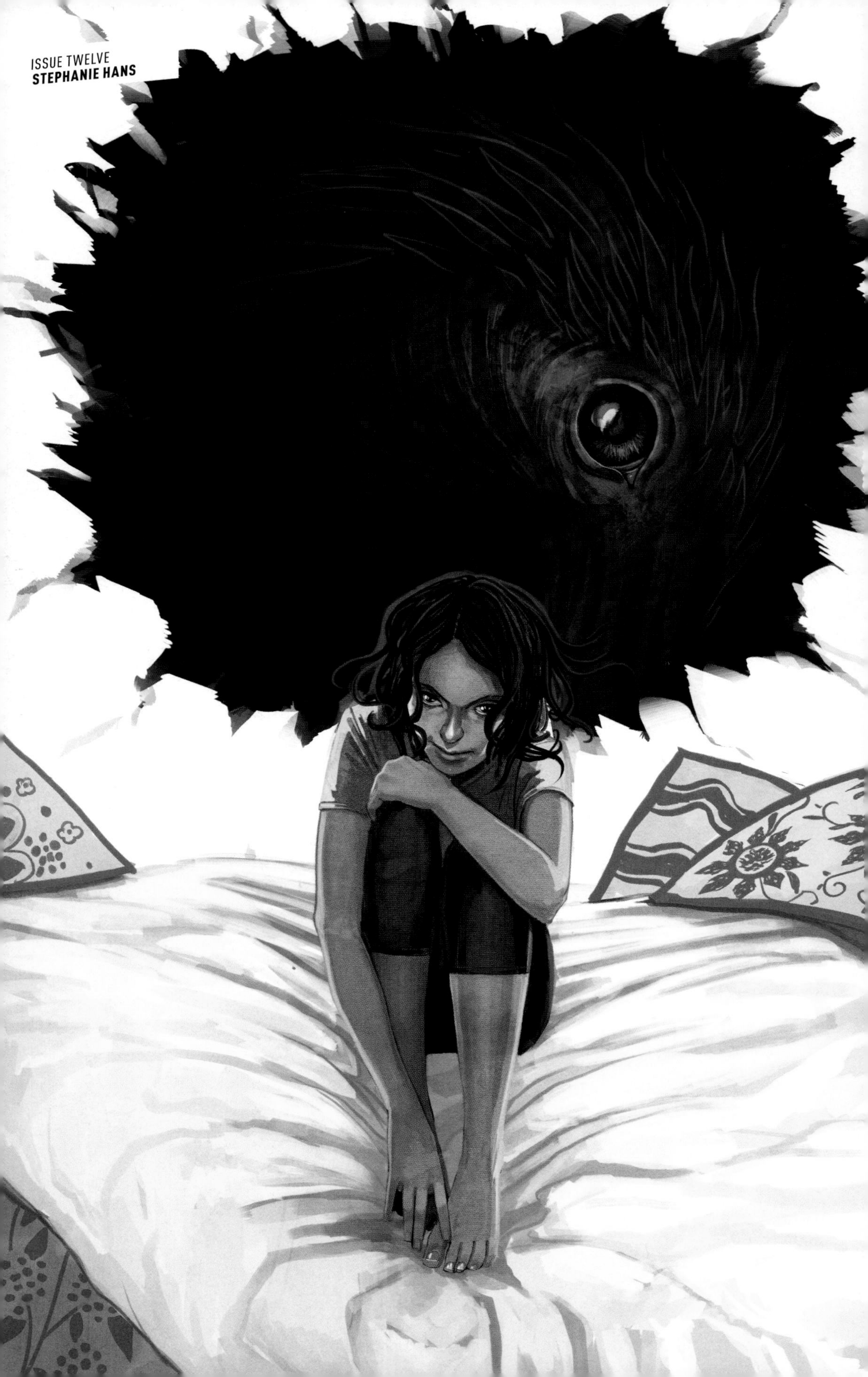

ISSUE THIRTEEN
STEPHANIE HANS

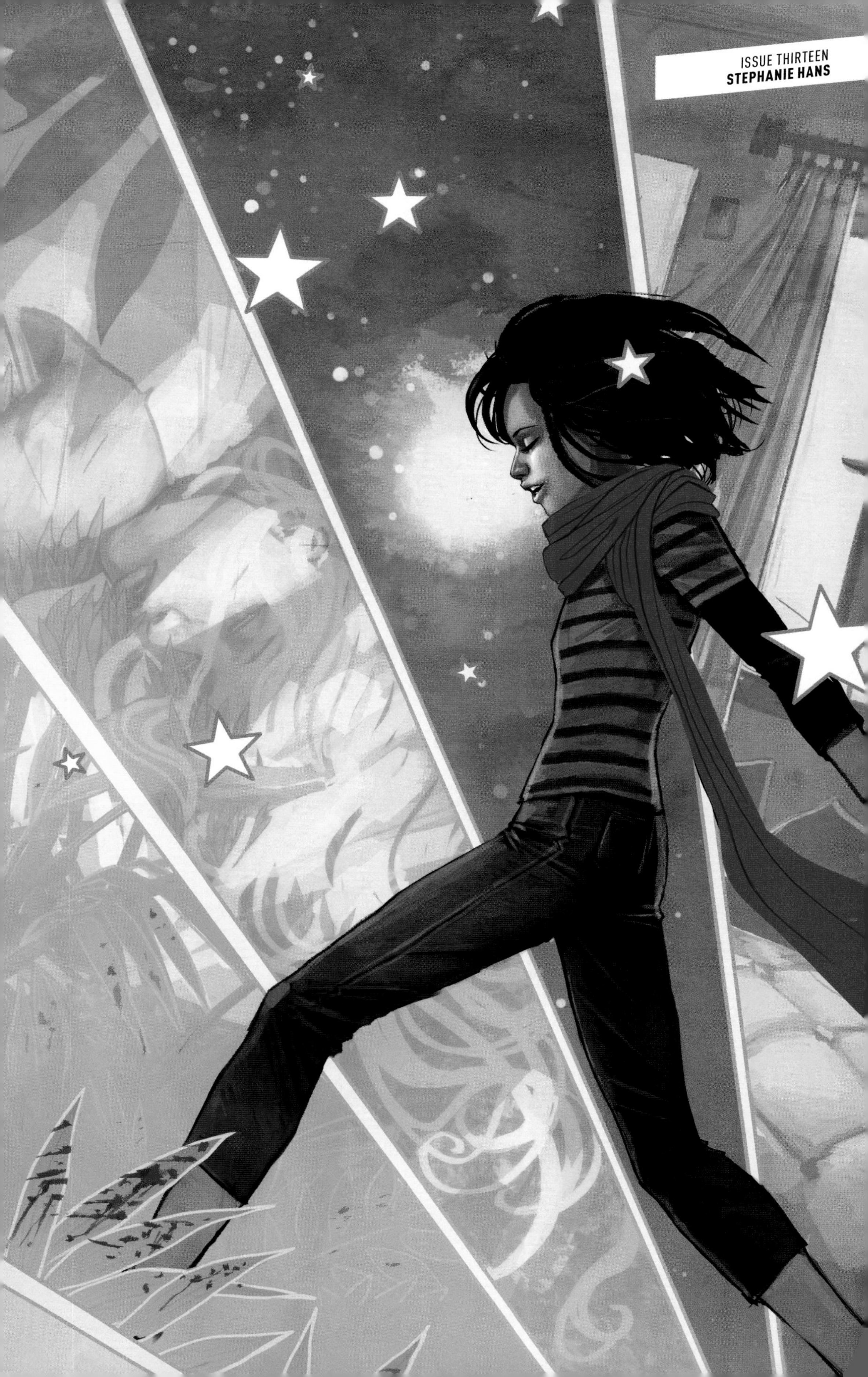

CHARACTER GALLERY
BY **ELENA CASAGRANDE**

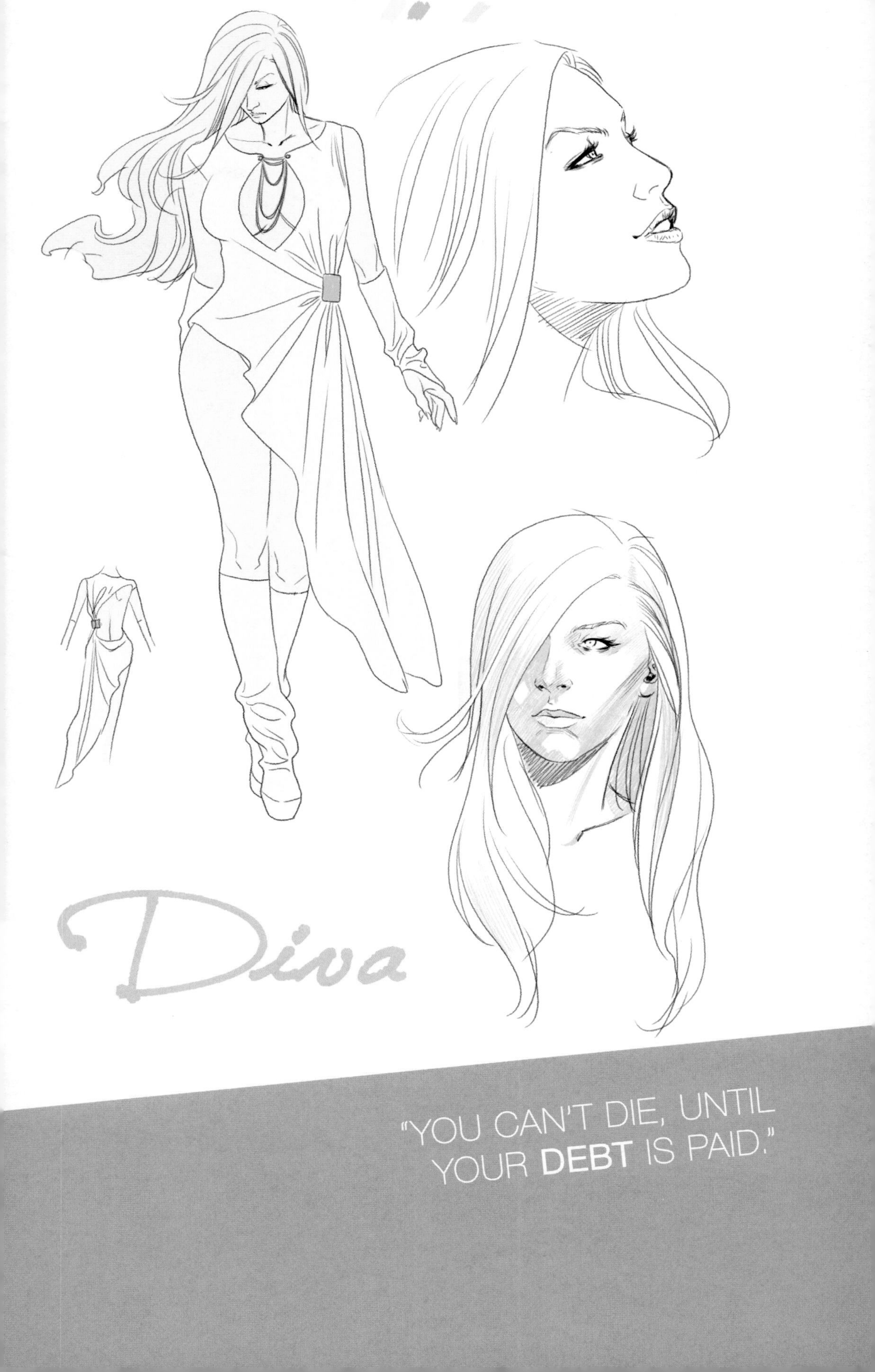
Diva

"YOU CAN'T DIE, UNTIL
YOUR **DEBT** IS PAID."

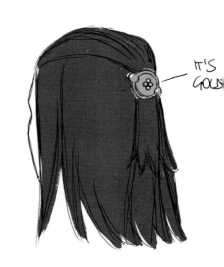

IT'S
GOLD

BACK

Terza

"LIKE ANY WEB, MADE OF LINES
SO **FINE** THAT YOU FORGET THEIR
INCREDIBLE STRENGTH."

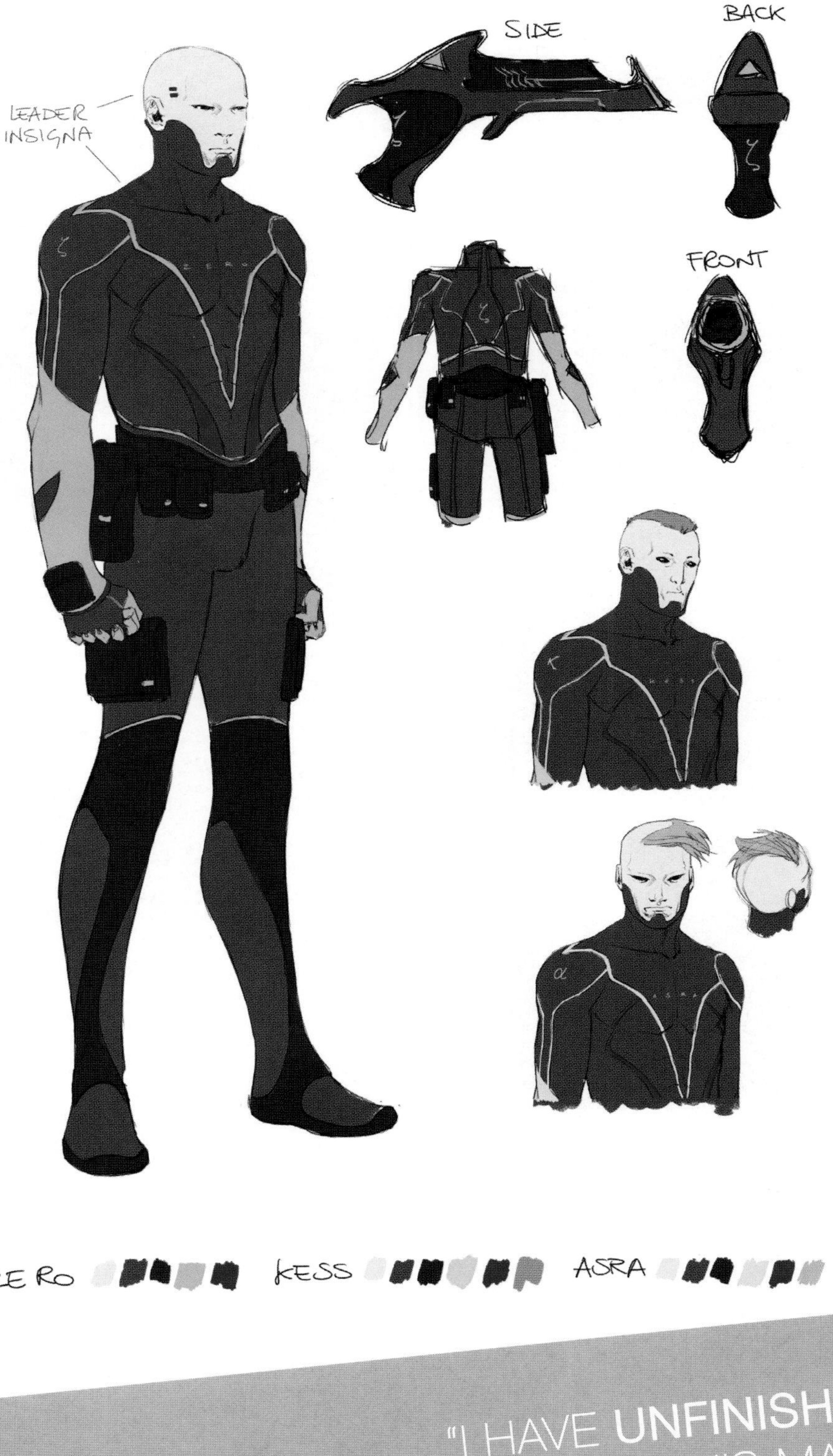
SIDE
BACK
LEADER
INSIGNA
FRONT
ZERO
KESS
ASRA

"I HAVE **UNFINISHED BUSINESS** WITH THIS MAN."

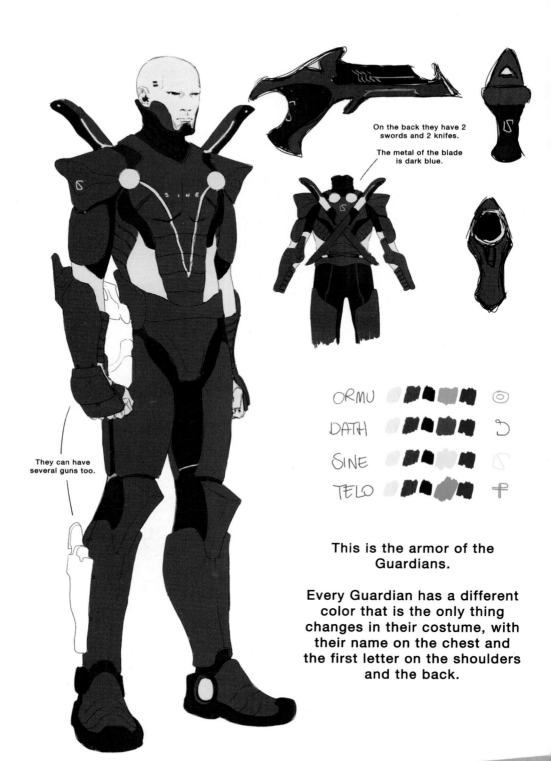

On the back they have 2 swords and 2 knifes.

The metal of the blade is dark blue.

They can have several guns too.

ORMU					◎
DATH					Ɔ
SINE					⼧
TELO					ⅎ

This is the armor of the Guardians.

Every Guardian has a different color that is the only thing changes in their costume, with their name on the chest and the first letter on the shoulders and the back.

"...THEY TRIED TO KILL THE MEMORY I WOULD BECOME."